U.S. History-Based Writing Lessons

Implementing the Structure and Style Writing Method™

Teacher Manual

by Lori Verstegen

Illustrated by Anthea Segger

First Edition © February 2017
Institute for Excellence in Writing, L.L.C.

Also by Lori Verstegen

Advanced U.S. History-Based Writing Lessons
All Things Fun and Fascinating
Ancient History-Based Writing Lessons
Bible Heroes Writing Lessons in Structure and Style™
Dress-Ups, Decorations, and Delightful Diversions
Medieval History-Based Writing Lessons
U.S. History-Based Writing Lessons Student Book

The purchaser of this book receives access to the following downloads:
the *Student Resource Packet*,
the *U.S. History-Based Writing Lessons Reproducible Checklists*,
the *U.S. History-Based Writing Lessons Blackline Masters*, and
the *U.S. History-Based Writing Lessons Sample Key Word Outlines*.
Go to IEW.com/USH-E. (See the blue page for complete download instructions.)

Copyright Policy
U.S. History-Based Writing Lessons
Implementing the Structure and Style Writing Method™
First Edition, February 2017

ISBN 978-1-62341-267-8

Institute for Excellence in Writing (IEW®)
8799 N. 387 Road
Locust Grove, OK 74352
800.856.5815
info@IEW.com IEW.com

Printed in the United States of America

Accessing Your Downloads

The purchaser of this book receives access to the following downloads:

- *Student Resource Packet**
- the optional *U.S. History-Based Writing Lessons Reproducible Checklists* e-book (35 pages)
- the optional *U.S. History-Based Writing Lessons Blackline Masters* e-book (17 pages)
- the optional *U.S. History-Based Writing Lessons Sample Key Word Outlines* e-book (12 pages)

To download these e-resources, please follow the directions below:

1. Go to our website: IEW.com
2. Log in to your online customer account. If you do not have an account, you will need to create one.
3. After you are logged in, go to this web page: IEW.com/USH-E
4. Click the red arrow, and then click the checkboxes next to the names of the files you wish to place in your account.
5. Click the "Add to my files" button.
6. To access your files now and in the future, click on "Your Account," and click on the "Files" tab (one of the gray tabs).
7. Click on each file name to download the files onto your computer.

Please note: You are free to download and print these e-books as needed for use within *your immediate family or classroom*. However, this information is proprietary, and we are trusting you to be on your honor not to share it with anyone. Please see the copyright page for further details. Thank you.

* If you would prefer to purchase *Student Resource Packet* as a preprinted packet, it is available at this web page: IEW.com/SRP-BL

If you have any difficulty receiving these downloads after going through the steps above, please call 800.856.5815.

Institute for Excellence in Writing
8799 N. 387 Road
Locust Grove, OK 74352

Contents

Welcome to *United States History-Based Writing Lessons*! We are thrilled to offer this Teacher's Manual in an exciting new format. It now includes reduced copies of the Student Book pages. Instructions to teachers, answers to questions, sample key word outlines, brainstorming ideas, review games, and helps for motivating students are inserted. This format allows a teacher to teach directly from the Teacher's Manual without the need of her own copy of the Student Book. Simply read through the Teacher's Manual and follow the special inserted instructions and helps.

Lesson instructions are directed to the student, but teachers should read over them with their students and help as necessary, especially with outlining and brainstorming.

It is assumed that teachers have attended IEW's *Teaching Writing: Structure and Style* seminar, either live or via DVD, and own the *Seminar Workbook*. Before each new unit, teachers should review the appropriate information in that workbook and DVD.

Introduction

The lessons in this book teach Structure and Style™ in writing. As they move through U.S. history themes, they incrementally introduce and review most of the models of structure and elements of style found in the Institute for Excellence in Writing's *Teaching Writing: Structure and Style*.

Student Book Contents

Have students look at and tab each section below in their books.

- **Scope and Sequence Chart** (pages 8–9)
- **The Lesson Pages**
  This is the majority of the text. The lesson pages contain the instructions, source texts, worksheets, and checklists you will need for each lesson.
- **Appendix I: Modified MLA Format**
- **Appendix II: Polished Draft Notebook and Keepsake**
  This appendix explains the polished draft notebook and includes a checklist that may be copied and used if teachers require polished drafts to be turned in for grading.
- **Appendix III: Student Samples**
  At least one student sample from IEW Units 2–9 is included to help clarify instructions and inspire you.
- **Appendix IV: Adding Literature**
  This appendix suggests various historical fiction novels to read alongside the lessons. It also includes templates of literature-response pages if teachers would like to assign such pages for students who will be adding the literature. These great stories will enhance students' understanding of American history as well as provide excellent models of structure and style.
- **Appendix V: Vocabulary (Chart, Quizzes, and Cards)**
  The vocabulary words are an important part of these lessons. You will be instructed to cut out one set of cards for some of the lessons. You should try to include some of these words in each composition you write. You will also be quizzed over the words periodically. The goal is that these great words will become part of your natural writing vocabulary.

U.S. History-Based Writing Lessons Blackline Masters

These optional, more advanced source texts, along with a few suggestions for more advanced Structure and Style that may be added to some of the lessons, will keep veteran IEW students progressing. (Sample key word outlines are also available for these. See the blue page at the front of this book for instructions for downloading both.)

*Structure and Style is a trademark of the Institute for Excellence in Writing, L.L.C

This Teacher's Manual includes an additional **Appendix VI: Motivating Students: Tickets and Games.** Some games require a little preparation, so be sure to read the Teacher's Manual a few days before class. Many games require the use of dice, so be sure to have some.

Customizing the Checklist
The total point value of each assignment is indicated at the bottom of each checklist. This total reflects only the basic items, not the more advanced additions. If these are used, add the appropriate amount of points, and write the new total on the custom total line.

Important: If students are not yet ready for a basic element on the checklist, simply have them cross it out. Subtract its point value from the total possible, and write the new total on the custom total line at the bottom.

If you would like to add elements to the checklist, assign each a point value, and add these points to the to the total possible, placing the new total on the custom total line. However, I like to make extra elements of style (e.g., vocabulary words and decorations) worth extra credit tickets instead (see Appendix VI). I find this to be more motivating to students than points toward their grades. I encourage all students to include vocabulary words.

Grading with the Checklist
To use the checklists for grading, do not try to add all the points earned. Instead, if an element is present, put a check in the blank or box next to it. If an element is missing, write the negative point value on its line or box. Total the negative points, and subtract them from the total points possible (or your custom total). *Hint: Use a different color of ink from the color the student used on the checklist.*

Introduction

Checklists

Each lesson includes a checklist that details all the requirements of the assignment for you and your teacher. You (students) should check off each element when you are sure it is included in your paper. Turn in the checklist with each assignment to be used by the teacher for grading.

More advanced additions are in gray boxes on the checklist. You will see *vocabulary words* in this box. This is because you are encouraged to use some vocabulary words in each composition you write. Doing so will help you master these quality words. Your teacher will decide how to reward you for using them. She may also sometimes ask you to add another element of style to the gray box that she would like you to try. If she will assign point values to these, she will have you write the new total points possible on the custom total line.

Teachers are free to adjust a checklist by requiring only the stylistic techniques that have become easy, plus one new one. "EZ+1"

Reproducible Checklists are available. View the blue page for download information.

Teacher's Manual

The Teacher's Manual includes all of the above (except the vocabulary cards) with added instructions for teachers, including sample key word outlines and brainstorming ideas, answers to questions, review games, vocabulary quizzes, and ideas for motivating students. Teachers may teach directly from this manual without their own copy of the Student Book.

The *Student Resource Packet*

The *Student Resource Packet* is a download used throughout these lessons. Please follow the instructions on the blue page for downloading this very helpful resource at no cost. If you prefer not to print so many pages, you may purchase a hard copy from IEW.

The Polished Draft Notebook

You should polish and illustrate each of your final drafts as soon as they have been checked and returned by your teacher. To do so, make the corrections noted, and add a picture. This last draft is referred to as "the polished draft" and does not have to be labeled. Polished drafts should be kept in a binder in clear sheet protectors *with the original, labeled "final draft" hidden behind each.* At the end of the year, you will have a collection of a variety of types of compositions that moves through major themes in U.S. history.

See Appendix II for more details about this notebook.

6 Institute for Excellence in Writing

In addition to the SRP, encourage students to bring a thesaurus to class. Most kids enjoy using an electronic thesaurus, but for those who prefer books, IEW offers a unique one entitled *A Word Write Now*. A more traditional one that I like for elementary students is *The Clear and Simple Thesaurus and Dictionary* by Harriet Wittles and Joan Greisman. For older students, I highly recommend *The Synonym Finder* by J.I. Rodale. You can buy multiple copies of the latter two (used) very cheaply on the Internet and have them available in class.

This schedule is provided to emphasize to parents and students, particularly in a class setting, that students should not expect to complete an entire lesson in one day. Spreading the work throughout the week will produce much better writing with much less stress. Parents teaching their own children at home should follow a similar schedule.

Suggested Weekly Schedule

In general, lessons are designed to be taught weekly and to be completed as follows.

Day 1:

1. Review concepts from previous lessons using activities in the Teacher's Manual.
2. Together, teacher and students read the new concept introduced in the lesson and do suggested activities. Then, follow Day 1 instructions to read the new source text, make a key word outline, and tell back the meaning of the notes.
3. Use the brainstorming page to discuss ideas for including elements of style.
4. Discuss the vocabulary words for the present lesson.
5. Experienced IEW students who are ready for a more advanced assignment can be instructed to additionally do the extra source text in *U.S. History-Based Writing Lessons Blackline Masters* if there is one, or add advanced elements of style.

Days 2–3:

1. Before returning to the new lesson, if work from a previous lesson has been returned with corrections to be made, polish this work with the help of a parent. Add a picture. Stylistic techniques do not need to be labeled. The polished draft will be placed in the polished draft notebook (see page 6) with the original, labeled final draft behind it, in the same sheet protector. *There is a polished draft checklist on page* 224.
2. Cut out and learn the vocabulary words for the present lesson. Review previous.
3. Review the key word outline from Day 1 of the new lesson. If a note is unclear, check the source text, and add what you need in order to make it clear. After you are sure you understand your notes, use the outline and the brainstorming ideas to write or type a composition *in your own words*. Try not to look back at the source text while you are writing. Include and label everything on the checklist. Let an editor proofread.

Day 4:

1. Review all vocabulary words learned thus far.
2. Write or type a final draft by making any corrections your editor asked you to make. (This will be fairly easy if the first draft was typed.) Check off each item on the checklist when you have included *and labeled* it.
3. Let an editor proofread again. He or she should check that all elements of Structure and Style are included and labeled as instructed on the checklist. Paperclip the checklist to your final draft to be turned in.

Labeling Dress-Ups

The lessons require one of each dress-up to be underlined in each paragraph. In addition, you may ask students to label each in the right margin using abbreviations (-ly, w-w, v, b/c, adj). Labeling will make grading simpler for teachers, and it will help students keep track of the elements to be sure that they use one of each.

Scope and Sequence

Lesson	Structural Model	Topic	Style (First Introduced)	Vocabulary	Literature Suggestions
1	**Unit 1: Note Making and Outlines**	Christopher Columbus Advanced: Europe Meets America		pillar, prosperity, transfixed, coax	*The Witch of Blackbird Pond* by Elizabeth George Speare Lessons 1–4
2	**Unit 2: Writing from Notes**	The Lost Colony Advanced: John White and Virginia Dare	-ly adverbs	resolve, endeavor, appalled, frivolous	
3		Jamestown Advanced: Slavery Arrives in America		askew, presume, flank, reverently	
4		The *Mayflower*	*who-which* clause title rule Advanced: Show emotions.	hostile, subside, perilous, secluded	
5	**Unit 3: Retelling Narrative Stories**	The Boston Massacre	alliteration	animosity, provoke, indignant, audacious	*Johnny Tremain* by Esther Forbes Lessons 5–10
6		The Boston Tea Party	strong verbs Advanced: similes	warily, vehemently, destined, confront	
7		The Shot Heard Round the World	conversation *because* clause	inevitable, squander, waver, diligent	
8		Borrowing a Conflict (original story)		cunning, contemplate, gravity, persevere	
9	**Unit 4: Summarizing a Reference**	Colonial Life Advanced: Care of the Sick	topic sentences and clinchers	compliant, obstinate, compel, deliberate	
10		The Declaration of Independence Advanced: Constitution	quality adjectives	solemn, tyrant, adept, enthrall	
11		The Louisiana Purchase	www.asia Ban *pretty/ugly, big.*	amiable, antagonist, distraught, awestruck	*The Sign of the Beaver* by Elizabeth George Speare
12		The Trail of Tears Advanced: Texas War for Independence	#2 prepositional opener	trite, formidable, obscure, laden	
13	**Unit 5: Writing from Pictures**	The Gold Rush	past perfect tense Advanced: dual dress-ups	incessant, zealous, trepidation, exemplary	*By the Great Horn Spoon!* by Sid Fleishman
14		Escape on the Underground Railroad	similes and metaphors		
15		The Battle	onomatopoeia	fathom, imperative, impotent, placidly	

Lesson	Subject and Structure	Topic	Style (First Introduced)	Vocabulary	Literature Suggestions
16	**Unit 6: Summarizing Multiple References**	The Civil War	fused outlines #3 -ly adverb opener	prominent, privily, affirm, espouse	*Rifles for Watie* by Harold Keith Lessons 16–20
17		Great Inventors: Thomas Edison	#4 -ing opener more banned words: *good, bad*	tedious, implement, scrutinize, potential	
18		Great Inventors: Alexander Graham Bell	Advanced: triple extension		
19		Great Inventors: Wright Brothers	3-paragraph model bibliography		
20	**Unit 7: Inventive Writing**	The Statue of Liberty: Hopes and Dreams, Part 1	question starter words #5 clausal opener	aspire, elated, auspicious, adverse	
21		Hopes and Dreams, Part 2	conclusion and introduction 4-paragraph model	revel, jaunty, encounter, lure	*Hattie Big Sky* by Kirby Larson Lessons 21–23
22		WWI: Soldiers			
23		Nationalism: The American Flag	(narrative: one paragraph) #6 VSS; 3sss		
24		Civil Rights: Freedom of Religion			Advanced: *Who Was Thomas Edison, Bell,* or *Wright Brothers?*
25	**Unit 8: Formal Essay Models**	Introduction and Conclusion to Inventor Paragraphs from Lessons 17–19	Advanced: anecdotal opener		
26		Space Race or Famous Astronaut, Part 1			*Journey to Topaz* by Yoshida Uchida Lessons 25–27
27		Space Race or Famous Astronaut, Part 2 Introduction and Conclusion	dramatic open-close: vss		
28	**Unit 9: Formal Critique**	*Journey to Topaz* Internment of Japanese-Americans			
29	Response to Literature: Character Analysis. Advanced: Optional Lesson: Theme Analysis	From a book you have read this year, choose a character, like Praiseworthy from *By the Great Horn Spoon.*			
30	**Vocabulary Story**				

Adapting the Schedule

Groups who follow a schedule with fewer than thirty weeks will have to omit some lessons. Because there are several lessons for each of the nine IEW units, this is not a problem. Teach the lessons that introduce new concepts, and omit some of those that do not.

Lesson 1: Christopher Columbus

Structures: IEW Unit 1: Note Making and Outlines
Style: introduction to style
Writing Topics: Christopher Columbus
Optional Student Reading Assignment: during Lessons 1–4: *The Witch of Blackbird Pond*

Teaching Writing: Structure and Style

Watch the sections for Unit 1 (Note Making and Outlines). At IEW.com/twss-help reference the TWSS Viewing Guides.

UNIT 1: NOTE MAKING AND OUTLINES

Lesson 1: Christopher Columbus

In this book you will learn many ways to make your writing more exciting and more enjoyable to read. You will learn to write with structure and with style.

Structure

What is *structure*? Think of a house. What had to happen before the house was built? The architect had to draw out the plans for the builder to follow. Without those plans, the builder might put a bathtub in the middle of the living room. We wouldn't want that, so we plan how everything will be arranged and in what order each part will be built.

Writing a paper is much the same. If we were just to begin writing without planning, our facts and details would probably not be arranged in the most logical way. Our composition would not be structured well and would not communicate our thoughts effectively. So in this course, you will "draw plans" for everything before you write. Your "plans" will be outlines, and they will follow a particular model for each type of composition.

Style

What comes to your mind when you hear the word *style*? Many people think of clothes. Clothes come in a variety of styles. You would dress differently to go to a wedding than you would to go out to play baseball. That's because formal events require a formal style of clothing, whereas casual events do not.

There are also different styles of language. Below are two sentences that communicate the same information in different styles. Which do you like better? Why?

> *He hit the ball!*
>
> *The determined Little Leaguer firmly smacked the spinning baseball with all his might!*

You probably like the second better because it is more descriptive. However, what if you were at the baseball game with your friend and the batter was your little brother? Which of the two sentences would be better for you to yell? Obviously, the first would be more appropriate. Your friend would probably think you were crazy if you jumped up and shouted the second one. Why the difference?

When you are speaking to people, they are there with you, experiencing the same scene and event as you are. You do not need to fill in the details. When you write, however, you must realize that the readers are not with you and cannot see, hear, or feel what is in your mind. You must help them see, hear, feel, and experience the scene you are writing about. IEW elements of style will help you do this.

Unit 1: Note Making and Outlines

Key Word Outlines

Before you begin to write, you will practice the first step of learning *structure* in writing: key word outlining.

Structure is how you organize the things you write. Key word outlining will help you gather information and organize it in your compositions.

When you outline, you will want to use or create some symbols or abbreviations to help you write quickly. There are some commonly accepted symbols listed for you in the *Student Resource Packet*. Below are a few symbols that we could use today. What do you think each means?

➔ ≠ ppl ⊙⊙ b/c

Practice key word outlining by following the assignment instructions on the following page.

➔ = lead to; go/went ≠ =different ppl = people ⊙⊙ = see or look b/c = because

Follow Day 1 instructions together. Then, read over Days 2-4, so students understand how to complete the lesson during the remainder of the week

The Assignment

Day 1:

1. With your teacher, read the paragraph on page 14. Then read it again. As you do, choose no more than three key words from each sentence that will best help you remember the meaning of the sentence. Write the words on the blank outline on page 15.

   Note: You may use symbols, abbreviations, and pictures freely. They do not count as words. However, be sure you can remember what they mean.
2. Cover the source text, and tell the meaning of each line of notes.
3. Note the vocabulary words for Lesson 1: *pillar, prosperity, transfixed, coax.*

Day 2:

1. Reread the paragraph on page 14. Then, turn the page so you cannot see it. Using only your key word notes on page 15, try to tell back the information in complete sentences *in your own words*. You should not memorize the source text word for word. Rather, you should let the key words remind you of the key ideas, and state the ideas in your own words.
2. Cut out and learn the vocabulary words for Lesson 1. Put them in a pencil pouch where you can easily retrieve them when writing or studying for a quiz.

Days 3–4:

1. Prepare to give an oral report from your key word outline. Practice telling back the information one line at a time. Look at a line; then look up and talk about it. Then look down at the next line, look up, and talk about it. Continue through the entire outline this way. Practice until the paragraph is smooth.
2. Review the vocabulary words.

Option for experienced Level B students: Complete the lesson in your Student Book first. If your parent or teacher assigns it, you can do the same with the extra paragraph, "Europe Meets America," in the *U.S. History-Based Writing Lessons Blackline Masters*.

Literature Suggestion

With Lessons 1–4 read *The Witch of Blackbird Pond* by Elizabeth George Speare.

Unit 1: Note Making and Outlines

Source Text

Christopher Columbus

In the 1400s, people of Europe wanted riches from the East Indies. Christopher Columbus believed that if the earth were round, he could reach the East by sailing west. He convinced the king and queen of Spain to give him three ships, and he set sail across the Sea of Darkness (the Atlantic Ocean). Some people thought he would fall off the edge of the world or be eaten by sea monsters. But on October 12, 1492, the sailors spotted land. They went ashore, and soon men very different from Europeans emerged from the bushes. Columbus called them Indians because he thought he was in the Indies. However, he had reached land that Europeans knew nothing about, the Americas.

Can you find out where Columbus landed?

Grammar notes: When pluralizing years, do not use an apostrophe. (This is a fairly new rule.) Capitalize direction words when they are used to refer to a region, but not when they are used simply as a direction.

Sample

Lesson 1: Christopher Columbus

Key Word Outline

I. *1400s, ppl. Eur., wanted, $$, E. Indies*

1. *CC, blvd., earth, round, sail, w E*
2. *K, Q, Spain, 3 ships, "Sea of Darkness"**
3. *thot, ↓ edge, sea, monster*
4. *Oct. 12, 1492, (⊘, ⊙⊙), land*
5. *ashore, (⊙⊙), ≠, men*
6. *called, "Indians," b/c thot, E. Indies*
7. *land, Eur., ⊘ know*

*Sea of Darkness counts as one word because it is the name of one thing.

Unit 2: Writing from Notes

Lesson 2: The Lost Colony

Structures: IEW Unit 2: Writing from Notes
Style: -ly adverb
Writing Topics: the lost colony
Optional Student Reading Assignment: during Lessons 1–4: *The Witch of Blackbird Pond*

Teaching Writing: Structure and Style

Watch the sections for Unit 2 (Writing from Notes). At IEW.com/twss-help reference the TWSS Viewing Guides.

UNIT 2: WRITING FROM NOTES

Lesson 2: The Lost Colony

Review

1. When making a key word outline, how many words may you write for each sentence of a source text?
2. What else may you use to help you remember ideas?
3. Share your "oral report" from Lesson 1.

symbols, abbreviations, pictures

Writing from Key Word Outlines

In Lesson 1 you wrote a key word outline from a paragraph about Christopher Columbus. You also may have done the same with the paragraph called "Europe Meets America" from the Advanced Lessons. In this lesson, you will learn to use a key word outline as a guide to write a paragraph. You will also practice using one of the IEW dress-ups.

Style: Fun with -ly Adverbs

There are many IEW elements of style. The first elements we will learn are called *dress-ups* because they will help you "dress up" your writing. The IEW dress-ups are descriptive words or phrases. Today we will have fun practicing one of these: the *-ly adverb*.

An -ly adverb is simply an adverb that ends in -ly. These words often tell *how* or *when* something happens or is done. Can you think of any such words? If you have trouble, you can find a list of many -ly adverbs in the *Student Resource Packet* (SRP).

Playing with -ly Adverbs

Play the -ly adverb game described in the Teacher's Manual. The box below contains possible -ly adverbs for the game, but you may think of others.

angrily	quietly	excitedly	eerily
sweetly	repetitively	hoarsely	snobbishly

-ly Adverb Game

Begin by explaining that -ly adverbs usually tell *how* or *when* something is done. In this game, we will play with several different ways you can *say* something.

Call one student up to the front of the room. Show him the -ly adverbs. He should choose one and say, "Come here, Johnny" in that way. The rest of the class should try to guess which -ly adverb describes the way he or she is speaking. The student who guesses correctly may then come up and do the same with a different -ly adverb.

Unit 2: Writing from Notes

Practice Using -ly Adverbs

Try adding an -ly adverb to each of the following sentences. Use the SRP for help.

1. *Confidently, bravely, audaciously, determinedly* Columbus set sail across the Sea of Darkness.

2. People thought Columbus would *ferociously, viciously, tragically surely, violently* be devoured by monsters.

3. Columbus *mistakenly, wrongly, presumably* thought he was in the East Indies.

The Assignment

Day 1:

1. Make a key word outline of the paragraph on page 20 by writing no more than three key words for each sentence. You may also use as many symbols and abbreviations as you need. Use the blank outline on page 21.
2. Cover the source text and tell the meaning of each line of notes.
3. Before you begin writing a paragraph from the outline, use page 22 to brainstorm ideas with your teacher for including -ly adverbs and vocabulary words. See the vocabulary words for Lesson 2: *resolve, endeavor, appalled, frivolous*. Learn them this week.
4. Using your key word outline as a guide, with your teacher's help, begin to write a paragraph *in your own words*. As you write, try to include some of the ideas for *-ly adverbs* and *vocabulary words* from your brainstorming.

Teachers, demonstrate by writing the beginning of a sample paragraph on the whiteboard as the students dictate it to you. Explain what double-spacing and indenting are. Explain that each line of notes does not necessarily have to equal one sentence. In other words, one note may be written in more than one sentence, or two notes may be combined into one sentence. The idea is to communicate the ideas in their own words. Encourage students to add an -ly adverb and a vocabulary word as you write their ideas on the board. (Look at the vocabulary words for Lessons 1 and 2.) Also encourage them to use their own words to communicate the ideas of the source text, not the exact words of the source text. Help as needed.

5. Go over the checklist on page 23. Note that you will need to underline one -ly adverb. (You may use more than one, but only underline one.) Also bold or label all vocabulary words you use for extra credit. (Put a ✔ in the box for each of these when you have done it.)
6. See Appendix I. It explains how to format your papers from this point forward. It is a slightly modified version of MLA format.

Days 2–4:

1. Review your outline. Be sure you understand everything on it. If a note is unclear, fix it before you work on your paragraph.
2. Finish writing your paragraph using your key word outline, your brainstorming ideas, and the checklist to guide you. Check off each item on the checklist when you are sure it is completed.
3. Paper clip the checklist with your paragraph. (Copy it if you do not want to tear it from the book.)
4. If your teacher assigns it, also write a paragraph from the outline you wrote in Lesson 1 about Christopher Columbus. Try to add and underline an -ly adverb.

Option for experienced Level B students: Complete the lesson in your Student Book first. If your parent or teacher assigns it, you can do the same with the extra paragraph, "John White and Virginia Dare," in the *U.S. History-Based Writing Lessons Blackline Masters*.

Unit 2: Writing from Notes

Source Text

The Lost Colony

In 1565, the Spanish established the first successful settlement in the New World: St. Augustine, Florida. Later, in 1587, about 120 Englishmen attempted to settle in the New World, too. They sailed to Roanoke Island, which is off the coast of what is now North Carolina. Soon they ran low on supplies, so they sent their governor, John White, to bring help from England. After many setbacks, the determined John White returned to find that the entire colony was gone! The only clue to the colonists' whereabouts was the name of an island, Croatoan, scribbled on the side of a tree. To this day, no one knows what happened to the people of what is now called the Lost Colony.

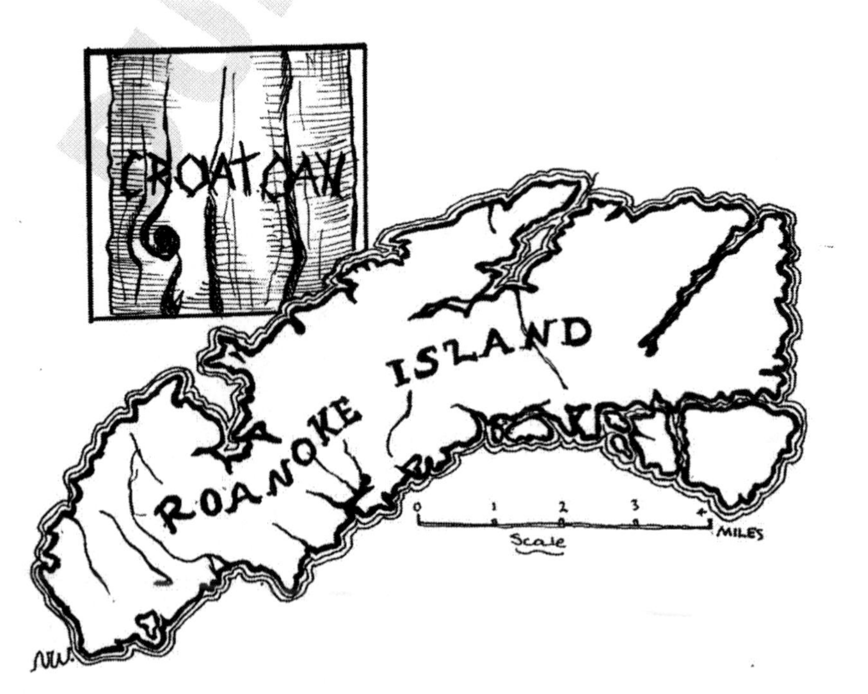

Sample

Lesson 2: The Lost Colony

Key Word Outline

I. *1565, Span., 1st, settlement, NW, St. Augustine, FL*

1. *1587, 120 Eng, ➔ NW, settle*
2. *Roanoke Isle, coast, N. Carolina*
3. *supplies ↓ Gov. John White, ➔ Eng., help*
4. *rtnd, settlement, gone!*
5. *Croatoan, scribbled, tree*
6. *?, happened, "Lost Colony"*

Brainstorming -ly Adverbs

Write ideas for adding -ly adverbs to each of the sentences below:

1. The Spanish *successfully, triumphantly, bravely, effectively* established the first settlement.

2. *Unfortunately, tragically, eventually, gradually,* the group ran low on supplies.

3. The colony *mysteriously, eerily, sadly, completely, unexpectedly* disappeared.

Other ideas:

Let students offer their own ideas.

Vocabulary Words

Try to use each of the following vocabulary words in a sentence that could be in your paragraph.

endeavored *The Englishmen endeavored to begin their own settlement in the New World.*

resolved *John White resolved to return with help.*

appalled *John White was appalled at what he discovered when he returned.*

Lesson 2: The Lost Colony

Lesson 2 Checklist: The Lost Colony

Name: ______________________________

STRUCTURE

☐	Name, lesson, and date in upper left-hand corner (See Appendix I.)	_____ (5 pts)
☐	Title centered on top line	_____ (5 pts)
☐	First line indented	_____ (5 pts)
☐	Composition double-spaced	_____ (5 pts)
☐	Checklist on top, final draft, rough draft, key word outline	_____ (5 pts)

STYLE Each paragraph must contain at least one of each element of style.

	Dress-Ups (underline one of each)	**(5 pts each)**
☐	-ly adverb	_____ (5 pts)

MECHANICS

☐	capitalization	_____ (1 pt)
☐	end marks and punctuation	_____ (1 pt)
☐	spelling and usage	_____ (2 pts)
☐	complete sentences (Does it make sense?)	_____ (1 pt)

	More Advanced Additions (optional unless your teacher requires them of you)	
☐	vocab word(s) (Label voc or bold.)	_____
☐	"John White and Virginia Dare" paragraph	_____

Total: _________/ 35

Custom Total: _________/___

Reproducible checklists are available (see blue page).

Unit 2: Writing from Notes

Lesson 3: Jamestown

Structures: IEW Unit 2: Writing from Notes
Style: reviewing -ly adverbs
Writing Topics: Jamestown
Optional Student Reading Assignment: during Lessons 1–4: *The Witch of Blackbird Pond*

UNIT 2: WRITING FROM NOTES

Lesson 3: Jamestown

Play a vocabulary game to prepare for the quiz next week. See the Teacher's Manual.

In this lesson you will again practice writing from a key word outline.

Vocabulary around the World would be a good choice. See Appendix VI.

The Assignment

Day 1:

1. Read the source text on page 26. With the help of your teacher, write a key word outline on page 27.
2. Cover the source text, and tell the meaning of each line of notes.
3. Before you write a paragraph from your notes, use page 28 to brainstorm ideas for including -ly adverbs and vocabulary words.
4. Look at the checklist on page 29. Make sure you understand everything on it.
5. Note the vocabulary words for Lesson 3: *askew, presume, flank, reverently.*

Days 2–4:

1. Review your outline. Be sure you understand everything on it. If a note is unclear, fix it before you write your paragraph.
2. Write your own paragraph about Jamestown, using your key word outline and your brainstorming ideas to guide you. Do not look at the source text.
3. Include and underline the elements of style on the checklist on page 29. Check off each item when you are sure you have completed it. Remember to paper clip the checklist to your paragraph.
4. Review all vocabulary words.

Study for Vocabulary Quiz 1. It will cover words from Lessons 1–3.

Option for experienced Level B students: Complete the lesson in your Student Book first. If your parent or teacher assigns it, you can do the same with the extra paragraph, "Slavery Arrives in America," in the *U.S. History-Based Writing Lessons Blackline Masters.*

Unit 2: Writing from Notes

Source Text

Jamestown

In 1607 a group of English gentlemen sailed to the New World hoping to find riches. They landed in Virginia and named their town Jamestown, after King James. The land was a swampy wilderness. The lazy gentlemen did not want to work. Within a few months about half of them had died. So Captain John Smith made a wise rule: "He who will not work will not eat!" They never found gold, but they did find tobacco. They sold it to England by the ton. Jamestown is now famous for being the first permanent English settlement in America.

Sample

Lesson 3: Jamestown

Key Word Outline

I. *1607, Eng. N.W., hoping, $$*

1. *landed, VA, named, Jamestown,* ♛
2. *swampy, wilderness*
3. *lazy, gentlemen, ⊘, work*
4. *Capt. Smith: ⊘ work, ⊘ eat*
5. *⊘ gold, found, tobacco*
6. *sold, Eng., ton*
7. *J----, 1st, perm, Eng., settl., N.W.*

Brainstorming

Write ideas for adding -ly adverbs.

Write several ideas on the lines below each sentence. Choose your favorite to write in the blank within the sentence.

1. They *foolishly* looked for riches instead of preparing for winter.

   -ly adverbs *greedily, frivolously, eagerly, foolishly, fervently*

2. *Snobbishly* they would not work.

   -ly adverbs *lazily, snobbishly, naturally, stubbornly, foolishly*

3. Smith *cunningly* made a rule.

   -ly adverbs *wisely, prudently, cunningly, finally, fortunately*

Vocabulary Word Ideas

Turn to page 254. It is a chart of the vocabulary words. Can you use any from Lessons 1–3 in a phrase that could be in your paragraph about Jamestown? (You may also look ahead and use future words if you like.)

Discuss ideas for vocabulary words. Here are some that work well. Offer a ticket for each word a student can use in a sentence that could be in the paragraph. (See Appendix VI for an explanation of tickets.)

John Smith was the pillar of Jamestown.

Tobacco brought prosperity to Jamestown.

The men presumed they would find riches.

John Smith was appalled at the men who would not work.

Lesson 3: Jamestown

Lesson 3 Checklist: Jamestown

Name: ______________________________

STRUCTURE

☐	Name, lesson, and date in upper left-hand corner (See Appendix I.)	____ (5 pts)
☐	Title centered on top line	____ (5 pts)
☐	Composition double-spaced	____ (5 pts)
☐	Checklist on top, final draft, rough draft, key word outline	____ (5 pts)

STYLE Each paragraph must contain at least one of each element of style.

	Dress-Ups (underline one of each)	**(5 pts each)**
☐	-ly adverb	____ (5 pts)

MECHANICS

☐	capitalization	____ (1 pt)
☐	end marks and punctuation	____ (1 pt)
☐	spelling and usage	____ (2 pts)
☐	complete sentences (Does it make sense?)	____ (1 pt)

	More Advanced Additions (optional unless your teacher requires them of you)	
☐	vocab word(s) (Label voc or bold.)	____
☐	"Slavery Arrives in America" paragraph	____

Total: ________ / 30

Custom Total: ________ /___

Reproducible checklists are available (see blue page).

Unit 2: Writing from Notes

Lesson 4: The *Mayflower* Mishap

Structures: IEW Unit 2: Writing from Notes
Style: *who-which* clause; title rule
Writing Topics: The *Mayflower*
Optional Student Reading Assignment: during Lessons 1–4: *The Witch of Blackbird Pond*

Lesson 4: The *Mayflower* Mishap

UNIT 2: WRITING FROM NOTES

Lesson 4: The *Mayflower* Mishap

Take Vocabulary Quiz 1.

The *Who-Which* Clause

In this lesson you will learn to add another dress-up to your paragraphs: a *who-which clause*. A *who* or *which* clause (*w-w clause*) is a clause that begins with either the word *who* or the word *which* and tells more information about a person, place, thing, or idea.

A *who* clause will tell more about a person. A *which* clause will tell more about a place, thing, or idea.

Jamestown, which is still prosperous today, was established by the English.

John Smith, who was resolved to help the settlement, enforced his rule.

Notice that each of the *who-which* clauses has a comma before and after it. That is because it is inserted into a sentence that was already complete. You could take it out of the sentence and still have a complete sentence left. Try it and see.

Ask a student to read each of the above sentences without the *who* or *which* clauses.

Warning: You cannot just insert the word *who* or the word *which* into a sentence to make a *who-which* clause. If you do, you will create a fragment.

For example, if you begin with *Jamestown is in Virginia*, and simply add the word *which*, notice what you have:

Jamestown, which is in Virginia,

This is a fragment. You must now add more information to make a complete sentence:

Jamestown, which is in Virginia, is the first permanent English settlement in America.

You will practice this dress-up when you brainstorm elements of style for your *Mayflower* story.

Unit 2: Writing from Notes

Five-Senses Words

The source text for this lesson is a story. You are going to add some of your own details to it. The key word outline is simply a guide. This is *your* story. You may add to the facts from the source text. A fun way to do this is to add more vivid descriptions. In the story for this lesson, there is a storm that will be fun to describe. The more vivid descriptions you can include, the better your reader will experience the storm. When you write your story, you will try to describe what the characters would see, hear, or feel in the storm like *bright flashes* of lightning, *booming* thunder, and *gusty* winds.

Turn to the five-senses words section in the SRP, and study the words there. Do you see how they each describe what something looks like, sounds like, feels like, smells like, or tastes like? Including these kinds of words in stories helps your reader imagine and even seem to experience the scenes.

There is much to do in this lesson. If your students are ready, consider assigning the outline at home, but be sure they feel confident enough to do so. Also, be sure they understand that each Roman numeral on the blank KWO represents a paragraph. This lesson's source text is two paragraphs.

Assignment

Day 1:

1. On page 35, make a key word outline of the story on page 34. (Your teacher might ask you to try this on your own at home.)
2. Before you begin writing a paragraph from the outline, use page 36 to brainstorm ideas with your teacher for including five-senses words and dress-ups.
3. See the vocabulary words for Lesson 4: *hostile, subside, perilous, secluded.* Learn them this week. Try to use some in your story.
4. See page 37 to see how to create a fun title for your story.
5. Using your key word outline as a guide, with your teacher's help begin to write your story *in your own words*. As you write, try to include extra details and descriptions from the brainstorming. Follow the checklist on page 38. Each dress-up must be in both of the two paragraphs.

Days 2–4:

1. Polish your Lost Colony paragraph from Lesson 2. (See Appendix II.) The chart of proofreading marks in the SRP may be helpful.
2. Finish writing your *Mayflower* story using your key word outline, your brainstorming ideas, and the checklist to guide you. Check off each item on the checklist when you are sure it is complete. Notice that there are two boxes for each dress-up. That is because both dress-ups are required in each paragraph. Turn in the checklist with your story.

   See page 6 for more detailed instructions.
3. If you are reading the literature, obtain *Johnny Tremain* by Esther Forbes for next week.

Option for experienced Level B students: Complete the lesson in your Student Book first. If your parent or teacher assigns it, try to add the advanced style (showing emotions) taught in the *U.S. History-Based Writing Lessons Blackline Masters*.

Note that the name of the ship, *Mayflower*, is in italics. Tell students that when they type names of ships, they should put them in italics. If they hand-write, ship names should be underlined.

Source Text

The *Mayflower* Mishap

In 1620 John Howland boarded an old creaky merchant ship called the *Mayflower* with a group of Englishmen who wanted to be able to worship God freely as they saw it. They headed across the vast Atlantic Ocean toward America. During the trip there was a terrible storm. Lightning flashed, thunder crashed, wind roared, and massive waves rocked the boat. The Pilgrims stayed below in the gun deck. It was crowded, and they were wet, cold, and scared.

John did not like being cooped up, so he climbed to the upper deck. Without warning the ship rolled, and he fell into the ocean. As he fell, he grabbed a hanging rope. As he dangled over the ocean, he screamed frantically for help. Luckily, the sailors had seen what had happened. They were able to grab him with a boat hook. Goodman Howland was relieved and grateful to be back on the boat. He returned to the gun deck where his friends were glad to see that he was safe. However, they knew that this journey to the New World would be a long and difficult one.

Sample

Lesson 4: The *Mayflower* Mishap

Key Word Outline

I. *1620, John Howland,* Mayflower, *w/ Eng. worship*

1. *➔ Amer.*
2. *storm*
3. *ϟ thunder, wind, waves*
4. *Pilgrims, ⬇ gun deck*
5. *crowded, scared*

II. *II. J.H., ⊘ like, cooped*

1. *ship, rolled,ocean*
2. *grabbed, rope*
3. *screamed, help*
4. *sailors, ⊙⊙*
5. *grabbed, w/ boat hook*
6. *☺ back, boat*
7. *gun deck, w/, friends ☺, ⊙⊙*
8. *knew, long, difficult*

Brainstorming Style

Words that help readers see, hear, feel, taste, and smell make stories more enjoyable. They create vivid images and help readers imagine the scenes as if they were there.

Look at the sample story on page 227. Notice the five-senses words.

Below is a list of elements of the storm in the story. In the first column, describe each with five-senses words. After each, tell what it would be doing, using five-senses words if you can. Try to add -ly adverbs to some. Use the five-senses words section of the SRP for help.

Five-Senses Words

Describe		Doing?	-ly Adverbs
heavy, roaring *cold, icy, pouring, swirling*	rain	*pelted and drenched the ship* *pounded, battered, beat, drummed*	*mercilessly* *continuously, savagely*
deafening, howling fierce, whirling, frigid	wind	*blasted, ripped, howled*	*incessantly, relentlessly*
rolling, roaring crashing, ear-piercing, deafening	thunder	*boomed, exploded, echoed, shook, bellowed*	*loudly, cruelly*
blinding, bright silver	lightning	*streaked, zigzagged, flashed, illuminated*	*blindingly, hazardously*
turbulent, massive towering, salty, foamy, frothy	waves	*crashed, exploded, tossed, drenched, swirled*	*vehemently, continuously, ruthlessly*

***Who-Which* Clauses**

Use some of the ideas you wrote above in a sentence with a *who-which* clause. Below are some examples. Notice how the *who-which* clause is set off by commas. Notice, too, that the words *who* or *which* are underlined. That is how you will indicate a *who-which* clause when you use one.

The tiny ship, which was tossed violently by the massive waves, struggled to stay afloat.

John Howland, who was being thrashed by towering waves, prayed for mercy.

1. The *ear-piercing* thunder, which *continually boomed*, shook the helpless ship.

2. The *deafening* wind, which *blasted the ship*, frightened the children.

3. Write your own: *Let the students offer ideas.*
   The roaring rain, which pelted the ship, seemed never ending.

The Title Rule

The last thing you will add to your final draft of the *Mayflower* story is a title. We want a title that will grab the readers' attention and make them want to read the story. Therefore, you should try to be a little creative with your titles.

The title repeats or reflects two to three key words from the last sentence. For example, the source text ended with, "They knew this journey to the New World would be a long and difficult one." The key words are underlined.

Here are some possible ways to repeat or reflect two to three of the key words from the last sentence:

Repeating words: "A Difficult Journey"

Reflecting some words: "A Challenging Journey"

"Adventure on the Trip to the New World"

Note: You may change your last sentence to help you create an intriguing title.

Remember the title rule:

The title repeats or reflects two to three key words from the last sentence.

Write your own ideas for a title.

A New World Ahead

Praying for Safety

Unit 2: Writing from Notes

Lesson 4 Checklist: The *Mayflower* Mishap

Name: ______________________________

STRUCTURE

☐	Name, lesson, and date in upper left-hand corner (See Appendix I.)	_____ (5 pts)
☐	Title centered and repeats or reflects 2–3 key words from last sentence	_____ (5 pts)
☐	Composition double-spaced	_____ (5 pts)
☐	Checklist on top, final draft, rough draft, key word outline	_____ (5 pts)

STYLE Each paragraph must contain at least one of each element of style.

¶ 1	¶ 2	Dress-Ups (underline one of each)	(5 pts each)
☐	☐	-ly adverb	_____ (10 pts)
☐	☐	*who-which* clause	_____ (10 pts)

MECHANICS

☐	capitalization	_____ (1 pt)
☐	end marks and punctuation	_____ (1 pt)
☐	spelling and usage	_____ (2 pts)
☐	complete sentences (Does it make sense?)	_____ (1 pt)
☐	Name of ship, *Mayflower*, is in italics or underlined.	_____ (5 pts)

¶ 1	¶ 2	More Advanced Additions (optional unless your teacher requires them of you)	
☐	☐	vocab word(s) (Label voc or bold.)	_____
☐	☐	Show emotions.	_____

Total: _________/ 50

Custom Total: _________/___

Teachers are free to adjust a checklist by requiring only the stylistic techniques that have become easy, plus one new one. "EZ+1." Reproducible checklists are available (see blue page).

Lesson 5: The Boston Massacre

Structures: IEW Unit 3: Retelling Narrative Stories

Style: decoration – alliteration

Writing Topics: the Boston Massacre

Optional Student Reading Assignment: during Lessons 5–10: *Johnny Tremain*

Teaching Writing: Structure and Style

Watch the sections for Unit 3 (Retelling Narrative Stories). At IEW.com/twss-help reference the TWSS Viewing Guides.

UNIT 3: RETELLING NARRATIVE STORIES

Lesson 5: The Boston Massacre

Review

1. How do you create an intriguing title?
2. Share the title of your *Mayflower* story from Lesson 4.
3. Share the *who-which* clause in your *Mayflower* story.
4. Share some five-senses words from your *Mayflower* story.

Use the title rule: Repeat or reflect 2–3 key words from the last sentence.

The Story Sequence Chart

The next several lessons will focus on story writing. You will use a new method of note-taking that will help you appreciate the important elements of a story. Every story, regardless of how long it is, contains the same basic elements.

Setting and Characters

Stories usually begin by introducing readers to the time and place of the story. This is called the *setting*. Descriptions of the setting often include five-senses words to help the reader feel as if they are there. They also help create the mood of the story. For example, a sad story might begin with gray skies and fog. A suspenseful story might begin with booming thunder, howling wind, and creaking doors.

What is the setting of "The *Mayflower* Mishap" story from Lesson 4?

Atlantic Ocean on the *Mayflower*, 1620

Also at their beginnings, stories must introduce their readers to the main people (or animals) of the story—the *characters*.

Who is the main character of "The *Mayflower* Mishap" story?

John Howland

Conflict or Problem

Then, for a story to be captivating, it must move into the next important element—the *conflict*. This is the problem, want, or need of the main character(s). Stories without some sort of problem to overcome or need to be met are not very interesting. Most of the action of the story is simply how the conflict is dealt with—what the characters do, say, think, or feel with respect to the conflict.

What is the main conflict of "The *Mayflower* Mishap"?

John falls overboard and needs to be rescued.

The sailors rescue John with a boat hook, so he is returned to ship to continue the difficult journey.

Poor decisions have consequences.
perseverance

Unit 3: Retelling Narrative Stories

Climax and Resolution

If there is a conflict or problem, there must be a way to solve it! We call the event that leads to the problem being solved the *climax* of the story. It is often the most exciting part of the story. We call the result of the climax (how the problem works out) the *resolution*.

What are the climax and resolution of "The *Mayflower* Mishap"?

Characters and readers often learn something about truths in life from a story. These are themes. Common themes include ideas such as good overcomes evil, and virtues such as courage, honesty, perseverance, and compassion are rewarded. A theme gives the story a sense of purpose. Some themes are subtle, or a story might not even have a theme. In the case of a story without any theme, you don't need to worry a great deal; that doesn't necessarily mean that the story has no point at all. However, if your instructor tells you that a narrative story assignment must have a theme, by all means include one.

What is one theme of "The *Mayflower* Mishap"?

The Assignment

Day 1:

1. Read "The Boston Massacre" on the following page. Then, with the help of your teacher, complete the outline on page 43. Do not take notes from each sentence. Simply answer the Story Sequence Chart questions. Your outline should be brief. You can add more details when you actually write your own version of the story.

   You do not have to outline the background. It is simply for your information.

   Note: Notes do not necessarily need to be placed on the line across from the questions they answer. For example, in Section I, it does not matter whether you introduce the setting or the characters first. You may also need more than one line to answer one question. You may be able to answer two questions on one line.

2. Students, take turns telling back the story, using one line of the outline at a time.
3. Begin to brainstorm ideas for elements of style on pages 44–45. You will learn a new element of style. It is the simplest of the IEW decorations: alliteration.
4. Go over the checklist on page 47. Note that each of the three sections of the story should include all dress-ups you have learned; however, the new decoration (alliteration) is only required once anywhere in the story.
5. Discuss vocabulary words for Lesson 5: *animosity, provoke, indignant, audacious.* Review words from previous lessons. How can you use some in your story?

Consider having a "best title" contest with this story. Tell the students the class will vote on the best title next week. Hint: Alliteration will make titles fun.

Days 2–4:

1. Polish your Jamestown paragraph from Lesson 3. (See Appendix II.)
2. Write your own version of the story, using only your key word outline and brainstorming ideas to guide you. *Write in your own words. Add plenty of description, but do not change historical facts.* You do not have to include the background information.
3. Include and label everything on the checklist. Each of the three sections of your story should use all dress-ups. Follow the suggested schedule on page 7.

Literature Suggestion

With Lessons 5–10 read *Johnny Tremain* by Esther Forbes.

Background: After the *Mayflower*, many more Englishmen sailed to America. Their settlements grew into thirteen colonies, governed by the king of England. Some colonists did not want to be ruled by a king so far away. The king, therefore, sent soldiers to America to keep law and order. The colonists did not like that either. The following story takes place when tensions were rising between the king and the colonists.

Unit 3: Retelling Narrative Stories

Source Text

The Boston Massacre

It was an unusually cold, bleak day in Boston in 1770. John and Hugh were standing guard on King Street. They were British soldiers. At the moment all was quiet, but John and Hugh were anxious. They knew there were many colonists, especially the Sons of Liberty, who were angry at King George for his unfair laws and taxes. They resented his soldiers being there, so they had been harassing and provoking them. The two nervously watched the streets.

It wasn't long before a colonist began trying to stir up trouble by taunting John. Hugh confronted the colonist and eventually became so angry that he struck him in the face with the butt of his gun. The colonist let out a cry, and a mob of angry colonists rushed over. The group grew larger and larger. Captain Preston, with several soldiers, went over to maintain order, but this only angered the mob more. They began throwing ice chunks, sticks, and clubs. They were yelling, "Kill them!"

The mob grew more and more violent until a club hit a soldier. He responded by firing his musket into the mob. The mob rushed closer, waving their clubs, and several soldiers panicked. They fired into the crowd. Several colonists were hit before the mob ran away. Five of those hit died. More trouble was sure to follow this bloody event.

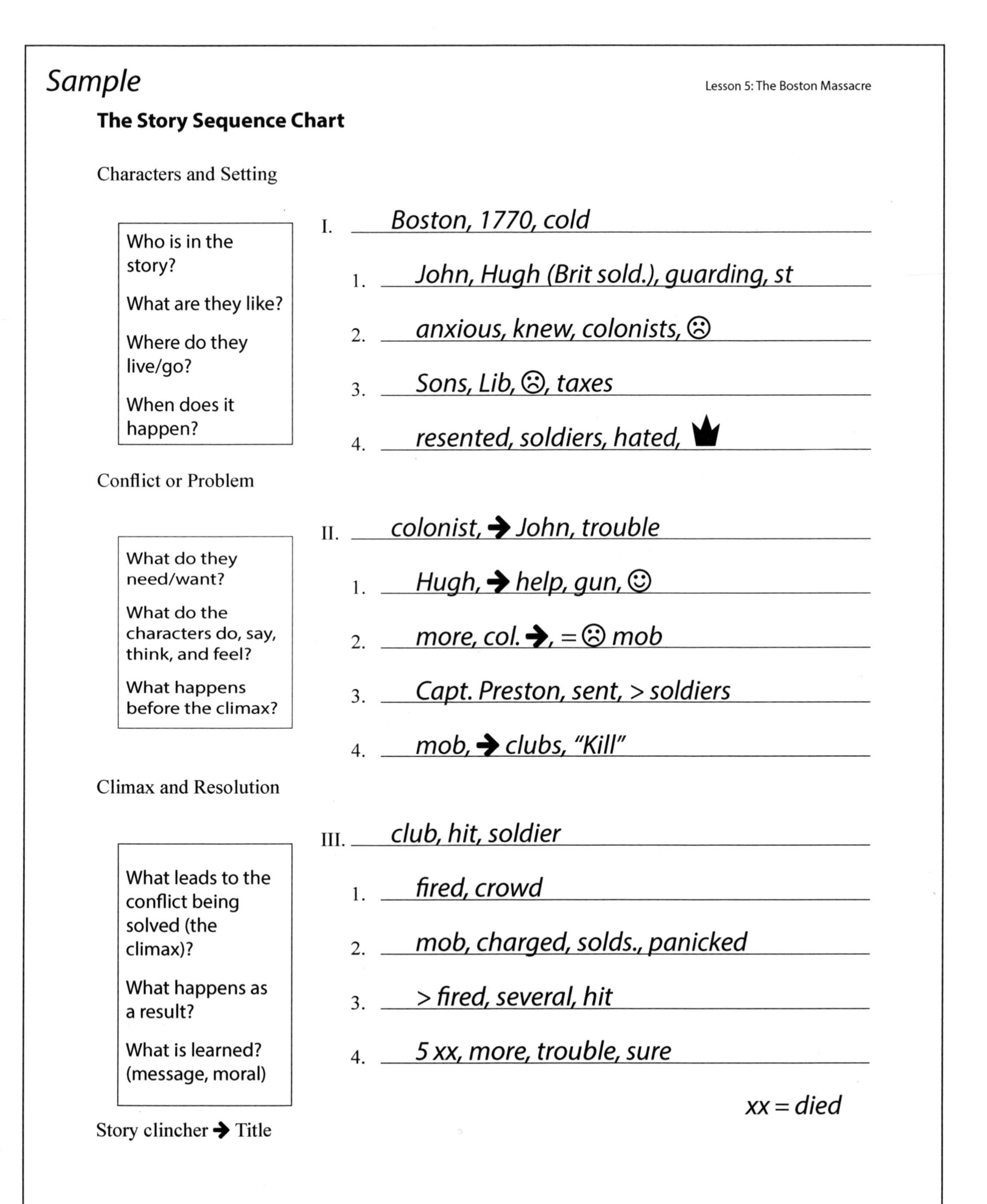

Sample

The Story Sequence Chart

Characters and Setting

Who is in the story? What are they like? Where do they live/go? When does it happen?	
I.	*Boston, 1770, cold*
1.	*John, Hugh (Brit sold.), guarding, st*
2.	*anxious, knew, colonists, ☹*
3.	*Sons, Lib, ☹, taxes*
4.	*resented, soldiers, hated, ♛*

Conflict or Problem

What do they need/want? What do the characters do, say, think, and feel? What happens before the climax?	
II.	*colonist, ➔ John, trouble*
1.	*Hugh, ➔ help, gun, ☺*
2.	*more, col. ➔, = ☹ mob*
3.	*Capt. Preston, sent, > soldiers*
4.	*mob, ➔ clubs, "Kill"*

Climax and Resolution

What leads to the conflict being solved (the climax)? What happens as a result? What is learned? (message, moral)	
III.	*club, hit, soldier*
1.	*fired, crowd*
2.	*mob, charged, solds., panicked*
3.	*> fired, several, hit*
4.	*5 xx, more, trouble, sure*

xx = died

Story clincher ➔ Title

You may want to let students work in pairs to come up with ideas. Be sure they all share their ideas.

Brainstorming Style

Describing the Setting

As you begin your story, help your readers feel as if they are there by including five-senses words. Also, use such words to help show the mood of the story. For example, a happy story might have bright sunshine, birds singing, and people smiling. But this story is not a happy story. What things could make you sense that trouble is near?

Write at least two sentences that describe the setting and help create the mood of the story. What would you see, hear, or feel on King Street as the story begins?

Example: *It was a cold, icy day in Boston in 1770. Hugh and John were shivering as fierce winds blasted sleet at their frozen faces.*

*The air was **freezing**, and **heavy** fog **clouded** the streets of **Boston**. **Icy** snow **crunched** under the feet of two British soldiers, Hugh and John were pacing back and forth to stay warm.*

Who-Which Clauses

Combine these two thoughts into one sentence using a *who* clause.

One colonist became especially irate. He threw a club at a soldier.

One colonist, who became especially irate, threw a club at a soldier.

-ly Adverbs

Add ideas for -ly adverbs to each of these sentences.

1. Hugh and John watched *warily, anxiously, suspiciously, intently, nervously*.
2. The two soldiers *carefully, closely, constantly* monitored the roads.
3. The mob *viciously, foolishly, angrily, indignantly, suddenly* yelled, "Kill them!"

Lesson 5: The Boston Massacre

Decorations: Alliteration

We have learned two of the IEW dress-ups that work well in any type of writing: -ly adverbs and *who-which* clauses. In stories, another kind of element of style is especially useful: decorations. Decorations are a bit fancier than dress-ups and add more sophistication and fun to stories.

In this lesson you will try the simplest of the decorations: alliteration. In this course alliteration is simply using three or more words close together that begin with the same sound. Our ear likes the repetition of sound. For example, which sentence sounds better to you?

The angry soldier prepared to fire his gun.

The raging redcoat readied his rifle.

Most people would like the sound of the second sentence better because of the repetition of the *r* sound.

Try to fill in the blanks below with words that begin with the given sound.

1. It was a d *dark, dreary*, d *drizzly, damp* day.
2. The wind w *whooshed, whipped* w *wildly, woefully* ly.
3. The soldiers stood s *silently, steadfastly* ly and s *solemnly, seriously* ly.
4. The captain could not control the m *massive, militant*, m *monstrous, mad* mob.

Because decorations are fancier than dress-ups, you will not be required to use alliteration in every paragraph of your story. You will only be required to use alliteration once anywhere in this story.

Vocabulary Word Ideas

Many vocabulary words will work well in this story. Write some ideas for including some. You may look ahead, too. Words for Lesson 6 will work well. You may look at the vocabulary chart on pages 254–255 for help.

Have students open to pages 254–255. How many words can they use in a sentence of the story? Give a ticket for each idea offered.

Vocabulary Word Ideas

The colonists provoked the soldiers.

The soldiers presumed that they were in danger.

The colonists were appalled that the soldier struck the patriot.

The crowd became hostile.

The gravity of the situation became clear.

The soldiers did not have time to contemplate before firing.

Conflict between the soldiers and patriots was inevitable.

Animosity grew as the indignant colonists continued to audaciously provoke the soldiers.

Unit 3: Retelling Narrative Stories

This picture is based on an engraving made by Paul Revere, which he called, "The Bloody Massacre Perpetrated in King-Street on March 5th, 1770." It was not an accurate depiction of the event. It was meant to stir up anger against the British.

Be sure students understand that both dress-ups have three boxes to check because each of the three sections of the story must include both dress-ups.

Alliteration has only one box because only one is required anywhere in this story.

Lesson 5 Checklist: The Boston Massacre

Name: ______________________________

STRUCTURE

☐	Name, lesson, and date in upper left-hand corner (See Appendix I.)	_____ (3 pts)
☐	Title centered and repeats or reflects 2–3 key words from story clincher	_____ (5 pts)
☐	Composition double-spaced	_____ (3 pts)
☐	Story follows Story Sequence Chart.	_____ (5 pts)
☐	Each paragraph (section of the story) contains at least four sentences.	_____ (5 pts)
☐	Checklist on top, final draft, rough draft, key word outline	_____ (3 pts)

STYLE Each paragraph must contain at least one of each element of style.

¶ 1	¶ 2	¶ 3	**Dress-Ups (underline one of each)**	**(3 pts each)**
☐	☐	☐	-ly adverb	_____ (9 pts)
☐	☐	☐	*who-which* clause	_____ (9 pts)

Decoration ("dec" in margin or italics if typed)

☐	alliteration *(allit)*	_____ (3 pts)

MECHANICS

☐	capitalization	_____ (1 pt)
☐	end marks and punctuation	_____ (1 pt)
☐	spelling and usage	_____ (2 pts)
☐	complete sentences (Does it make sense?)	_____ (1 pt)

More Advanced Additions (optional unless your teacher requires them of you)

☐ vocab word(s) (Label voc or bold.) _____

Total: _________/ 50

Custom Total: _________/___

Teachers are free to adjust a checklist by requiring only the stylistic techniques that have become easy, plus one new one. "EZ+1." Reproducible checklists are available (see blue page).

If you will have a best title contest, have students note that on this checklist.

Unit 3: Retelling Narrative Stories

Lesson 6: The Boston Tea Party

Structures: IEW Unit 3: Retelling Narrative Stories

Style: strong verb

Writing Topics: the Boston Tea Party

Optional Student Reading Assignment: during Lessons 5–10: *Johnny Tremain*

After you let students share their alliterations, collect the Boston Massacre stories. If you did the best title contest, write each title on the whiteboard, so students do not know which title belongs to which student. Read each title. Let students vote for their favorite two. (I have them close their eyes and raise their hands, but instead you could have them write their choices on paper.) Students may not vote for their own. The top title receives ten tickets. The next two receive five.

UNIT 3: RETELLING NARRATIVE STORIES

Lesson 6: The Boston Tea Party

Review

1. Share the alliteration from your Boston Massacre story.
2. Review the elements of the Story Sequence Chart. Fill in the blanks below.

I. When and where the story takes place *setting*

Who the story is about *characters*

II. The problem, want, or need *conflict*

What happens *problem*

III. What leads to the problem being solved? *climax*

The end result *resolution*

What can be learned *message or moral*

Teachers, provide sticky tabs or sticky notes; have students tab the strong verb section in the SRP.

Unit 3: Retelling Narrative Stories

Strong Verbs

In this lesson you will learn another IEW dress-up: *strong verbs*. Every sentence has a verb, but not all verbs are *strong* verbs. Strong verbs are words that show *action* that is easily pictured. They tell what someone or something is *doing*. For example, *zoom*, *shriek*, and *devour* are all strong verbs because they are easy to picture.

Some verbs are boring and are not easy to picture. For example, what is the verb in the following sentence?

The boy went onto the ship.

Does *went* show much action? Can you easily and clearly picture *went*? No, it communicates very little. But what about *dashed*?

The boy dashed onto the ship.

Can you picture *dashed* better than *went*? What does it communicate?

Verbs like *went* are boring and will, therefore, not be allowed when you write for this class. In the box below are the verbs that you may not use from this point forward.

Banned Verbs

go/went say/said

To help you avoid these banned verbs, there are lists of substitutes for them in the strong verbs section of the SRP. Look at some of those examples of strong verbs.

Find better words to use in the sample sentence:

The boy <u>*charged, stumbled, cartwheeled, trudged*</u> onto the ship.

How does each choice change the image of the sentence?

Find some stronger verbs to replace *said* in this sentence:

demanded
begged shrieked
whispered
boomed

"Give me the key," he said.

How does each change the image created?

Lesson 6: The Boston Tea Party

The Assignment

Day 1:

1. Read the story, "The Boston Tea Party" on the following page. Then, with the help of your teacher, complete the outline.

   Note: You may change the characters and add more detail to your story, as long as you do not change the historical facts. Read the student sample on page 229. From whose perspective is this story told?

2. Students take turns telling back the story, using one line of the outline at a time.
3. Brainstorm ideas for elements of style on pages 54–55.
4. Go over the checklist on page 56. Note that each of the three sections of the story should include all dress-ups; however, the decoration (alliteration) is only required once anywhere.
5. Look at vocabulary words for Lesson 6: *warily*, *vehemently*, *destined*, *confront*. Review all.

Days 2–4:

1. Polish your *Mayflower* Mishap story from Lesson 4.
2. Write your own version of the Boston Tea Party story, using only your key word outline and brainstorming ideas to guide you. *Write in your own words.*

   Remember, you may change the characters and add more detail to your story, as long as you do not change the historical facts.

3. Include and label everything on the checklist on page 56. Paperclip the checklist to your story.

Study for Vocabulary Quiz 2. It will cover words from Lessons 1–6.

Option for experienced Level B students: Complete the lesson in your Student Book first. If your parent or teacher assigns it, try to add the advanced style (similes) taught in the *U.S. History-Based Writing Lessons Blackline Masters*.

Unit 3: Retelling Narrative Stories

Source Text

The Boston Tea Party

On a cold December evening in 1773, the streets of Boston were crowded with people. Ten-year-old Paul was among them. He was there because his older brother, who belonged to the Sons of Liberty, had told him that something exciting was going to happen. He knew it had something to do with the three ships sitting in the harbor loaded with British tea, but he did not know what it was. He couldn't wait to find out.

As he stood there, Paul thought about what his father had told him. Colonists were refusing to buy the tea on the ships because England was charging a tax on it. They did not believe England had the right to tax them. They told England to take the tea back. But the Royal Governor of Boston would not let the ships sail back to England. He said the king's orders must be obeyed, and the tea must be unloaded by December 16. That was tonight.

Suddenly the crowd began to stir. Almost one hundred "Indians" cut through. As they passed, Paul saw that they were not Indians at all. They were the Sons of Liberty dressed like Indians. Their faces were rubbed with soot and painted with red and blue stripes. They were carrying axes! Paul watched as they boarded the ships. Then came whack! Whack! Whack! The "Indians" were chopping open the wooden chests. In the moonlight, the crowd watched smashed boxes drop over the sides of the ships into the ocean. Soon the scent of tea filled the night air. Cheers broke out and the crowd began to chant, "Rally Indians! Bring your axes, and tell King George we'll pay no taxes!" Paul knew King George would understand this message.

Sample

Lesson 6: The Boston Tea Party

The Story Sequence Chart

Characters and Setting

Who is in the story? What are they like? Where do they live/go? When does it happen?

I. *Dec., p.m., 1773, Boston*

1. *streets, crowded, noisy*
2. *Paul, 10 y-o, anxious*
3. *older, bro., Sons of Lib.*
4. *told, exciting, Brit., tea*

Conflict or Problem

What do they need/want? What do the characters do, say, think, and feel? What happens before the climax?

II. *colonists, refused, tea*

1. *Eng., ⊘ right, tax ☹*
2. *Royal, Gov. x, send, back*
3. *king, obeyed, unload*
4. *Dec. 16, tonight!*

Climax and Resolution

What leads to the conflict being solved (the climax)? What happens as a result? What is learned? (message, moral)

III. *≈100, Ind., cut, = Sons of Lib.*

1. *➔ ships, chopped, crated*
2. *🡻 tea, ocean*
3. *crowd, cheered, "Rally . . . "*
4. *knew, KG, understand, message*

Story clincher ➔ Title

Let students work in pairs. Have them all share their ideas.

Brainstorming Style

Describing the Setting

When you write a story, help your readers feel as if they are there. Help them see, hear, feel, smell, or taste things in the setting.

On the lines below, write two sentences that will help your readers see, hear, feel, taste, or smell the streets of Boston on the December night of the Boston Tea Party. (Realize that Boston is a harbor city. What might you see, hear, taste, or smell at a harbor?) You should be able to use your sentences in your story.

Example: (Five-senses words are in bold.)

*The **hazy** moonlight **peeked** through **dark** clouds and **reflected** off the **white** sails of the ships. People **shuffled** down the **icy** streets, **chatting** about the tea.*

Seagulls squawked overhead.

The icy wind reeked of fish and tea.

The ships were bobbing shadows.

Strong Verbs and -ly Adverbs

Cross out the banned verbs. In the first column following each sentence, write at least two stronger verbs that could replace the banned verb. Can you add -ly adverbs to the verbs?

	Strong Verbs	-ly Adverbs
The royal governor *said* that the king must be obeyed and the tea must be unloaded.	*insisted, demanded,*	*resolutely,*
	boomed	*vehemently*
The "Indians" *went* through the crowd.	*cut, paraded*	*determinedly,*
		quietly
The crates of tea *went* into the ocean.	*plunged, splashed,*	*haphazardly,*
	plummeted	*aimlessly*

Decorations: Alliteration

Add alliteration once anywhere in this story. If you need help, try filling in at least two of the blanks in this sentence with words that begin with the s sound. (Remember that some words that begin with a c can make the s sound. These words would count in the *s* alliteration.)

The ___stone city___ streets were s___slick silent___ with s___sleek spectators___

Vocabulary Word Ideas

Many vocabulary words will work well in this story. Look at page 254–255. Discuss ideas for including some vocabulary words in your story. This will help prepare you for the quiz next week.

Write some vocabulary words in phrases that could be used in your story.

___

___

___

Vocabulary Word Ideas

Colonists were appalled (or indignant) at the taxes.

They were provoked.

Much animosity existed between the king and the colonists.

An obstinate king presumed they would buy the tea.

Colonists resolved not to buy.

They irreverently tossed the tea.

They wore cunning disguises.

The king couldn't fathom their determination.

While watching, the crowd was transfixed.

I offer two tickets for each vocabulary word students use correctly in this story.

Unit 3: Retelling Narrative Stories

Lesson 6 Checklist: The Boston Tea Party

Name: ______________________________

STRUCTURE

- ☐ Name, lesson, and date in upper left-hand corner (See Appendix I.) _____ (5 pts)
- ☐ Title centered and repeats or reflects 2–3 key words from story clincher _____ (5 pts)
- ☐ Composition double-spaced _____ (5 pts)
- ☐ Story follows Story Sequence Chart. _____ (5 pts)
- ☐ Each paragraph (section of the story) contains at least four sentences. _____ (5 pts)
- ☐ Checklist on top, final draft, rough draft, key word outline _____ (5 pts)

STYLE Each paragraph must contain at least one of each element of style.

¶ 1	¶ 2	¶ 3	**Dress-Ups (underline one of each)**	**(3 pts each)**
☐	☐	☐	-ly adverb	_____ (9 pts)
☐	☐	☐	*who-which* clause	_____ (9 pts)
☐	☐	☐	strong verb	_____ (9 pts)

Decoration ("dec" in margin or italics if typed)

- ☐ alliteration *(allit)* _____ (3 pts)

MECHANICS

- ☐ capitalization _____ (1 pt)
- ☐ end marks and punctuation _____ (1 pt)
- ☐ spelling and usage _____ (2 pts)
- ☐ complete sentences (Does it make sense?) _____ (1 pt)
- ☐ banned words: go/went, say/said _____ (-1 pt)

More Advanced Additions (optional unless your teacher requires them of you)

- ☐ vocab word(s) (Label voc or bold.) _____
- ☐ simile or metaphor _____

Total: __________/ 65

Custom Total: __________/___

Teachers are free to adjust a checklist by requiring only the stylistic techniques that have become easy, plus one new one. "EZ+1." Reproducible checklists are available (see blue page).

Lesson 7: "The Shot Heard Round the World"

Structures: IEW Unit 3: Retelling Narrative Stories
Style: *because* clause; decoration – conversation
Writing Topics: the beginning of the American Revolutionary War
Optional Student Reading Assignment: during Lessons 5–10: *Johnny Tremain*

UNIT 3: RETELLING NARRATIVE STORIES

Lesson 7: "The Shot Heard Round the World"

Begin with Vocabulary Quiz 2.

In this lesson you will follow the same method as the previous two lessons to write another story. This time we will add another dress-up, the *because* clause. We will also discuss the use of conversation in stories because the source text includes conversation between the characters.

The *Because* Clause

The *because* clause is a clause (a group of words with a subject and a verb) that begins with the word *because*. Even though a *because* clause has a subject and a verb, it is not a complete sentence. Adding the word *because* to a sentence makes it an incomplete thought:

The colonists refused to buy British tea. (a sentence)

Because the colonists refused to buy British tea, (not a sentence)

An entire *because* clause must be added to a sentence that is already complete. It may be added before or after the complete sentence. Comma rules: If the *because* clause comes first, follow it with a comma. Do not put a comma before a *because* clause.

To check that you have a complete sentence, remove the word *because*. You should have two sentences left. What are the two sentences in the examples below?

The Revolutionary War was inevitable because America was destined to be free.

Because America was destined to be free, the Revolutionary War was inevitable.

A *because* clause helps add more detail to a sentence. It also helps explain why something happens. Try to add a *because* clause to each paragraph you write. When you do, underline the word *because*, and observe the comma rules.

Practice

Add more detail to each sentence by adding a *because* clause. You may add the clause to the beginning or the end of the sentence. Underline the word *because*. That is how you will indicate it in your paragraphs.

1. The redcoat sneered at the minuteman.

The redcoat sneered at the minuteman because he did not even have a uniform.

2. John would be the perfect spy.

Because he was only a boy, John would be the perfect spy.

Decoration: Conversation

Generally, stories are more engaging when characters talk to each other. This is called conversation or dialogue. The story you will write this week includes conversation, so you should understand how to punctuate and format it.

The SRP explains the rules for punctuating dialogue. Study those rules.

In this story, work on adding conversation. When you do, remember that *said* is a banned verb, so choose stronger verbs to describe how each comment is being spoken.

The Assignment

Day 1:

1. On page 62 outline the story on the following page in the same way you outlined previous stories. When you outline, remember that you need just the bare-bones key ideas to answer each Story Sequence Chart question. You can add details as you brainstorm and write.

   You may change the characters and some of the details in the story. For example, many students have enjoyed writing from the perspective of a son or daughter of a minuteman who follows his or her father to Lexington Green. Others have proposed ideas for how the first shot was fired (a squirrel knocking over a gun, a minuteman dropping his gun, etc.)

   However, do not change the historical facts, and do include the words of Captain John Parker and the British officer, because these are famous words in history. Quote them exactly.

2. Look at the new vocabulary words for Lesson 7: *diligent, squander, waver, inevitable.* Discuss ways you could use them in your story.

Days 2–4:

1. Polish your Boston Massacre story from Lesson 5.
2. Write your own version of "The Shot Heard Round the World" story, using only your key word outline and brainstorming ideas to guide you. *Write in your own words.*
3. Include and label everything on the checklist on page 65. Paper clip the checklist to your story.

Note: You will need to use all dress-ups in each section of this story. Since you will use dialogue, you will begin new paragraphs within sections. *To keep sections clearly separated, add extra space (double double-space) between them, like the source text does.*

Source Text

The Shot Heard Round the World

John was a farmer who lived in Massachusetts in 1775. He lived with his wife, Sarah, and their two small sons near Lexington. His village had always been small and peaceful, but recently King George had sent soldiers, and turmoil had taken over the land. One day, he returned home quite upset.

"Taxes, taxes, taxes on everything! What is King George doing? And his blasted redcoats are everywhere! Adams and Hancock are right. We need to store up arms to protect ourselves," he told Sarah.

"Do you think it will come to a war?" Sarah worriedly asked.

"I hope not, but we must be prepared. I've joined the minutemen who are hiding ammunition in Concord. We will be ready to fight if we have to."

In April the minutemen learned that the British were planning to seize their store of ammunition. Late one night there was a loud voice outside John's door. He leaned out the window and saw Paul Revere.

"Hurry, John," he said, "the regulars are coming out!"

John knew that meant that the redcoats were headed for Concord. He woke Sarah and told her, "I must go to Lexington. We must stop the redcoats from reaching our arms."

When John reached Lexington Green, there were about seventy other minutemen ready to face the redcoats. They waited anxiously. Then, early the next morning about seven hundred British troops arrived.

"Do not fire unless fired upon," Captain John Parker ordered the minutemen, "but if they mean to have a war, let it begin here!"

"Disperse, ye rebels," the British officer ordered.

The minutemen did not budge. John's heart was pounding. He prayed that the soldiers would turn back, but as the officer was speaking to the leaders of the minutemen, a shot rang out—then another, and another. When the shooting stopped, eight or nine minutemen were dead, and the redcoats were marching to Concord. Along the way more minutemen met them, and more fighting broke out. The British finally marched back to Boston. The minutemen had saved some of their arms, but they had also begun the Revolutionary War.

No one knows who fired that first shot, but because it began the war, the whole world took note. It has been called "the shot heard round the world."

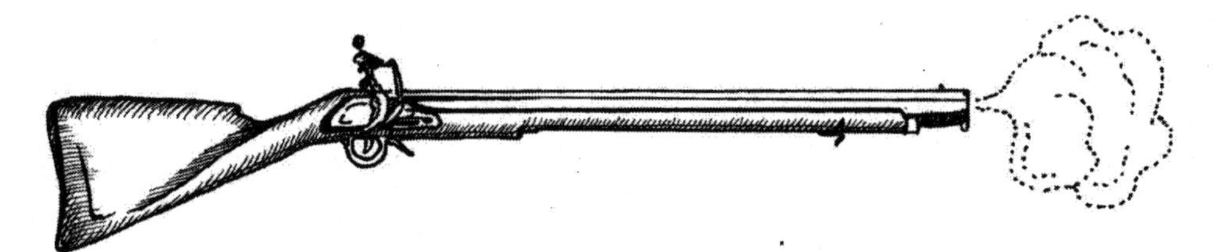

Students may copy the words of Captain Parker and the British officer from the source text because they are famous quotations.

Unit 3: Retelling Narrative Stories *Sample*

The Story Sequence Chart

Characters and Setting

Who is in the story? What are they like? Where do they live/go? When does it happen?	I. *Mass., 1775, near, Lexington* 1. *turmoil, b/c, taxes, redcoats (RC)* 2. *John, upset, "RC everywhere!"* 3. *"store, ammo, protect"* 4. *"joined, MM, ammo, Concord"*

Conflict or Problem

What do they need/want? What do the characters do, say, think, and feel? What happens before the climax?	II. *MM, disc., Brit., seize, ammo.* 1. *John, "I, ➔ Lexington w/MM"* 2. *70 MM, waited, 700 RC, appeared* 3. *Capt. Parker, "⊘ unless, fired"* 4. *Brit., officer, "Disperse rebels"*

Climax and Resolution

What leads to the conflict being solved (the climax)? What happens as a result? What is learned? (message, moral)	III. *MM, ⊘, budge, John, prayed* 1. *shot, more, shots* 2. *8 MM, dead, RC, Concord* 3. *MM, saved, ammo., started, Rev., War* 4. *? fired, 1st, "shot, round"*

Story clincher ➔ Title

Break students into three groups. Assign each group a scene to add conversation to (one scene from Section I and two from Section II). Each student should write his group's ideas. As they work, walk around the room. Check that they are formatting and punctuating the conversation correctly.

For fun, when everyone is done, let students act out the scene they wrote. That is, direct students to choose a character and read what the character says.

Brainstorming Style: Adding Conversation

You may work in groups for this activity.

Section I

Write a conversation in which John (or whoever you make your main character) explains to another character (wife, children, friend) why he joined the minutemen and that they are storing ammunition to be ready to fight for their rights. *Write ideas on your own paper. Remember to begin a new paragraph for each new speaker. Try to include a* because *clause in your conversation.*

"Sam, have you heard what the minutemen are up to?" asked Peter.

"They are collecting and storing ammunition at Concord," Sam responded.

"Will war come?" Peter asked with concern.

"I think it is likely. Many are angry at the king's taxes, the unjust laws, and his soldiers everywhere.

Section II

Write a conversation: What might John and his wife (or your characters, if you changed them) have said to each other as he was preparing to head for Lexington? What might he and his children have said to each other?

Or, what might the minutemen have said to each other as they waited for the redcoats or when they saw seven hundred approaching? *Try to include a* because *clause in your conversation.*

"I must go to Lexington with the other minutemen to save our arms. Sarah, please pack food and water for me," John declared.

"Dad, may I go with you? You taught me how to fire a gun," pleaded Tommy.

"No, son. Things could get dangerous, and if anything happened to you . . ."

"About seventy of us ready to face the redcoats if they show up," commented Sam.

"That is, if they show up. Are we sure they are coming?" Luke questioned.

"Over there!" one of the other men shouted. "Here they come!"

"That's a lot of red! How many do you suppose there are?" asked Peter.

"A lot more than seventy," responded Sam.

more minutemen as they marched

Vocabulary Word Ideas

The minutemen stood transfixed when they saw 700 British troops approaching.

The minutemen resolved to store their ammunition.

They had audaciously hid the ammunition.

Men confronted the redcoats without wavering.

The minutemen were appalled at the sight of eight dead.

America was destined for war.

Section III

In this section let's have some fun with another decoration, *alliteration*. Here is a basic sentence:

The tired redcoats looked around carefully for more minutemen as they marched.

Can you rewrite the sentence above to include alliteration with words that begin with a *w*? (***Hint***: Change *redcoats* to *warriors*. Then, what *w*- words could you use for "tired" and for "looked around carefully"? One of your vocabulary words from Lesson 6 is a possibility.)

The *weary, worn out* warriors *watched warily* for more minutemen as they marched.

(***Note***: Did you notice the alliteration with words that begin with *m*- in the original sentence? What are they?)

Other alliteration ideas: *Allow ideas for any section of the story.*

A wave of red rode rapidly toward them. They rapidly readied their rifles. They stood solemnly still. Soon the sun sank in the sky. The redcoats returned to Boston battered and bruised.

Vocabulary

Take out the vocabulary chart on page 254–255. How could some of the words be used in this story? To get started, fill in the blanks with the new vocabulary words for Lesson 7.

The minutemen were *diligent* in storing arms.

When confronted by seven hundred British troops, the minutemen did not *waver*.

After the shot was fired, war was *inevitable*.

Write more ideas for using vocabulary words from any lesson:

Lesson 7: "The Shot Heard Round the World"

Lesson 7 Checklist: The Shot Heard Round the World

Name: ______________________________

STRUCTURE

☐	Name, lesson, and date in upper left-hand corner (See Appendix I.)	____ (5 pts)
☐	Title centered and repeats or reflects 2–3 key words from story clincher	____ (5 pts)
☐	Composition double-spaced	____ (5 pts)
☐	Story follows Story Sequence Chart.	____ (5 pts)
☐	Each paragraph (section of the story) contains at least four sentences.	____ (5 pts)
☐	Checklist on top, final draft, rough draft, key word outline	____ (4 pts)

STYLE Each paragraph must contain at least one of each element of style.

¶ 1	¶ 2	¶ 3	Dress-Ups (underline one of each)	(3 pts each)
☐	☐	☐	-ly adverb	____ (9 pts)
☐	☐	☐	*who-which* clause	____ (9 pts)
☐	☐	☐	strong verb	____ (9 pts)
☐	☐	☐	*because* clause	____ (9 pts)

Decorations ("dec" in margin or italics if typed) (one per paragraph)

☐	alliteration *(allit)*	____ (2 pts)
☐	conversation	____ (2 pts)
☐	____________________	____ (2 pts)

MECHANICS

☐	capitalization	____ (1 pt)
☐	end marks and punctuation	____ (1 pt)
☐	spelling and usage	____ (1 pt)
☐	complete sentences (Does it make sense?)	____ (1 pt)
☐	banned words: go/went, say/said	____ (-1 pt)

More Advanced Additions (optional unless your teacher requires them of you)

☐	vocab word(s) (Label voc or bold.)	____
☐	simile or metaphor	____

Total: ________ / 75

Custom Total: ________ /___

Teachers are free to adjust a checklist by requiring only the stylistic techniques that have become easy, plus one new one. "EZ+1." Reproducible checklists are available (see blue page).

Unit 3: Retelling Narrative Stories

Lesson 8: Borrowing a Conflict

Structures: IEW Unit 3: Retelling Narrative Stories

Style: no new stylistic techniques

Writing Topics: an original story with a borrowed conflict

Optional Student Reading Assignment: during Lessons 5–10: *Johnny Tremain*

Students love the Alliteration Game! Divide the class into teams of 3–5 students. One at time, write the following words and blanks on the whiteboard. For each, give the teams one minute to create as much alliteration as possible. Words may be added before and after the original word. For example, if you write __________ *girls* __________________, it could turn into *Giddy girls giggled while gorillas gobbled grapes*. Allow them to use a thesaurus if they have one.

Teams get 1 pt. for each word that begins with the alliteration sound, so the sentence above would be worth 7 pts. Words must make sense. This is for the teacher to judge.

_________ bunnies _________

_________ toddlers _________

The _________ lion _________

(Add more of your own if you have time.)

UNIT 3: RETELLING NARRATIVE STORIES

Lesson 8: Borrowing a Conflict

Begin class by playing the Alliteration Game described in the Teacher's Manual.

In this lesson you will use what you have learned about stories to write your own story. You now know that every story must contain the basic elements of the Story Sequence Chart. Therefore, to help you write your story, first fill out a Story Sequence Chart on page 69 with your own ideas. The setting should be early America, and the characters should be appropriate for that setting.

To further help, you may "borrow" a conflict from a familiar story. To understand this better, read the sample story on page 231 of the Appendix. What familiar story did the student borrow a conflict from?

Other stories that may work well are listed below with possible changes to make them appropriate to early American times, but you may use any story you like.

"The Tortoise and the Hare"	A redcoat and a minuteman (or two minutemen) in some type of competition. It could be a race, but change the cause of the bragger losing. Do not make him take a nap. Or even better, make it a shooting competition.
"The Boy Who Cried Wolf"	The lookout who cried, "The redcoats are coming!"
"Rudolph the Red-Nosed Reindeer"	A young boy who wants to fight in the Revolution is made fun of by the others. By the end of the story, he is needed by George Washington because he is young.
"The Three Bears"	Three Hessians or British soldiers raid a colonist's home.

Other stories to consider: "The Milkmaid and Her Pail," "The Lion and the Mouse," "The Little Red Hen," "The Gingerbread Boy," or any Aesop fable or children's story.

For fun, break students into three groups. Give them 3–5 minutes to list familiar stories. At the end of the time, groups take turns reading one idea at a time. If another group has the same story written, both put an x by the title. If no one else wrote the same idea, they would circle it. Continue with each group reading one idea without an x at a time. The group with the most ideas circled wins.

Ideas

Little Red Riding Hood
The Fox and the Crow
Belling the Cat
The Crow and the Peacock
Jack and the Beanstalk
The Goose That Laid the Golden Egg
The Three Little Pigs
The Ants and the Grasshopper
The Country Mouse and the City Mouse
Midas and the Golden Touch
The Ugly Duckling
The Three Billy Goats Gruff
The Trojan Horse
Cinderella
Chicken Little
The Little Engine That Could

The Assignment

Day 1:

1. Choose a familiar story from which you can borrow a conflict. In a class setting, you may work in groups to get ideas flowing. What famous stories do all know? Make a class list.
2. Once you choose a story, use page 69 to outline your own version of it. Change the setting and characters. Try to make them early American.
3. Look at the vocabulary words for Lesson 8: *cunning, contemplate, gravity, persevere*. Can you think of ways to use any in your story? What about words from previous lessons?

Days 2–4:

1. Polish your "Boston Tea Party" story from Lesson 6.
2. Write your Borrowing a Conflict story. Be sure to include and label everything on the checklist on page 70. Attach the checklist to your final draft.
3. Study vocabulary words for Lessons 1–8.

Note: Bring a thesaurus to class next week.

Sample

Lesson 8: Borrowing a Conflict

The Story Sequence Chart

Characters and Setting

Questions	Notes
Who is in the story? What are they like? Where do they live/go? When does it happen?	I. *country, college, graduate* 1. *rural, dbl.-wide, trailer* 2. *gardened, own, food* 3. *city, cousin, visited* 4. *bustled, sophisticated, waiter*

Conflict or Problem

Questions	Notes
What do they need/want? What do the characters do, say, think, and feel? What happens before the climax?	II. *disagreed, city? country?* 1. *"Come, city, life, EZ!"* 2. *travelled, ➔ fancy, condo* 3. *subway, explosion! terrified, grad.* 4. *barely, escaped*

Climax and Resolution

Questions	Notes
What leads to the conflict being solved (the climax)? What happens as a result? What is learned? (message, moral)	III. *prefer, peaceful, lifestyle* 1. *live, simple, country* 2. *returned, trailer, garden* 3. *home, felt, happier* 4. *idea, ➔ raise, chickens!*

Story clincher ➔ Title

Unit 3: Retelling Narrative Stories

Lesson 8 Checklist: Borrowing a Conflict

Name: ______________________________

STRUCTURE

☐	Name, lesson, and date in upper left-hand corner (See Appendix I.)	_____	(5 pts)
☐	Title centered and repeats or reflects 2–3 key words from story clincher	_____	(5 pts)
☐	Composition double-spaced	_____	(5 pts)
☐	Story follows Story Sequence Chart.	_____	(5 pts)
☐	Each paragraph (section of the story) contains at least four sentences.	_____	(5 pts)
☐	Checklist on top, final draft, rough draft, key word outline	_____	(5 pts)

STYLE Each paragraph must contain at least one of each element of style.

	Dress-Ups (underline one of each)		**(5 pts each)**
☐ ☐ ☐	-ly adverb	_____	(15 pts)
☐ ☐ ☐	*who-which* clause	_____	(15 pts)
☐ ☐ ☐	strong verb	_____	(15 pts)
☐ ☐ ☐	*because* clause	_____	(15 pts)
	Decoration ("dec" in margin or italics if typed)		
☐	alliteration *(allit)*	_____	(3 pts)

MECHANICS

☐	capitalization	_____	(1 pt)
☐	end marks and punctuation	_____	(2 pts)
☐	spelling and usage	_____	(2 pts)
☐	complete sentences (Does it make sense?)	_____	(2 pts)
☐	banned words: go, went, say, said	_____	(-1 pt)

More Advanced Additions (optional unless your teacher requires them of you)

☐	vocab word(s) (Label voc or bold.)	_____
☐	simile or metaphor	_____
☐	conversation	_____

Total: __________/ 100

Custom Total: __________/___

Teachers are free to adjust a checklist by requiring only the stylistic techniques that have become easy, plus one new one. "EZ+1." Reproducible checklists are available (see blue page).

"Care of the sick"
Advanced Download paragraph

Lesson 9: Colonial Life

Structures: Unit 4: Summarizing a Reference

Style: reviewing stylistic techniques

Writing Topics: colonial life – church; law and order

Optional Student Reading Assignment: during Lessons 5–10: *Johnny Tremain*

Allow some students to share their "borrowing a conflict" story. Can the class guess which familiar story they borrowed the conflict from?

Teaching Writing: Structure and Style

Watch the sections for Unit 4 (Summarizing a Reference). At IEW.com/twss-help reference the TWSS Viewing Guides.

UNIT 4: SUMMARIZING A REFERENCE

Lesson 9: Colonial Life

Review

Stretch the following sentence as your teacher instructs:

The girl ate the last doughnut.

Summarizing a Reference

In this lesson you will learn to write reports by summarizing a reference. Reports do not have the same structure as stories, so the key word outlining method you will use will be different from the methods you have used thus far.

When you write a short report, most often you turn to an encyclopedia, textbook, or Internet article for information. These sources may have much more information than you need. In Lessons 9–12, you will read fairly lengthy sources and look for only enough information to create a summary. It is important to understand that you will not try to note every fact from your source text. You only want to look for the most important or most interesting facts. Remember, you will be "SOME-a-rizing."

Topic Sentences

When you write a report, your facts must be organized into paragraphs. Every paragraph must have a clear topic. A topic is what the paragraph is about. Begin each paragraph with a *topic sentence* that reveals its topic.

A topic sentence should not say anything like "In this paragraph I will tell you about ... " or "The topic of this paragraph is ... ". It should simply make a statement about the topic.

Clinchers

It is also a good technique to end a paragraph by reminding the reader of the topic. You do this in the last sentence by repeating or reflecting (using words that mean the same thing) two to three key words from the topic sentence. We call this last sentence the *clincher*.

Remember the topic-clincher rule:

The topic sentence and clincher sentence of a paragraph must repeat or reflect two to three key words.

Practicing Elements of Style

Instruct students to write the sentence on a sheet of paper turned sideways, with space between words. Then, one at a time, direct them to do the following:

1. Change the boring verb to a strong verb.
2. Add a *because* clause. Remember the comma after the clause if it is not at the end of the sentence.
3. Add a *who-which* clause. Remember the commas if needed.
4. Add an -ly adverb.
5. Try to add alliteration. When everyone is finished, have some students read theirs.

Example: Because no one was watching, the audacious *girl greedily gobbled* the donut that had been left for her brother, who was now indignant.

Topic Sentences

Ask the kids what they are interested in. Choose one idea to break into topics. For example, if they say they are interested in horses, ask what topics this subject could be broken into? (wild, domesticated, training, care, breeds, and more). So, if I begin a paragraph with "there are many breeds of horses," what will this paragraph discuss? How could you begin a paragraph about caring for horses?

Clinchers

For example, for the above topic sentence about breeds, a clincher could be this: Each of the many breeds is special in its own way.

Sample Report with Topic Sentences and Clinchers

Notice and highlight the key words in the topic sentences and clinchers of this report.

The First Thanksgiving

After sixty-three days at sea, the *Mayflower* finally reached the New World. It did not arrive in Virginia as planned, but it reached what is now the state of Massachusetts. Before landing, the Pilgrim men had a meeting. They signed an agreement to obey all the laws made for the colony. This was called The *Mayflower* Compact. Then they began to search for a place to build a settlement. They chose Plymouth, a harbor discovered a few years earlier by Captain John Smith. On December 10, 1620, they finally walked onto the new land and thanked God for a safe journey.

The first winter was colder and more difficult than any the Englishmen had ever experienced. It was too late to plant crops, so the Pilgrims had little food. Many of them were sick or exhausted from the long voyage. More than half of the Pilgrims died. At one point in time, there were only six or seven people well enough to take care of the sick and bury the dead. The Pilgrims prayed continually for help to persevere through that dreadful winter.

Then in the spring, the Pilgrims were relieved and thankful when some Indians visited Plymouth and helped them. Surprisingly, two of them, Samoset and Squanto, could speak English. They showed the Pilgrims how to plant corn, and they showed them the best places to fish and hunt. They also brought their chief, Massasoit, who made a peace treaty with the Plymouth colony. By summer the Pilgrims had houses built to protect them from the next winter, they had a bountiful harvest, and they were at peace with the Indians. They decided to have a feast to thank God. Massasoit arrived with ninety Indians. Together the Pilgrims and Indians celebrated the first "Thanksgiving" in the New World.

The Assignment

Day 1:

1. Read Source Text 1 on the following page. It is more than one paragraph, but you will have to choose the facts you want from it in order to write ONE summary paragraph.

   On the top line of the blank KWO, page 75, write key words that will help you write a topic sentence. What will the paragraph be about?

2. Next, reread the source text, and look for *no more than seven* of the most important or most interesting facts. You cannot write everything there is in the source text in one summary paragraph. *You will have to leave some information out. You are summarizing.*

   To help you remember each fact you choose, write no more than three key words on one line of the blank outline.

3. Without looking at the source text, tell back the meaning of each line of your notes. Remember, it may take more than one sentence to tell back the meaning of a line of notes. If you do not understand one of your notes, fix it so that you do.
4. Brainstorm elements of Structure and Style together using page 76.
5. If there is time, outline the Source Text 2 on page 78. If not, do for homework.

Days 2–4:

1. Polish your "Shot Heard Round the World" story from Lesson 7.
2. Write ONE paragraph about church in colonial times using only your key word outline and brainstorming ideas to guide you. *Write in your own words.*
3. Include and label everything on the checklist on page 77.
4. If your parent or teacher assigns it, repeat the process to write one paragraph about law and order in colonial times using pages 78–81.
5. Learn the new vocabulary words for Lesson 9. Review all.

Option for experienced Level B students: Complete the lesson in your Student Book first. If your parent or teacher assigns it, repeat the above process for a third paragraph: Care of the Sick in Colonial Times.

You will most likely have to help students quite a bit at first. Most students find limiting their notes difficult until they see it modeled. See the sample key word outline for help. Many details in the source text are unnecessary. Let students choose the ones they think are most important or most interesting, but limit them. Ask them which facts they can do without.

Unit 4: Summarizing a Reference

Source Text 1

Colonial Life: Church

In the New England colonies, life centered in the church and religious beliefs. The Bible, as the people understood it, was their guide. Even children were expected to read the entire Bible several times. On Sundays everyone attended the church, called the meetinghouse, for almost the whole day. However, families did not sit together. Men sat on one side and women on the other. Native Americans and slaves also had a separate section. Services were long. A sermon could last from two to five hours. There was a service in the morning and one again in the afternoon, and everyone went to both. After the services, the minister told all the news of the week.

The meetinghouse was not fancy. Often it was cold and damp. The benches were hard and uncomfortable, too. So, there was a watchman called the tithing-man. He had a long stick with a hard ball at one end and a fox's tail at the other. Children who misbehaved received a bop on the head. Adults who fell asleep were tickled with the tail. If someone whispered or smiled, the tithing-man would report them. They would be fined. The tithing-man, and others, also made sure no one left early. No one could leave until the minister and his wife had gone. Sunday was a long day devoted to God in colonial America.

Bibliography

Day, Nancy. *Your Travel Guide to Colonial America*. Minneapolis: Runestone Press, 2001. Print.

McGovern, Ann. *If You Lived in Colonial Times*. New York: Scholastic Books, 1992. Print.

Sample

Lesson 9: Colonial Life

Key Word Outline

I. *church, important, colonial Xs*

1. *life, centered, [church symbol], Bible*
2. *Sunday, all, church*
3. *services, long (2–5 hrs.), a.m. + p.m.*
4. *tithing-man, rod, ⊙ ⊙*
5. *children, misbehave, bop*
6. *adults, sleep, foxtail*
7. *whisper = fine*

Clincher

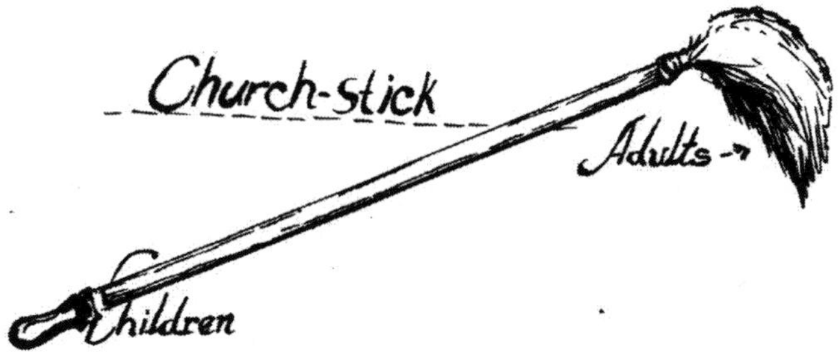

Church-stick

Adults

Children

The X is my symbol for times because it is the times symbol in math.

Walk around and help students as necessary. Have students share their ideas with the class.

Brainstorming

You will need to include all the dress-ups listed on the checklist, but our brainstorming will focus on the *because* clause and the new skill of using topic sentences and clinchers.

Topic Sentences and Clinchers

Write an idea for a topic sentence for this paragraph. Use or reflect two to three key words from your key word outline that tell the topic of the paragraph. Highlight them as you will in your paragraph.

*In **colonial times** everyone was expected to attend **church**.*

***Church** was extremely important in **colonial times**.*

Now write a possible clincher to match the above topic sentence. Highlight the two to three words you repeat or reflect.

*No one missed **church** on **Sundays**.*

***Sundays** were devoted to **church** in the colonies.*

Because Clause

Write a sentence with a *because* clause that you could use in your paragraph. Underline the word *because*.

Remember the punctuation rule: Use a comma after the entire clause (unless it is the end of the sentence), but do not use a comma before the clause.

On Sundays everyone attended church <u>because</u> all were devoted to their religion.

Lesson 9: Colonial Life

Lesson 9 Checklist: Colonial Life: Church

Name: ______________________________

STRUCTURE

☐	Name and date in upper left-hand corner	_____ (1 pt)
☐	Title centered and repeats or reflects 2–3 key words of clincher	_____ (1 pt)
☐	Composition double-spaced	_____ (1 pt)
☐	Topic-clincher key words repeat or reflect (highlighted or bold).	_____ (5 pts)
☐	Each paragraph contains at least 4 sentences.	_____ (2 pts)
☐	Checklist on top, final draft, rough draft, KWO	_____ (1 pt)

STYLE Each paragraph must contain at least one of each element of style.

	Dress-Ups (underline one of each)	**(5 pts each)**
☐	-ly adverb	_____ (5 pts)
☐	*who-which* clause	_____ (5 pts)
☐	strong verb	_____ (5 pts)
☐	*because* clause	_____ (5 pts)
	Decoration ("dec" in margin or italics if typed)	
☐	alliteration *(allit)*	_____ (5 pts)

MECHANICS

☐	capitalization	_____ (1 pt)
☐	end marks and punctuation	_____ (1 pt)
☐	spelling and usage	_____ (1 pt)
☐	complete sentences (Does it make sense?)	_____ (1 pt)
☐	banned words: go, went, say, said	_____ (-1 pt)

	More Advanced Additions (optional unless your teacher requires them of you)	
☐	vocab word(s) (Label voc or bold.)	_____
☐	simile or metaphor	_____

Total: _________/ 40

Custom Total: _________/___

Teachers are free to adjust a checklist by requiring only the stylistic techniques that have become easy, plus one new one. "EZ+1." Reproducible checklists are available (see blue page).

Unit 4: Summarizing a Reference

Source Text 2

Colonial Life: Law and Order

Law and order were important in colonial America. The colonists had strict laws with harsh punishments for breaking them. For example, people could be fined heavily for lying, calling people names, or making rude remarks. One man in Virginia spoke badly of the governor. His tongue was punctured, and then he was banished from the community.

The most common punishments for crimes were intended to cause public shame. For example, some criminals were whipped at the whipping post in front of the meetinghouse. Others were placed in stocks with a card around their necks that told their crime. People who passed by would throw rotten food and mud at them. Another punishment was to burn the name of the crime onto the guilty person's hand. Public hanging was also a common punishment for stealing. A man who stole just one silver spoon could be hanged.

Less serious offenses also had cruel consequences. Women who talked back to their husbands were tied to a stool and dunked in water in a public display. Children who did not behave in school received a whipping from the schoolmaster. Students who talked in class had a stick, called a whispering stick, put into their mouths. Students who did not pay attention had to wear either a dunce cap or a sign that said "Idle Boy." The colonists kept strict law and order.

Bibliography

Day, Nancy. *Your Travel Guide to Colonial America.* Minneapolis: Runestone Press, 2001. Print.

McGovern, Ann. *If You Lived in Colonial Times.* New York: Scholastic Books, 1992. Print.

Sample

Lesson 9: Colonial Life

Key Word Outline

I. *col., kept, strict, law & ord.*

1. *punishments, harsh, breaking*
2. *> fine, lies, name-calling*
3. *most, public, shame*
4. *whipping, stocks, hanging*
5. *women, disrespect, husb., dunk*
6. *children, talk, sch., whisp. sticks*
7. *⊘ attention = dunce cap*

Clincher

Unit 4: Summarizing a Reference

Brainstorming

You will need to include all the dress-ups listed on the checklist, but our brainstorming will keep focusing on the *because* clause and the new skill of using topic sentences and clinchers.

Topic Sentences and Clinchers

Write an idea for a topic sentence for this paragraph. Use or reflect two to three key words from your key word outline that tell the topic of the paragraph. Highlight them as you will in your paragraph.

*Colonists maintained **law** and **order** by enforcing harsh **punishments** for misbehavior.*

*Colonists kept **strict law** and **order**.*

Now write a possible clincher to match the above topic sentence. Highlight the words you repeat or reflect.

*Fear of these dreaded **punishments** helped keep **law** and **order** in the colonies.*

***Laws** were very **strict** in the **colonies**.*

Because Clause

Write a sentence with a *because* clause that you could use in your paragraph. Underline the word *because*.

Jail was not a common punishment <u>because</u> colonists believed public humiliation worked better to make people behave.

Lesson 9: Colonial Life

Lesson 9 Checklist: Colonial Life: Law and Order

Name: ______________________________

STRUCTURE

☐	Name and date in upper left-hand corner	_____ (1 pt)
☐	Title centered and repeats or reflects 2–3 key words from clincher	_____ (1 pt)
☐	Composition double-spaced	_____ (1 pt)
☐	Topic-clincher repeats or reflects 2–3 key words (highlighted or bold).	_____ (5 pts)
☐	Each paragraph contains at least four sentences.	_____ (2 pts)
☐	Checklist on top, final draft, rough draft, KWO	_____ (1 pt)

STYLE Each paragraph must contain at least one of each element of style.

	Dress-Ups (underline one of each)	**(5 pts each)**
☐	-ly adverb	_____ (5 pts)
☐	*who-which* clause	_____ (5 pts)
☐	strong verb	_____ (5 pts)
☐	*because* clause	_____ (5 pts)
	Decoration ("dec" in margin or italics if typed)	
☐	alliteration *(allit)*	_____ (5 pts)

MECHANICS

☐	capitalization	_____ (1 pt)
☐	end marks and punctuation	_____ (1 pt)
☐	spelling and usage	_____ (1 pt)
☐	complete sentences (Does it make sense?)	_____ (1 pt)
☐	banned words: go, went, say, said	_____ (-1 pt)

	More Advanced Additions (optional unless your teacher requires them of you)	
☐	vocab word(s) (Label voc or bold.)	_____
☐	simile and metaphor	_____
☐	"Care of the Sick" paragraph	_____

Total: _________/ 40

Custom Total: _________/___

Teachers are free to adjust a checklist by requiring only the stylistic techniques that have become easy, plus one new one. "EZ+1." Reproducible checklists are available (see blue page).

Unit 4: Summarizing a Reference

Lesson 10: The Declaration of Independence

Structures: Unit 4: Summarizing a Reference
Style: quality adjective
Writing Topics: colonial life – church; law and order
Optional Student Reading Assignment: during Lessons 5–10: *Johnny Tremain*

UNIT 4: SUMMARIZING A REFERENCE

Lesson 10: The Declaration of Independence

Review

1. Play a review game such as the Question Bag Game or Tic-Tac-Toe.
2. Read your topic sentences and clinchers from the colonial life paragraphs.

In this lesson you will follow the procedure taught in Lesson 9 to write a paragraph about the Declaration of Independence. You will also learn to add a new dress-up to your paragraph: the quality adjective.

The Assignment

Day 1:

1. Read the source text on the following page. It is fairly long, so your job will be to choose only some of the facts in order to summarize the information. As you read, put a * (an asterisk) by the facts you believe are most important or most interesting.
2. On the blank outline on page 85, write key words for a topic.
3. Reread the source text. Note four to seven facts you wish to include.
4. In your own words, tell back the meaning of each line of your notes.
5. On page 87 learn a new dress-up: quality adjectives. Then, brainstorm ideas for adding elements of Structure and Style.

Days 2–4:

1. Polish your story from Lesson 8.
2. Use your key word outline to write your 1-paragraph summary of the Declaration of Independence.
3. Remember to highlight words in your topic sentence and clincher that tell the topic of the paragraph. Attach the checklist on page 88.
4. Learn the new vocabulary words for Lesson 10. Review all. Try to use some in your paragraph.
5. If you are reading the literature, obtain *The Sign of the Beaver* by Elizabeth George Speare for next week.

Option for experienced Level B students: Complete the lesson in your Student Book first. If your parent or teacher assigns it, repeat the above process for a second paragraph: The Constitution.

Students will likely need much help. Teachers should model the note-making process and help limit the facts they choose. Help them look for the interesting or important ideas and facts. Ask them which facts they can do without. Write a sample key word outline on the whiteboard.

Unit 4: Summarizing a Reference

Source Text

The Declaration of Independence

The Declaration of Independence is the document that declared America to be its own independent nation. It was written when the thirteen American colonies belonged to England. King George ruled them through his governors and kept order by sending his soldiers. When he began to tax Americans heavily and take away some of their rights, the colonists became angry. When they asked King George for fair treatment, he did not listen. Instead, he sent more soldiers. So Americans decided to declare themselves free from his rule. They formed a Congress made up of men from each of the colonies.

This Congress chose Thomas Jefferson to write the document that would declare America to be a free, independent country. It took him seventeen days. In it he stated that all men have God-given rights like "Life, Liberty, and the pursuit of Happiness." He said that if a government takes away those rights, the people have the right to overthrow it. Then he listed many charges against King George to show that he was a tyrant. He declared America free from the king and from England. Congress made only a few changes to what he wrote before they adopted it on July 4, 1776. Every member signed the document, even though they knew it was treason. The Declaration of Independence proclaimed America's independence and inspired the colonists to fight for freedom. It was the beginning of a new nation.

Sample

Lesson 10: The Declaration of Independence

Key Word Outline

I. *Dec. Ind., decl., Amer., free*

1. *B4, Eng, controlled, w/gov., soldiers*
2. *, taxed, 0 fair, 0 listen*
3. *Congress, T. Jefferson, write, Dec.*
4. *17 days, stated, men w/rts*
5. *"life, liberty, pursuit of happiness"*
6. *gov't, take, rts, OK, ppl, overthrow*
7. *Cong., adopted, July 4, 1776*

Clincher

Unit 4: Summarizing a Reference

Brainstorming Structure

You will need to include all the dress-ups listed on the checklist, but our brainstorming will continue to focus on the *because* clause and the important skill of using topic sentences and clinchers.

Topic Sentences and Clinchers

Write an idea for a topic sentence for this paragraph. Use or reflect the two to three key words on your key word outline that tell the topic of the paragraph. Highlight them as you will in your paragraph.

*When **Americans** wanted to have their own country, they wrote the Declaration of **Independence**.*

Now write a possible clincher to match the above topic sentence. Highlight two to three key words you repeat or reflect.

***America** became a new, **free nation**.*

Lesson 10: The Declaration of Independence

Brainstorming Style

Quality Adjectives

As you write your paragraph, look for a place to add a new dress-up: the quality adjective. An adjective is a word that describes a noun—a person, place, thing, or idea. Adjectives tell things like *what color, what size, what shape, what kind, what emotion, how many*. Most adjectives can be put into phrases like these:

the _____________ *pen*   *the* _____________ *person*

Can you think of some adjectives to describe the things you see around you? What adjectives could you use to describe the following nouns in your summary paragraph?

the *unjust, unreasonable, obstinate* king

the *angry, indignant, determined* colonists

the *bold, inspiring, renowned* Declaration of Independence

Because Clause

Write a sentence with a *because* clause that you could use in your paragraph. Underline the word *because*.

The colonists were angry because King George seemed tyrannical.

____

Unit 4: Summarizing a Reference

Lesson 10 Checklist: The Declaration of Independence

Name: ______________________________

STRUCTURE

☐	Name and date in upper left-hand corner	_____ (1 pt)
☐	Title centered and repeats or reflects 2–3 key words from clincher	_____ (1 pt)
☐	Composition double-spaced	_____ (1 pt)
☐	Topic-clincher repeats or reflects 2–3 key words (highlighted or bold).	_____ (5 pts)
☐	Each paragraph contains at least four sentences.	_____ (2 pts)
☐	Checklist on top, final draft, rough draft, key word outline	_____ (1 pt)

STYLE

Each paragraph must contain at least one of each element of style.

	Dress-Ups (underline one of each)	**(5 pts each)**
☐	-ly adverb	_____ (5 pts)
☐	*who-which* clause	_____ (5 pts)
☐	strong verb	_____ (5 pts)
☐	*because* clause	_____ (5 pts)
☐	quality adjective	_____ (5 pts)
	Decoration ("dec" in margin or italics if typed)	
☐	alliteration *(allit)*	_____ (5 pts)

MECHANICS

☐	capitalization	_____ (1 pt)
☐	end marks and punctuation	_____ (1 pt)
☐	spelling and usage	_____ (1 pt)
☐	complete sentences (Does it make sense?)	_____ (1 pt)
☐	banned words: go, went, say, said	_____ (-1 pt)

	More Advanced Additions (optional unless your teacher requires them of you)	
☐	vocab word(s) (Label voc or bold.)	_____
☐	simile or metaphor	_____
☐	"The Constitution" paragraph	_____

Total: __________/ 45

Custom Total: __________/___

Teachers are free to adjust a checklist by requiring only the stylistic techniques that have become easy, plus one new one. "EZ+1." Reproducible checklists are available (see blue page).

Lesson 11: The Louisiana Purchase

Structures: Unit 4: Summarizing a Reference

Style: www.asia.b clause

Writing Topics: the Louisiana Purchase

Optional Student Reading Assignment: during Lessons 11–12: *The Sign of the Beaver*

UNIT 4: SUMMARIZING A REFERENCE

Lesson 11: The Louisiana Purchase

Review

Play a vocabulary review game from the Teacher's Manual.

In this lesson we will continue summarizing from a reference, but before we do, we will practice more with the new dress-up from Lesson 10, the quality adjective. You will also learn a new dress-up, the www.asia.b clause.

Banned Words

In Lesson 10 you learned about adjectives. Descriptive words like adjectives make your writing more enjoyable; however, there are some adjectives that are overused or boring. You do not want to use those. Look at the sentences below. Underline the adjectives. Which are boring adjectives? Which are more precise?

The big mountains were pretty. *The towering mountains were majestic.*

Words that you may not use when you write for this class are listed below.

Banned Adjectives
pretty/ugly big

Those adjectives are banned because they are vague. They do not paint clear pictures in your reader's mind. Take out your SRP. Look for quality adjectives that you can substitute for banned adjectives.

When you write, be sure *not* to use those words. When you are tempted to use one of them, use a thesaurus or the *Student Resource Packet* to help you replace it with a stronger word.

Practice

Replace the banned words with quality adjectives in the sentences below.

1. The pretty stream was filled with big fish.

The (sparkling, flowing, magnificent) stream was filled with (fat, enormous, giant, massive) fish.

2. The villain was evil and ugly.

The villain was (malicious, harmful) and (hideous, grotesque, beastly, repulsive.)

The Assignment

Day 1:

1. Read the source text on the following page. As you read, put an asterisk by the facts you believe are most important or most interesting. Also circle any banned words you notice. You may not use them when you write.
2. On the blank outline on page 93, write key words for a topic.
3. Reread the source text. Note four to seven facts you wish to include.
4. In your own words, tell back the meaning of each line of your notes.
5. On page 94 you will learn a new dress-up, the www.asia.b clause.
6. On page 94 brainstorm ideas for elements of style.
7. Optional: Discuss ideas for the adjective poem on page 96.

Days 2–4:

1. Polish your Colonial Life report from Lesson 9.
2. Use your key word outline to write a 1-paragraph summary of the Louisiana Purchase.
3. Remember to highlight two to three key words in your topic sentence and clincher that tell the topic of the paragraph. Follow and attach the checklist on page 95.
4. Optional: Write the adjective poem on pages 96–97.
5. Learn the new vocabulary words for Lesson 11. Review all. Try to use some in your paragraph.

Literature Suggestion

With Lessons 11–12 read *The Sign of the Beaver* by Elizabeth George Speare.

You will most likely have to help students quite a bit at first. Most students find limiting their notes difficult until they see it modeled. See the sample key word outline for help. Many details in the source text are unnecessary. Let students choose the ones they think are most important or most interesting, but limit them. Ask them which facts they can do without.

Unit 4: Summarizing a Reference

Source Text

The Louisiana Purchase

Everyone enjoys getting a good deal. Thomas Jefferson, our third president, got a great deal for America! When he first took office in 1801, America included the land along the East Coast, stretching only as far west as the Mississippi River. The land west of the great river belonged to France. Its emperor, Napoleon Bonaparte, hoped to build a big French empire in what was known as the Louisiana Territory. He controlled important parts of the Mississippi River and sometimes hindered America's ability to use it to trade goods. So Jefferson sent men to France to try to buy New Orleans, an important port city, from him. When they arrived in 1803, Napoleon was in desperate need of money for wars he was fighting. To the surprise of Jefferson's men, Napoleon wanted to sell not just New Orleans, but the entire Louisiana Territory. He sold all 828,000 square miles for just $15 million. That's less than four cents per acre! This big purchase almost doubled the size of the United States. When Jefferson sent Lewis and Clark to explore and map it, they found that it was very pretty land, rich with resources. What an amazing purchase!

Bibliography

Dethloff, Henry C. "Louisiana Purchase." *The World Book Encyclopedia.* International ed. 2001. Print.

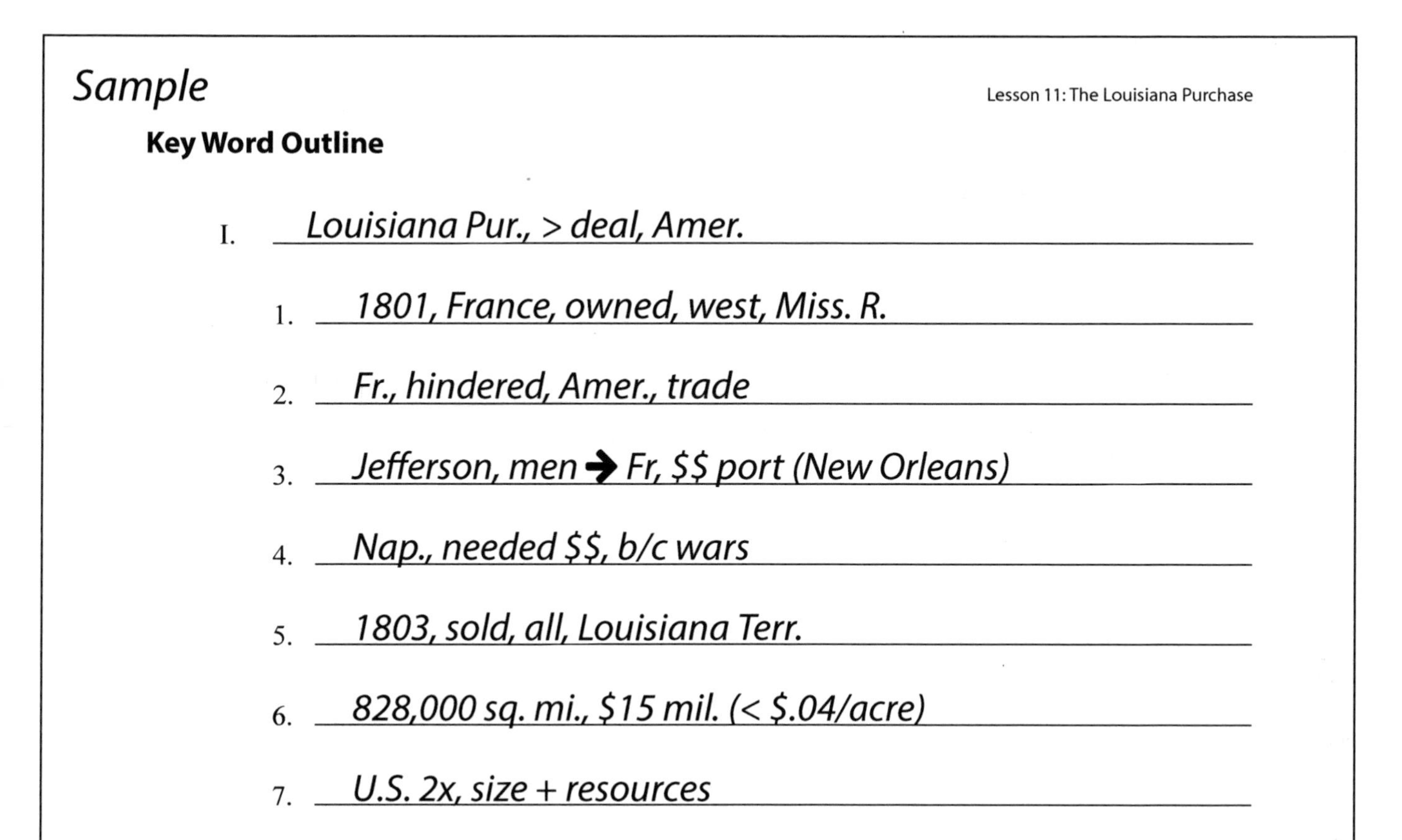

Sample

Lesson 11: The Louisiana Purchase

Key Word Outline

I. *Louisiana Pur., > deal, Amer.*

1. *1801, France, owned, west, Miss. R.*
2. *Fr., hindered, Amer., trade*
3. *Jefferson, men ➔ Fr, $$ port (New Orleans)*
4. *Nap., needed $$, b/c wars*
5. *1803, sold, all, Louisiana Terr.*
6. *828,000 sq. mi., $15 mil. (< $.04/acre)*
7. *U.S. 2x, size + resources*

Clincher

www.asia.b Clause

You have been using a *because* clause for a while. Now you will learn to form the same type of clause with other words. This acronym will help you remember them: www.asia.b. Each letter is the first letter of one of the words shown below that can begin a clausal dress-up:

when while where as since if although because

p. 109

A www.asia.b clause helps you add more detail to a sentence. Memorize these words.

Example: *The United States almost doubled in size* when *President Thomas Jefferson purchased the Louisiana Territory.*

Brainstorming

Clauses

1. Finish this sentence by using a www.asia clause. (Do not use *because* since you have already been practicing using it.)

   President Jefferson was delighted *when Napoleon wanted to sell all of the Louisiana Territory.*

2. Write a sentence with a *who* or *which* clause that you might use in your summary paragraph Remember the commas.

   Napoleon, who needed money for fighting wars, sold all his land.

   The Louisiana Purchase, which doubled the size of the United States, was rich with resources.

Quality Adjectives

Write ideas for quality adjectives that could replace the banned adjectives.

The Louisiana Purchase was a big, pretty territory, rich with resources.

The Louisiana Purchase was a (spacious, vast,) (breathtaking, beautiful) territory, rich with resources.

Adjective Poem

For more practice with quality adjectives, try the adjective poem described on page 96. You can illustrate it and use it as the cover of your polished draft notebook.

Lesson 11: The Louisiana Purchase

Lesson 11 Checklist: The Louisiana Purchase

Name: ______________________________

STRUCTURE

☐	Name and date in upper left-hand corner	_____ (1 pt)
☐	Title centered and repeats or reflects 2–3 key words from clincher	_____ (1 pt)
☐	Composition double-spaced	_____ (1 pt)
☐	Topic-clincher repeats or reflects 2–3 key words (highlighted or bold).	_____ (5 pts)
☐	Each paragraph contains at least four sentences.	_____ (2 pts)
☐	Checklist on top, final draft, rough draft, key word outline	_____ (1 pt)

STYLE Each paragraph must contain at least one of each element of style.

	Dress-Ups (underline one of each)	**(5 pts each)**
☐	ly adverb	_____ (5 pts)
☐	*who-which* clause	_____ (5 pts)
☐	strong verb	_____ (5 pts)
☐	quality adjective	_____ (5 pts)
☐	www.asia.b clause	_____ (5 pts)
	Decoration ("dec" in margin or italics if typed)	
☐	alliteration *(allit)*	_____ (5 pts)

MECHANICS

☐	capitalization	_____ (1 pt)
☐	end marks and punctuation	_____ (1 pt)
☐	spelling and usage	_____ (1 pt)
☐	complete sentences (Does it make sense?)	_____ (1 pt)
☐	banned words: go, went, say, said, pretty, ugly, big	_____ (-1 pt)

	More Advanced Additions (optional unless your teacher requires them of you)	
☐	vocab word(s) (Label voc or bold.)	_____
☐	simile or metaphor	_____

Total: _________/ 45

Custom Total: _________/___

Teachers are free to adjust a checklist by requiring only the stylistic techniques that have become easy, plus one new one. "EZ+1." Reproducible checklists are available (see blue page).

Unit 4: Summarizing a Reference

Quality Adjectives "America" Poem

Use the model below to help you write a poem about America that is filled with quality adjectives. You may make some changes to the model; it is a general guide. See page 234 for a sample poem.

But first, brainstorm on the following page. Find possible adjectives for each line in the poem. Use the adjective lists in your SRP and a thesaurus for help. Remember to think of the five senses; what does each *look* like, *sound* like, *feel* like, or *smell* like (*taste* won't apply)?

America, Land of ...

1 or 2 adjectives	seashores	(*that*, *of*, or *with*)	______________
1 or 2 adjectives	forests	(*that*, *of*, or *with*)	______________
1 or 2 adjectives	mountains	(*that*, *of*, or *with*)	______________
1 or 2 adjectives	rivers	(*that*, *of*, or *with*)	______________
1 or 2 adjectives	plains	(*that*, *of*, or *with*)	______________

(You may add others, such as cities, towns, farms, churches, historical landmarks, etc.)

America, Land of ...

1 or 2 adjectives describing people who are ______________________________

1 or 2 adjectives describing people who are ______________________________

"The free and the brave."

"God bless America,

my Home Sweet Home."

That, *of*, or *with* phrases are optional. To include them, choose one of the three words and follow it with a phrase to complete a thought. Notice the examples in the sample poem on page 234.

Lesson 11: The Louisiana Purchase, Part 2

Brainstorming

List adjectives to describe each thing below.

seashores	forests	mountains
warm	*frosty*	*majestic*
sandy	*piney*	*snowcapped*
serene	*misty*	*massive*
shimmering	*tranquil*	*breathtaking*

rivers	plains	people
roaring	*golden*	*patriotic*
refreshing	*vast*	*diverse*
clear	*fruited*	*hardworking*
sapphire	*waving*	*hopeful*

Alliteration

Try to put some words together to form alliteration, for example, *rapid, raging rivers*. Find examples of alliteration in the sample poem on page 234.

Try to use alliteration in the poem. Do not overuse it. Unlike dress-ups, decorations should be used sparingly, or your writing will be unnatural.

Note: The poem will be the cover of your polished draft notebook, so place your name and the school year toward the bottom of the page. Make the title very large and bold, as it will be the title of your book. See the sample poem in the Appendix, page 234.

Illustrate your final draft, or copy it onto specialty paper. Be sure to include everything on the checklist on page 98.

Lesson 11, Part 2 Checklist: The "America" Poem

Name: ______________________________

STRUCTURE

☐	Name and school year follows poem.	_____ (1 pt)
☐	Title of poem "America" is large and bold.	_____ (1 pt)
☐	Poetry form (first word of each line is capitalized)	_____ (4 pts)

STYLE Each paragraph must contain at least one of each element of style.

☐	Contains at least ten quality adjectives.	_____ (10 pts)
☐	Strong verbs are underlined.	_____ (5 pts)
	Decoration ("dec" in margin or italics if typed)	**(5 pts each)**
☐	alliteration *(allit)*	_____ (5 pts)

MECHANICS

☐	capitalization	_____ (1 pt)
☐	end marks and punctuation	_____ (1 pt)
☐	spelling and usage	_____ (1 pt)
☐	complete sentences (Does it make sense?)	_____ (1 pt)
☐	banned words: pretty, ugly, big, go, went, say, said	_____ (-1 pt)

Total: _________/ 30

Custom Total: _________/___

Reproducible checklists are available (see blue page).

Lesson 12: The Trail of Tears

Structures: Unit 4: Summarizing a Reference
Style: #2 prepositional opener
Writing Topics: the Trail of Tears
Optional Student Reading Assignment: during Lessons 11–12: *The Sign of the Beaver*

UNIT 4: SUMMARIZING A REFERENCE

Lesson 12: The Trail of Tears

Review

Play a vocabulary review game from the Teacher's Manual to prepare for the quiz next week.

See Appendix VI. "Lightning" is a favorite with my classes and covers all the words quickly.

Sentence Openers

In this lesson you will learn a different kind of element of style. To help you appreciate it, read the following two versions of part of a report about the Indian Removal Act of 1830. What is the difference between them? Which sounds better?

Version 1

White men wanted fertile Native American lands. There was gold there. They passed a law. It was called the Indian Removal Act of 1830. It opened land west of the Mississippi River. The greedy men forced the Native Americans to live there.

Version 2

2 In the early 1800s white men wanted fertile Native American lands. There was gold there. Cleverly, they passed a law called the Indian Removal Act of 1830. It opened land west of the Mississippi, and the greedy men forced the Native Americans to live there.

The first sentence begins with "In the early 1800s" in front of the subject. In the third sentence the word *cleverly* is placed in front of the subject. The final two sentences are combined using the word *and*.

In Version 1, all the sentences begin with the subject and are about the same length. This makes writing boring. One way to make your writing more sophisticated is to begin some of your sentences with something other than the subject and to use sentences of differing lengths—some short, some medium, and some long. Can you see how Version 2 accomplished both of these things?

The #2 Prepositional Opener

In this lesson, learn the *#2 prepositional* opener that begins a sentence with a prepositional phrase. So that you can indicate it when you use it, it is given a number. (You will learn more sentence openers later that will be given other numbers.)

Here is the #2 prepositional opener from Version 2 on the previous page:

2 *In the early 1800s white men wanted fertile Native American lands.*

Note that the preposition begins a phrase placed in front of a complete sentence. This is the structure of a #2 prepositional opener. If your prepositional phrase has five words or more, follow it with a comma. A comma is optional but usually not recommended with shorter phrases.

SRP

Practice

transitional comma

Some Prepositions
about above across after around at before behind by down during for from in inside into near of off on outside over past through to under up with within without

Write a sentence with a #2 prepositional opener. Label it by writing a *2* in the left margin. Do *not* underline the sentence opener.

2 *With different kinds of sentences, writing becomes more engaging.*

The Assignment

Day 1:

1. Read the source text on the following page.
2. On the blank outline on page 103, write key words for a topic sentence.
3. Reread the source text. Note four to seven key facts.
4. In your own words, tell back the meaning of each line of your notes.
5. On page 104, brainstorm ideas for elements of style.

Days 2–4:

1. Polish your Declaration of Independence report from Lesson 10.
2. Use your key word outline to write a 1-paragraph summary of "The Trail of Tears."
3. Remember to highlight two to three key words in your topic sentence and clincher that tell the topic of the paragraph. Follow and attach the checklist on page 105.
4. Learn the new vocabulary words. Review all previous words. Try to use some in your paragraph.
5. If you are reading the literature suggestions, obtain *By the Great Horn Spoon!* by Sid Fleischman for next week.

Option for experienced Level B students: Complete the lesson in your Student Book first. If your parent or teacher assigns it, repeat the above process for a second paragraph: The Alamo, from the Blackline Masters.

Study for Vocabulary Quiz 3. It will cover words from Lessons 1–12.

You will most likely have to help students quite a bit at first. Most students find limiting their notes difficult until they see it modeled. See the sample key word outline for help. Many details in the source text are unnecessary. Let students choose the ones they think are most important or most interesting, but limit them. Ask them which facts they can do without.

Unit 4: Summarizing a Reference

Source Text

The Trail of Tears

Native Americans will never forget the "Trail of Tears." In the early 1830s more than 100,000 Native Americans lived on millions of acres in southeast America. This land had been their home for generations before the white men arrived. However, as more and more white men came, many of them desired this land. Gold had been found in Georgia, and the land was fertile. It could be used for huge cotton plantations that would make the men rich. In 1830 President Andrew Jackson signed the Indian Removal Act. This made some land in the Louisiana Territory (what is now Oklahoma) Indian Territory. The Removal Act gave the government the power to trade this land for the land the Native Americans were currently on. The original intent was to trade fairly and peacefully. However, most Native Americans did not want to move, so the president sent U.S. troops to force their removal. The most brutal evacuation was of the Cherokees in 1838. When they resisted, the government sent seven thousand soldiers. The soldiers looted their homes and marched about fifteen thousand Cherokees at gunpoint over twelve hundred miles. More than five thousand died on this journey. It will forever be remembered as the "Trail of Tears."

Bibliography

"Trail of Tears." *History.com*. A&E Televison Network. N.d. Web.

Sample

Lesson 12: The Trail of Tears

Key Word Outline

I. *"Trail of Tears," ☹, Nat. Amer., ⊘ forget*

1. *white 👤, wanted, land*
2. *gold, fertile, 4 cotton, $$*
3. *1830, Pres. A. Jackson, Indian Removal Act*
4. *= land, Louis. Purch., Ind. territory*
5. *Nat. Am., ⊘ want, ➔, U.S. troops, forced*
6. *most, brutal, Cherokees*
7. *@ gunpoint, >1200 miles, >5000 XX*

Clincher

If time permits, discuss using vocabulary words. Examples:

White men desired the prosperity the land could bring them. They vehemently resolved to take the land.

Along the journey they encountered hostile conditions. The white men devised cunning plans to take land.

Many Native Americans could not persevere through the perilous journey. The U.S. government and its troops were too formidable to resist. On the trip, they were laden with the few possessions they could carry.

shamefully, mercilessly, greedily, scandalously, heartlessly/ evacuated, removed, dislocated, uprooted

Brainstorming

#2 Prepositional Opener

Indicate each by placing a *2* in the left margin. Do not underline.

In order to grab Native American land, white men passed the Indian Removal Act.

Along the way, many Native Americans died.

Strong Verbs with -ly Adverbs

Add two ideas for a strong verb and an -ly adverb that would work in this sentence:

The U.S. government *selfishly* ly *expelled* Cherokees from their land.

cruelly ly *forced*

Clauses

1. Write a sentence with a *who* or *which* clause that you might use in your summary paragraph. Remember the commas.

   The Native Americans' land, which was fertile, was coveted by white men.

2. Write a sentence with a www.asia.b clause that you might use in your summary paragraph.

   The Native Americans faced many hardships as they traveled.

Quality Adjectives

Describe the following with quality adjectives:

the *dejected, cheated, scorned* Native Americans

the Native Americans' *productive, desirable* land

the *untrustworthy, deceitful, greedy* white men

Lesson 12: The Trail of Tears

Lesson 12 Checklist: The Trail of Tears

Name: ______________________________

STRUCTURE

☐	MLA format (see Appendix I)	_____ (5 pts)
☐	Title centered and repeats or reflects 2–3 key words from clincher	_____ (3 pts)
☐	Topic-clincher repeats or reflects 2–3 key words (highlighted or bold).	_____ (5 pts)

STYLE

Each paragraph must contain at least one of each element of style.

	Dress-Ups (underline one of each)	**(5 pts each)**
☐	-ly adverb	____ (5 pts)
☐	*who-which* clause	____ (5 pts)
☐	strong verb	____ (5 pts)
☐	*because* clause	____ (5 pts)
☐	quality adjective	____ (5 pts)
	Sentence Openers (numbered)	**(3 pts each)**
☐	[2] prepositional	_____ (3 pts)
	Decoration ("dec" in margin or italics if typed)	**(5 pts each)**
☐	alliteration *(allit)*	_____ (5 pts)

MECHANICS

☐	capitalization	_____ (1 pt)
☐	end marks and punctuation	_____ (1 pt)
☐	spelling and usage	_____ (1 pt)
☐	complete sentences (Does it make sense?)	_____ (1 pt)
☐	banned words: go, went, say, said, pretty, ugly, big	_____ (-1 pt)

	More Advanced Additions (optional unless your teacher requires them of you)	
☐	vocab word(s) (Label voc or bold.)	_____
☐	simile or metaphor	_____
☐	The Alamo paragraph	_____

Total: _________/ 50

Custom Total: _________/___

Teachers are free to adjust a checklist by requiring only the stylistic techniques that have become easy, plus one new one. "EZ+1." Reproducible checklists are available (see blue page).

Unit 4: Summarizing a Reference

Lesson 13: The Gold Rush

Structures: Unit 5: Writing from Pictures

Style: reviewing stylistic techniques

Writing Topics: the Gold Rush

Optional Student Reading Assignment: during Lessons 13–15: *By the Great Horn Spoon!*

Teaching Writing: Structure and Style

Watch the sections for Unit 5 (Writing from Pictures). At IEW.com/twss-help reference the TWSS Viewing Guides.

UNIT 5: WRITING FROM PICTURES

p. 235 HBW before outline

Lesson 13: The Gold Rush

Begin with Vocabulary Quiz 3.

In the following two lessons, you will not have a source text from which you can take notes. Instead, you will have three pictures to guide you. The background of the pictures for this lesson is the California Gold Rush. Gold was discovered in California in 1848. News traveled all over the country as well as across the Atlantic. In 1849 thousands of people left all they had and headed to California, hoping to strike it rich. The trips were difficult whether by wagon trains, clipper ships, or steamboats. In California, mining towns sprang up quickly. Miners worked hard axing and panning, but most did not find much gold. When the mines were emptied, miners left, and towns became ghost towns. However, many people stayed in California and made it their new home.

Follow the assignment instructions, but first read about the past perfect tense, *which is an advanced concept.*

central fact past tense

Details: past perfect

Clincher past tense

Past Perfect Tense

The story you will be writing for this lesson should be written in past tense. However, you may also need to use the past perfect tense.

The past perfect tense is formed by placing the word *had* in front of a past tense verb. The past perfect tense is used when you want to write about what happened before what you are writing about in past tense. When writing from pictures, you must begin each paragraph with what you see in each picture. For the first picture of this lesson, you might write something like this:

> *John and Mary stood transfixed at the exciting news posted on the store wall.*

Then, if you want to tell what happened before that, such as why they are at the store, you must switch to past perfect by putting the word *had* in front of the past tense verbs.

> *John and Mary stood transfixed at the exciting news posted on the store wall. They* ***had walked*** *into town hoping to find work so that they could pay off the debt on their home. They* ***had almost lost*** *hope. Now, here was the answer to their troubles!*

Notice that the end of the last sentence switched back to regular past tense. Why?

The scene has switched back to what is in the picture.

Practice

SRP p. 38

Add a past perfect tense sentence that could logically follow this sentence:

> *They were ready to begin their journey.*

They had packed everything they could into their covered wagon.

Adding clinchers is the most difficult part of writing from pictures. Be sure to discuss ideas for each picture. For example, perhaps the central fact of Picture 1 tells this: ***John and Mary*** *read a sign that told them there was* ***gold*** *in* ***California***.

The middle of the paragraph could discuss how they decided to go to California, so they packed up. The paragraph could tell what they did to get ready, what they decided to take with them, and what (and whom) they would leave behind. The clincher might be something like this: *Now that they were packed,* ***they*** *were on their way to* ***California*** *and* ***gold****!*

If the central fact of the second paragraph tells that John and Mary reached the **raging river**, it could end with them being glad the **raging river** was behind them.

If the central fact of the third paragraph tells that John and Mary felt disappointed when they reached the first **town in California**, the middle could have them continue on to other towns. The final clincher might be something like this: *There were* ***many towns still waiting*** *to be* ***explored*** *in the* ***large state***.

The Assignment

Day 1:

1. Look at the three pictures on page 109. On the top blank next to the first picture, note what is happening in the picture (the central fact) in key words.

   On the other lines by the first box, you will note what is happening by answering questions. In a class setting, outline together. The teacher will write your ideas on the whiteboard, but you should not copy them into your book because you will do your own later.
2. Repeat the above steps for the remaining two pictures.
3. Brainstorm some elements of style on page 110.
4. Begin orally composing a class version of the story you outlined together. The teacher should write just enough of it on the whiteboard to be sure everyone understands the process. Read the sample story on page 235.

Days 2–4:

1. Polish the Louisiana Purchase paragraph from Lesson 11.
2. Outline a story from the pictures in the same way we did in class; then, write your story in three paragraphs. Each should begin with the central fact of one of the pictures and end with a clincher that reflects two to three key words. Highlight the repeated or reflected words.
3. Add all the elements of style listed on the checklist.
4. Cut out and learn vocabulary words for Lesson 13.

Option for experienced Level B students: Learn an advanced dress-up: dual adjectives, verbs, or -ly adverbs from the *U.S. History-Based Writing Lessons Blackline Masters*.

Literature Suggestion

With Lessons 13–15 read *By the Great Horn Spoon!* by Sid Fleischman.

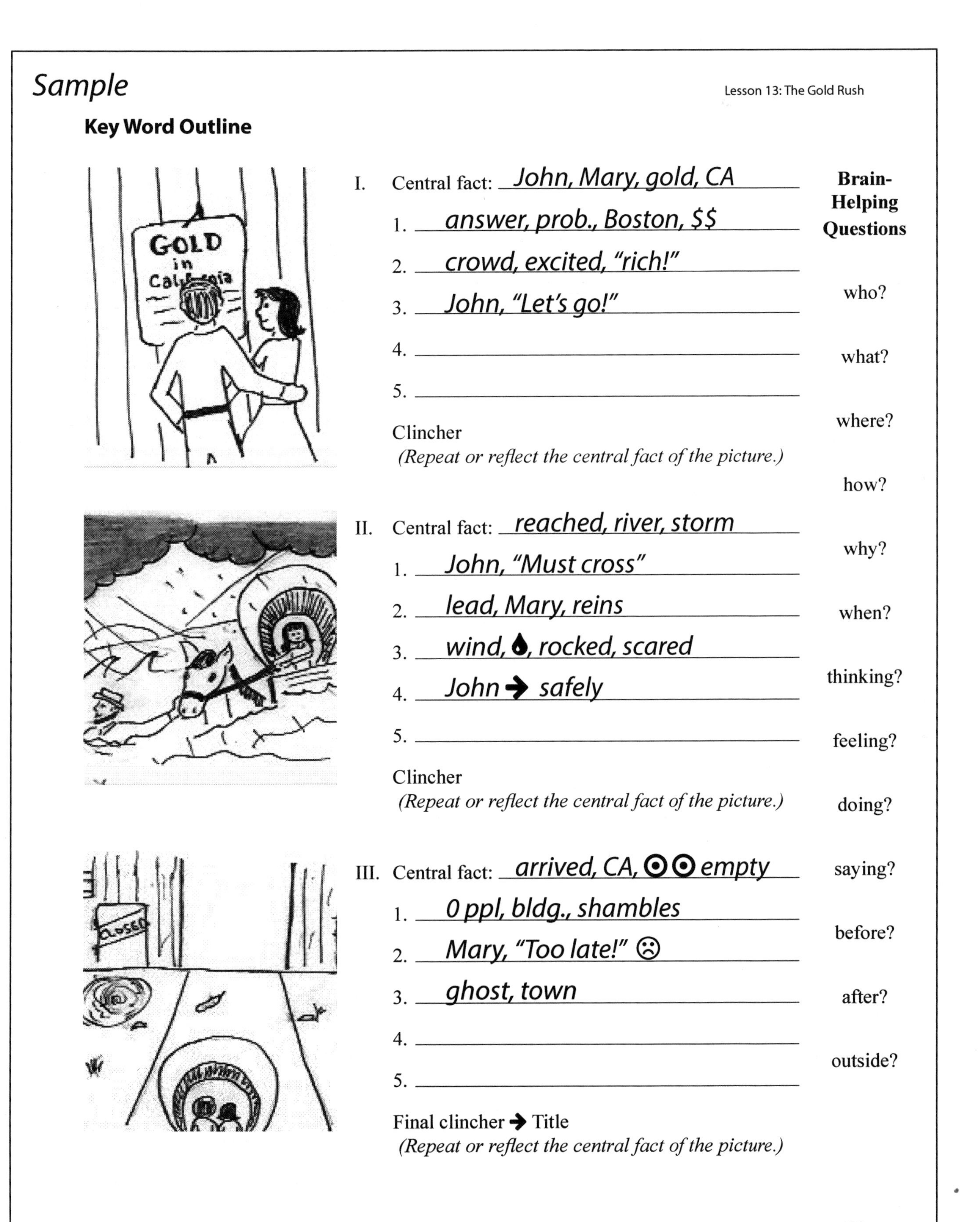

Sample

Lesson 13: The Gold Rush

Key Word Outline

I. Central fact: *John, Mary, gold, CA*

1. *answer, prob., Boston, $$*
2. *crowd, excited, "rich!"*
3. *John, "Let's go!"*
4. ______
5. ______

Clincher
(Repeat or reflect the central fact of the picture.)

II. Central fact: *reached, river, storm*

1. *John, "Must cross"*
2. *lead, Mary, reins*
3. *wind, 💧, rocked, scared*
4. *John ➔ safely*
5. ______

Clincher
(Repeat or reflect the central fact of the picture.)

III. Central fact: *arrived, CA, ⊙⊙ empty*

1. *0 ppl, bldg., shambles*
2. *Mary, "Too late!" ☹*
3. *ghost, town*
4. ______
5. ______

Final clincher ➔ Title
(Repeat or reflect the central fact of the picture.)

Brain-Helping Questions

who?
what?
where?
how?
why?
when?
thinking?
feeling?
doing?
saying?
before?
after?
outside?

U.S. History-Based Writing Lessons: Student Book

109

Let students offer ideas.

Unit 5: Writing from Pictures

Brainstorming

#2 Prepositional Opener

Write an idea for a #2 sentence. Label it by placing a *2* in the left margin. Do not underline.

2 In the morning, John and Mary walked to town.

2 With wind howling and water raging, John struggled to lead the wagon through the river.

Quality Adjectives

Describe these nouns. Think of different parts of the story, the five senses, and emotions.

your characters *I. hopeful II. nervous, determined III. disappointed, worried*

the wagon *I. rickety II. heavy, unstable III. creaky, slow*

the town *deserted, eerie, quiet*

Strong Verbs and -ly Adverbs

What would these things be doing at any part of the story? Think of strong verbs. Add -ly adverbs if you can.

the river *swirled, churned, roared ferociously, vehemently*

the horse *struggled, panicked, labored, frantically, diligently*

Decoration Ideas: Conversation

Since this is a story, you should add some conversation. What would your characters say to one another? Write one idea for conversation.

Have students work in pairs and then share ideas with the class. Here is one idea.

"John, I'm too scared to cross. What if we get caught in a whirlpool?" Mary cried.

John assured her: "The horses are strong, and the water is not deep. Look, it is only up to my chest. Hold the reins."

"I'll try," Mary replied. "But if the water is too strong, please turn us back."

Lesson 13: The Gold Rush

Lesson 13 Checklist: The Gold Rush

Name: ______________________________

STRUCTURE

☐	MLA format (see Appendix I)	_____ (2 pts)
☐	Title centered and repeats or reflects 2–3 key words from final clincher	_____ (5 pts)
☐	Clincher repeats or reflects 2–3 key words of central fact (highlighted or bold).	_____ (5 pts)

STYLE Each paragraph must contain at least one of each element of style.

¶ 1	¶ 2	¶ 3	**Dress-Ups (underline one of each)**	**(1 pt each)**
☐	☐	☐	-ly adverb	_____ (3 pts)
☐	☐	☐	*who-which* clause	_____ (3 pts)
☐	☐	☐	strong verb	_____ (3 pts)
☐	☐	☐	www.asia.b clause	_____ (3 pts)
☐	☐	☐	quality adjective	_____ (3 pts)
¶ 1	**¶ 2**	**¶ 3**	**Sentence Openers (numbered; one of each as possible)**	**(3 pts each)**
☐	☐	☐	[2] prepositional	_____ (9 pts)

	Decorations ("dec" in margin or italics if typed) (one per paragraph)	**(5 pts each)**
☐	alliteration *(allit)*	_____ (5 pts)
☐	conversation	_____ (5 pts)
☐	____________	_____ (5 pts)

MECHANICS

☐	capitalization	_____ (1 pt)
☐	end marks and punctuation	_____ (1 pt)
☐	spelling and usage	_____ (1 pt)
☐	complete sentences (Does it make sense?)	_____ (1 pt)
☐	banned words: go, went, say, said, pretty, ugly, big	_____ (-1 pt)

	More Advanced Additions (optional unless your teacher requires them of you)	
☐	vocab word(s) (Label voc or bold.)	_____
☐	simile or metaphor	_____
☐	dual adjectives, verbs, or -ly adverbs	_____

Total: __________/ 55

Custom Total: __________/___

Teachers are free to adjust a checklist by requiring only the stylistic techniques that have become easy, plus one new one. "EZ+1." Reproducible checklists are available (see blue page).

Unit 5: Writing from Pictures

Lesson 14: Escape on the Underground Railroad

Structures: Unit 5: Writing from Pictures

Style: decorations – simile or metaphor

Writing Topics: the Underground Railroad

Optional Student Reading Assignment: during Lessons 13–15: *By the Great Horn Spoon!*

UNIT 5: WRITING FROM PICTURES

Lesson 14: Escape on the Underground Railroad

Review

1. Share sentences from your Gold Rush story in which you used the past perfect tense.
2. Share a #2 prepositional opener from your Gold Rush story. Then, play Preposition Round Robin from the Teacher's Manual.

In this lesson you will write another story from pictures. First, learn a new decoration.

Similes and Metaphors

Similes and metaphors describe something by comparing it to something else. A simile says that one thing is like or as something else. A metaphor does not use *like* or *as*. It simply writes as if one thing is another. If you have been reading *By the Great Horn Spoon!* as suggested for Lessons 13–15, you have seen many similes and metaphors. Here are some examples:

"the two gold ships, *linked together like sausages*" (simile)

"The grains of dust sparkled *like yellow fire*." (simile)

"At night the chorus of snorting and snoring *was a sea-going grand opera*." (metaphor)

"At night the sky *became their textbook*." (metaphor)

You will be required to use a simile or metaphor in your story with this lesson. The brainstorming page will help you with this.

Background: The Underground Railroad

Prior to the Civil War, a network of people formed to help slaves escape to freedom in the North and Canada. They called their network the Underground Railroad. The Underground Railroad consisted of former slaves who had escaped as well as white men and women who opposed slavery. The former slaves were often the ones who led runaways in their flight. They were called conductors. The most famous conductor was Harriet Tubman.

People who housed and hid runaways were called station masters, and their homes were called stations. Often their homes had secret hiding places such as spaces between walls or under the floor. The people of the Underground Railroad used many secret codes and signals to let runaways know where, how, and when to flee. For example, code words in songs might have told them when it was time to flee. Owl hoots or quail calls might have directed slaves to a conductor. The people of the Underground Railroad also used clever disguises and tricks to help slaves. However, most journeys took many weeks or even months. Runaways were often on their own, guided only by the Big Dipper for much of the time. The trips were filled with hardships and danger. Despite all this between 1830 and 1862, thousands of slaves escaped to freedom on the Underground Railroad.

Preposition Round Robin

Give students one minute to study the list of prepositions on page 100. Then, have them all stand. In turn, each student has 10 seconds to name a preposition. As each preposition is named, write it on the whiteboard, and give the student who said it a ticket (or point). Students who are successful remain standing; however, if a student cannot think of a preposition, gives a word that is not a preposition, or gives a preposition already on the whiteboard, he or she must sit down. Continue until only one student remains standing. If you get down to two or three students, and none can give you another preposition, they tie. Winners get 5 tickets extra.

The Assignment

Day 1:

1. Look at the three pictures on page 115. On the top blank next to the first picture, note what is happening in the picture (the central fact) in key words.

   On the other lines by the first box, you will note what is happening by answering questions. In a class setting, outline together. The teacher will write the students' ideas on the whiteboard, but you should not copy them into your book because you will do your own later.

2. Repeat the above steps for the remaining two pictures.
3. Brainstorm some elements of style on page 116.
4. Begin orally composing a class version of the story you outlined together. The teacher should write just enough of it on the whiteboard to be sure everyone understands the process.

Days 2–4:

1. Polish the "Trail of Tears" paragraph from Lesson 12.
2. Outline a story from the pictures in the same way you did in class; then, write your story in three paragraphs. Each should begin with the central fact of one of the pictures.
3. As you fill in details for each picture, add the elements of style listed on the checklist. Don't forget to try the new decoration: the simile or metaphor. Also, remember to highlight words in each central fact that tell what is happening in each picture. Add clinchers as well. Follow and attach the checklist.
4. There are no new vocabulary words for Lesson 14.

The Drinking Gourd

Key Word Outline

I. Central fact: Amos, Mary, running

1. baby, had, sold
2. waited, signal, night
3. nervous, following, Big Dipper
4. hope, conductor, soon

Clincher
(Repeat or reflect the central fact of the picture.)

II. Central fact: Quaker, w/wagon, signaled

1. knew, safe, approached
2. hid, base, wagon
3. hunters, "seen, runaways?"
4. look, wagon, ⊘, find

Clincher
(Repeat or reflect the central fact of the picture.)

III. Central fact: → river, edge

1. another, Quaker, w/raft
2. family, boarded, relieved
3. lay, flat, prayed
4. dogs, far, back
5. reached, shore, free!

Final clincher → Title
(Repeat or reflect the central fact of the picture.)

Brain-Helping Questions

who?
what?
where?
how?
why?
when?
thinking?
feeling?
doing?
saying?
before?
after?
outside?

Brainstorming

Quality Adjectives

Use adjectives to describe what the runaways might see, hear, or feel during their flight (for example: *eerie night* shadows, *hazy* glow of the moon, *soft rustling* leaves, *hot, muggy* air).

thick gray fog; soft dim moonlight; shimmering stars; dark silhouettes; obscured forms; pitch black night; croaking frogs; melodic chirping crickets; distant howling dogs; steady, rhythmic sloshing footsteps; soft, damp ground; prickly thorns; oozing mud; soft grass; slippery moss; jagged rocks

Strong Verbs

Use strong verbs to tell what the following might do in the story. Can you add an -ly adverb to some of your strong verbs?

the runaways *hearts raced uncontrollably; watched warily; held their breath anxiously*

wagon *jerked forward; stopped suddenly; bounced and rocked*

slave hunters *pursued relentlessly; scoured angrily; scowled indignantly*

dogs *trailed; sniffed; ran; bayed, howled viciously, ferociously*

Decoration Ideas: Similes and Metaphors

Can you finish these ideas using similes or metaphors?

In the night, the trees looked like *spooky strangers; eerie monsters; scarecrows*

The North Star shone like *a beacon of hope; a diamond; an angel*

The long black river looked like *a serpent; never-ending road; a whip*

The Big Dipper was *a trustworthy friend, a sparkling compass*

Other ideas *Allow students to work in groups and share more ideas.*

Lesson 14: Escape on the Underground Railroad

Lesson 14 Checklist: Escape on the Underground Railroad

Name: ______________________________

STRUCTURE

☐	MLA format (see Appendix I)	_____ (2 pts)
☐	Title centered and repeats or reflects 2–3 key words from final clincher	_____ (5 pts)
☐	Clincher repeats or reflects 2–3 key words of central fact (highlighted or bold).	_____ (5 pts)

STYLE

Each paragraph must contain at least one of each element of style.

¶ 1	¶ 2	¶ 3	**Dress-Ups (underline one of each)**	**(1 pt each)**
☐	☐	☐	-ly adverb	_____ (3 pts)
☐	☐	☐	*who-which* clause	_____ (3 pts)
☐	☐	☐	strong verb	_____ (3 pts)
☐	☐	☐	www.asia.b clause	_____ (3 pts)
☐	☐	☐	quality adjective	_____ (3 pts)
¶ 1	**¶ 2**	**¶ 3**	**Sentence Openers (numbered; one of each as possible)**	**(3 pts each)**
☐	☐	☐	[2] prepositional	_____ (9 pts)
			Decorations ("dec" in margin or italics if typed) (one per paragraph)	**(5 pts each)**
☐	☐	☐	alliteration *(allit)*, conversation, simile, or metaphor	_____ (15 pts)

MECHANICS

☐	capitalization	_____ (1 pt)
☐	end marks and punctuation	_____ (1 pt)
☐	spelling and usage	_____ (1 pt)
☐	complete sentences (Does it make sense?)	_____ (1 pt)
☐	banned words: go, went, say, said, pretty, ugly, big	_____ (-1 pt)

More Advanced Additions (optional unless your teacher requires them of you)

☐	vocab word(s) (Label voc or bold.)	_____
☐	dual adjectives, verbs, or -ly adverbs	_____

Total: __________/ 55

Custom Total: __________/___

Teachers are free to adjust a checklist by requiring only the stylistic techniques that have become easy, plus one new one. "EZ+1." Reproducible checklists are available (see blue page).

Unit 5: Writing from Pictures

Lesson 15: The Battle

Structures: Unit 5: Writing from Pictures
Style: literary device – onomatopoeia
Writing Topics: a Civil War battle
Optional Student Reading Assignment: during Lessons 13–15: *By the Great Horn Spoon!*

UNIT 5: WRITING FROM PICTURES

Lesson 15: The Battle

Review

1. Play a vocabulary review game.
2. Share the simile or metaphor in your Underground Railroad story.

See Appendix VI. "Find the Card" is a good choice.

When each student reads, ask the class to decide whether the thought contains a simile or a metaphor.

In this lesson you will write from pictures once more. The background for the pictures in this lesson is the Civil War.

The Civil War

The Civil War was a war in which Americans fought Americans from 1861–1865. When Abraham Lincoln was elected president, the southern states feared that slavery would eventually be outlawed. Even though Lincoln had said that he would not interfere with slavery in the South, many Northerners spoke out against it as an evil practice, and Lincoln belonged to the anti-slavery Republican party. In addition, more states were entering the Union, and if they were anti-slavery, the southern states would be outnumbered in Congress.

The South had many huge cotton and tobacco plantations that depended upon slave labor. So the southern states tried to leave the Union to form their own separate nation called the Confederate States of America. They even elected their own president, Jefferson Davis. However, President Lincoln did not believe the South had the right to leave the country, so he did not remove U.S. soldiers from the South. Soon the Civil War began. Both sides fought for what they believed was a just cause. The Civil War was America's bloodiest and deadliest war ever, killing about 620,000 men and boys.

Just for Fun: Onomatopoeia

An element of style that might be fun to try with this story is onomatopoeia. This is the use of words that sound like what they mean. For example, *meow*, *buzz*, and *honk* are words that sound like what they mean. When describing the battle scene in your story, there will be opportunities to use onomatopoeia.

If you will be reading *Rifles for Watie*, as will be suggested in Lesson 16, you will find many examples of onomatopoeia.

"hoofs *stomping*, harness *jingling*"

"the *spat*, *spat*, *spat* of his quick blows"

"*Clonk!* A thousand colored lights exploded in Jeff's head."

"*Tramp, tramp, tramp, tramp.*"

Unit 5: Writing from Pictures

The Assignment

Day 1:

1. Look at the three pictures on page 121. On the top blank next to the first picture, note what is happening in the picture (the central fact) in key words.

   On the other lines by the first box, you will note what is happening by answering questions. In a class setting, outline together. The teacher will write your ideas on the whiteboard, but you should not copy them into your book because you will do your own later.

2. Repeat the above steps for the remaining two pictures.
3. Brainstorm some elements of style on page 122.
4. Begin orally composing a class version of the story you outlined together. The teacher should write just enough of it on the whiteboard to be sure everyone understands the process.

Days 2–4:

1. Polish the Gold Rush story from Lesson 13.
2. Outline a story from the pictures in the same way we did in class; then write your story in three paragraphs. Each should begin with the central fact of one of the pictures.
3. As you fill in details for each picture, add the elements of style listed on the checklist.
4. Cut out and learn vocabulary words for Lesson 15.
5. If you are doing the literature suggestions, obtain *Rifles for Watie* by Harold Keith for next week.

Lesson 15: The Battle

Key Word Outline

I. Central fact: David, drummer, w/Union
1. too, young, infantry
2. long, march, ➔ battle
3. heard, artillery, ahead
4. men, yelling, bullets
5. grabbed, rifle

Clincher
(Repeat or reflect the central fact of the picture.)

II. Central fact: artillery, men, shot
1. David, alone, @cannon
2. drum, down, fired
3. > battle, blasts, chaos
4. enemy, eventually, retreated

Clincher
(Repeat or reflect the central fact of the picture.)

III. Central fact: presented, w/medal, valor
1. promoted, soldier
2. traded, gun, rifle
3. fought, bravely, rest
4. home, town, cheered

Final clincher ➔ Title
(Repeat or reflect the central fact of the picture.)

Brain-Helping Questions

who?
what?
where?
how?
why?
when?
thinking?
feeling?
doing?
saying?
before?
after?
outside?

Brainstorming

Quality Adjectives

Use quality adjectives to describe the things that you would see, hear, and feel on a battlefield. Write adjectives that would describe how your characters might feel at different parts of your story.

soldiers *I. eager, zealous, wary II. frantic, battered, injured III. proud, resolved*

the boy *I. patriotic, hopeful II. determined, resolute III. humble, honored*

the yells *I. zealous, patriotic II. horrific, agonizing III. (cheers) jubilant, victorious*

other ideas *shiny, new drum; silver bayonets; whizzing bullets; brave act*

Strong Verbs

Use strong verbs to tell what the following might do in the story. Can you add an -ly adverb to some of your strong verbs?

bullets *whizzed incessantly, buzzed, flew, struck mercilessly, swarmed*

cannons *blasted vehemently, boomed loudly, exploded violently, smoked*

soldiers *dreamed of glory, marched steadfastly, charged ferociously*

the boy *beat his drum rhythmically and solemnly, loaded and fired diligently*

Decoration Ideas

Just for Fun: Onomatopoeia (See page 119.)

Try to use onomatopoeia for any sounds associated with the following:

marching *stomp, tramp, slush, thump*

cannon *boom, blast, roar*

bullets *buzz, whiz, whoosh, zing*

Alliteration

Can you add words to any of the above to form alliteration? (***Example***: If you wrote *fought* as a verb for soldiers, you could add *The few frantic soldiers fought fiercely*.

Cannons blasted then bolted as they boomed.

Lesson 15: The Battle

Lesson 15 Checklist: The Battle

Name: ______________________________

STRUCTURE

☐	MLA format (see Appendix I)	_____ (5 pts)
☐	Title centered and repeats or reflects 2–3 key words from final clincher	_____ (2 pts)
☐	Clincher repeats or reflects 2–3 key words of central fact (highlighted or bold).	_____ (5 pts)

STYLE Each paragraph must contain at least one of each element of style.

¶ 1	¶ 2	¶ 3	Dress-Ups (underline one of each)	(1 pt each)
☐	☐	☐	-ly adverb	_____ (3 pts)
☐	☐	☐	*who-which* clause	_____ (3 pts)
☐	☐	☐	strong verb	_____ (3 pts)
☐	☐	☐	www.asia.b clause	_____ (3 pts)
☐	☐	☐	quality adjective	_____ (3 pts)
¶ 1	**¶ 2**	**¶ 3**	**Sentence Openers (numbered; one of each as possible)**	**(3 pts each)**
☐	☐	☐	[2] prepositional	_____ (9 pts)
			Decorations ("dec" in margin or italics if typed) (one per paragraph)	**(5 pts each)**
☐	☐	☐	alliteration *(allit)*, conversation, simile, or metaphor	_____ (15 pts)

MECHANICS

☐	capitalization, punctuation, spelling, grammar	_____ (4 pts)
☐	banned words: go, went, say, said, pretty, ugly, big	_____ (-1 pt)

More Advanced Additions (optional unless your teacher requires them of you)

☐	vocab word(s) (Label voc or bold.)	_____
☐	dual adj, verbs, or -ly adverbs	_____
☐	onomatopoeia	_____

Total: _________/ 55

Custom Total: _________/___

Teachers are free to adjust a checklist by requiring only the stylistic techniques that have become easy, plus one new one. "EZ+1." Reproducible checklists are available (see blue page).

Unit 5: Writing from Pictures
124
Institute for Excellence in Writing

Lesson 16: The Civil War

Structures: Unit 6: Summarizing Multiple References

Style: #3 -ly adverb opener

Writing Topics: a Civil War battle

Optional Student Reading Assignment: during Lessons 16–20: *Rifles for Watie*

Teaching Writing: Structure and Style

Watch the section for Unit 6: Summarizing Multiple References. At IEW.com/twss-help reference the TWSS Viewing Guides.

UNIT 6: SUMMARIZING MULTIPLE REFERENCES

Lesson 16: The Civil War

Review

Share a decoration from your battle story from Lesson 15.

Summarizing Multiple References

When you are asked to write a research report, your teacher will require that you use several sources from which to gather facts. The IEW method for note taking and outlining will help you to do this successfully. In this lesson you will write a 1-paragraph report, but you will have more than one source text. This means you will first take notes from each source; then, you will pick and choose the notes you would like to put into a key word outline from which you will write the paragraph. Follow these steps:

The Assignment

Day 1:

1. Read Source 1, "Civil War" on page 126. On your own paper, formatted like page 128, write three key words to help you remember each of the facts you think are the most interesting or most important.
2. Repeat Step 1 with Source 2, "America's Deadliest War," on page 127. Do not note facts that you already noted from the first source.
3. Once you have notes from both sources, you will have to organize them into one *fused outline* on page 128. Remember that report paragraphs need topic sentences. What main idea about the Civil War would make a good topic sentence?
4. To make your fused outline, under the topic line, note no more than seven facts. Arrange the notes in an order that makes sense.
5. Use the fused outline to tell back, in complete sentences, the ideas you will include in your paragraph.
6. Study page 129 to learn a new sentence opener: the #3 -ly adverb opener.

Students will have more room for notes if they use two sheets of paper: one for the notes from both sources and the other for the fused outline.

Days 2–4:

1. Polish your "Escape on the Underground Railroad" story from Lesson 14.
2. Use your fused outline to write a paragraph. Follow and attach the checklist.
3. Cut out and learn the vocabulary words for Lesson 16. Review all.

Literature Suggestion

With Lessons 16–21 read *Rifles for Watie* by Harold Keith.

Source Text 1

Civil War

When we think of war, usually we think of one country fighting against another country. But in a civil war citizens of the same country fight against one another. In America's Civil War the northern states and the southern states fought against each other. Because of this, more Americans died in this war than in any other war America has ever fought. And the war cost the country $15 million. So what were they fighting for? There were many complicated issues, but basically the North was fighting to keep the United States together. They were called the Union. The South was fighting for the right to leave the United States and become its own nation: the Confederate States of America. Southerners did not want to stay in the United States because they believed the government would eventually take away their right to own slaves. Their economy depended upon slave labor, so they fought fiercely. But after four long years and much bloodshed and destruction across the land, the South finally surrendered. The United States would remain united.

Lesson 16: The Civil War

Source Text 2

America's Deadliest War

The Civil War was a war in which Americans fought Americans from 1861–1865. When Abraham Lincoln was elected president, the southern states feared that slavery would eventually be outlawed. Even though Lincoln had said that he would not interfere with slavery in the South, many northerners spoke out against it as an evil practice. In addition, more states were entering the Union, and Lincoln and the North did not want to allow slavery in them. If the new states were anti-slavery, the southern states would be outnumbered in Congress. The South had many huge cotton and tobacco plantations that depended upon slave labor. So the southern states tried to leave the Union to form their own separate nation called the Confederate States of America. They even elected their own president, Jefferson Davis.

However, President Lincoln did not believe the South had the right to leave the country. U.S. soldiers remained in the South to maintain control of federal forts. When southerners attacked Union troops at Fort Sumter and forced their surrender, the Civil War began. Both sides fought for what they believed was a just cause. The war was America's bloodiest and deadliest war ever, killing about 620,000 men and boys.

Unit 6: Summarizing Multiple References

Key Word Outline

Topic: The Civil War

Source 1: "Civil War"

1. *civil war = citizens, fight*
2. *US, N vs. S > xx, any, war*
3. *N, keep, Union, together*
4. *S, formed, own, Confed. States of Amer.*
5. *b/c, thot, US, ⊘ slavery*
6. *S, economy, depended, slaves*
7. *fought, 4 yrs, > bloodshed*

Source 2: "America's Deadliest War"

1. *1861–1865, b/c, Lincoln, elected*
2. *S, feared, 0 slaves*
3. *S, elected, Jefferson Davis, Pres.*
4. *N, ⊘, remove, troops, S*
5. *S vs. Union, troops, Ft. Sumter*
6. *Civil War, bloodiest, 620,000 xx*

Choose some of the notes you took from both sources, and put them in a logical order.

Fused Outline

I. *1861–1865, Amer., fought, Civil War*

1. *620,000 👤, xx, b/c N, fought, S*
2. *S, wanted, own, Confed. States of Amer.*
3. *feared, Lincoln, 0 slavery*
4. *S, econ., needed, slaves*
5. *N, keep, Union, together*
6. *⊘, remove, troops, S*
7. *S, attacked, troops, Ft. Sumter, 1st*

Clincher

Lesson 16: The Civil War

The #3 -ly Adverb Opener

Before you write from your fused outline, learn a new sentence opener. A #3 -ly adverb opener is a sentence that begins with an -ly adverb. Here is an example:

Tragically, America lost hundreds of thousands of men.

An -ly adverb as the first word of a sentence cannot count as an -ly dress-up anymore. It will be your #3 sentence opener. You will now, therefore, need to have two -ly adverbs in each paragraph you write—one at the beginning of a sentence (#3 opener) and one in the middle of a sentence (dress-up).

The -ly opener should not be underlined, but the dress-up should be. A *3* in the left margin is the only indicator for the -ly opener.

Comma Guidelines for the #3 -ly Adverb Opener

The opening -ly adverb takes a comma if you can convert it into the phrase "It is ____ that" with the adjective form of that adverb in the blank. Consider these examples:

Notably, historians call the Civil War the first modern war.

We can just as easily say this: It is notable that historians call the Civil War the first modern war. Therefore, the -ly adverb takes a comma.

Clumsily men used glass plate photography to document battles.

We cannot say this: It is clumsy that men used glass plate photography to document battles. In this case, then, no comma is needed.

Add a #3 -ly adverb opener to the sentences below.

1. *Tragically, Ironically, Sadly* Americans fought Americans.

2. *Vehemently, Wholeheartedly* both sides fought for what they believed was right.

Write your own idea for a sentence with a #3 -ly adverb opener.

Technologically the Civil War is classified as modern warfare.

Unit 6: Summarizing Multiple References

Lesson 16 Checklist: The Civil War

Name: ______________________________

STRUCTURE

☐	MLA format (see Appendix I)	_____ (6 pts)
☐	Title centered and repeats or reflects 2–3 key words from clincher	_____ (1 pt)
☐	Topic-clincher repeats or reflects 2–3 key words (highlighted or bold).	_____ (5 pts)

STYLE Each paragraph must contain at least one of each element of style.

	Dress-Ups (underline one of each)	**(3 pts each)**
☐	-ly adverb	_____ (3 pts)
☐	*who-which* clause	_____ (3 pts)
☐	strong verb	_____ (3 pts)
☐	quality adjective	_____ (3 pts)
☐	www.asia.b clause	_____ (3 pts)
	Sentence Openers (numbered; one of each as possible)	**(2 pts each)**
☐	[2] prepositional	_____ (2 pts)
☐	[3] -ly adverb	_____ (2 pts)
	Decorations ("dec" in margin or italics if typed) (Choose one.)	**(5 pts each)**
☐	alliteration *(allit)*, simile, or metaphor	_____ (5 pts)

MECHANICS

☐	capitalization, punctuation, spelling, grammar	_____ (4 pts)
☐	banned words: go, went, say, said, pretty, ugly, big	_____ (-1 pt)

	More Advanced Additions (optional unless your teacher requires them of you)	
☐	vocab word(s) (Label voc or bold.)	_____
☐	dual adj, verbs, or -ly adverbs	_____

Total: __________/ 40

Custom Total: __________/___

Teachers are free to adjust a checklist by requiring only the stylistic techniques that have become easy, plus one new one. "EZ+1." Reproducible checklists are available (see blue page).

Lesson 17: Great Inventors: Thomas Edison

Structures: Unit 6: Summarizing Multiple References

Style: #4 -ing opener

Writing Topics: Thomas Edison

Optional Student Reading Assignment: during Lessons 16–20: *Rifles for Watie*

UNIT 6: SUMMARIZING MULTIPLE REFERENCES

Lesson 17: Great Inventors: Thomas Edison

Review

1. Play a vocabulary review game from the Teacher's Manual.
2. What is a fused outline? What must a fused outline begin with? End with?

In the next three lessons, you are going to again use more than one source of information to help you write a report. This time you will write a three-paragraph report, one paragraph at a time. Before you begin, learn a new sentence opener: the #4 -ing opener.

The #4 -ing Opener

A #4 sentence opener is a sentence that begins with an -ing phrase.

The -ing word must be an action word that begins a phrase.

The -ing phrase must be followed by a comma and a complete sentence.

The subject of that sentence must be doing the -ing phrase.

Notice how all of the above are true in this sample sentence:

4 *Desiring to make the world a better place, inventors work feverishly.*

Imposter #4s

The #4 -ing opener can be tricky. There are some imposters, such as sentences that begin with prepositions that end in -ing.

During the 1900s, America saw many new inventions.
(This would be a #2 prepositional opener.)

Some adjectives end in -ing: *Dazzling light filled the sky.*

Note that in the above sentence there is no phrase followed by a comma followed by a complete sentence. *Dazzling* is simply describing the lights.

Sometimes an -ing word is the subject of a sentence. In this case, again, there will not be a phrase followed by a comma followed by a complete sentence.

Talking came from the machine.

Watch out for imposters.

Try to write your own #4 -ing opener (about anything).

Play "Hangman" with these definitions:

WORTHY OF IMITATION (exemplary)

NEVER-ENDING (incessant)

A fused outline is an outline that combines selected notes from more than one source into one outline. It begins with key words for a topic.

The #4 -ing Opener

The #4 -ing opener is a challenging stylistic technique. If your students are not yet ready to use it, have them cross it off the checklist until the time when they have practiced it, and it has become easy. EZ+1.

Teachers, walk around the room and help as necessary. Check for sentence structure and a comma. Here is an example:

4 *Following the checklist diligently, a student can be confident in his work.*

You will most likely have to help students quite a bit. Teachers should model the note taking process and help students limit the facts they choose. Help them look for the main, important ideas and facts. Ask them which facts they can do without. Write sample notes on the whiteboard.

Unit 6: Summarizing Multiple References

The Assignment

Day 1:

1. Read Source 1, "The Wizard of Menlo Park," on page 134. On your own paper, formatted like page 136, write three key words to help you remember each of the facts you think are the most interesting or most important. Limit your notes to no more than seven facts.
2. Repeat Step 1 with Source 2, "An Amazing Inventor," on page 135. Do not note facts that you already noted from the first source.
3. Once you have notes from both sources, you will have to organize them into one fused outline on page 136. Remember that report paragraphs need topic sentences. What main idea about Thomas Edison would make a good topic sentence?
4. To make your fused outline, under the topic line, note seven facts. Arrange the notes in an order that makes sense.
5. Use the fused outline to tell back in complete sentences the ideas you will include in your paragraph.
6. Use page 137 to learn two banned adjectives and write ideas for a #4 -ing opener.

Days 2–4:

1. Polish your Civil War story ("The Battle") from Lesson 15.
2. Use your fused outline (not your notes) to write one paragraph about Thomas Edison. Follow and attach the checklist on page 138. If your teacher decided not to have you include the #4 -ing opener, cross it off your checklist.
3. Cut out and learn the vocabulary words for Lesson 17. Review all.

Option for experienced Level B students: Find a third source text of your own from which to take notes. Fuse those notes into the fused outline from class before writing your paragraph.

Study for Vocabulary Quiz 4. It will cover words from Lessons 1–17.

Lesson 17: Great Inventors: Thomas Edison

Thomas Alva Edison 1841–1931

Unit 6: Summarizing Multiple References

Source Text 1

The Wizard of Menlo Park

From the mid-1800s through the early 1900s, many new inventions changed America—and the world—forever. One of the most prolific inventors of that time was Thomas Edison. However, the most important thing he created was probably not a particular invention. It was his concept of a research laboratory where a team of engineers and mechanics could work together on ideas and inventions. His most famous research laboratory was in Menlo Park, New Jersey. It became known as "the Invention Factory." In Edison's labs he and his team produced more than a thousand patented inventions, including the phonograph (Edison's personal favorite), the first practical electric light bulb, the dynamo for generating electricity, and the motion picture camera.

Edison became known for his perseverance. After many failed experiments, he once stated, "I have not failed. I've just found ten thousand ways that don't work." He also once said, "Our greatest weakness is giving up. The most certain way to succeed is always to try just one more time." Edison certainly succeeded in creating many wonderful inventions. Because of this, he was called "the Wizard of Menlo Park."

Bibliography

Newman, John J. and John H. Schmalbach. *United States History: Preparing for the Advanced Placement Examination*. New York: AMSCO School Publications, 2010.

Lesson 17: Great Inventors: Thomas Edison

Source Text 2

An Amazing Inventor

Thomas Edison is probably America's most famous inventor. He was successful because he worked hard and never gave up. As a young man he worked as a telegraph operator, but he studied electricity and experimented on his own time. Eventually he set up his own shop for working on inventions. At first, he and his team worked on improving other people's inventions, like the typewriter, the telegraph, and the telephone. Soon, though, he built a laboratory in Menlo Park, New Jersey, where he worked on his own inventions. He wanted to build a "talking machine." Some of his workers laughed at his idea, but before long his phonograph was repeating "Mary had a little lamb," the first words ever recorded and played back. After that he spent close to two years trying to develop a practical electric light bulb. He sent men all over the world to find the best material for the filament—one that would glow for a long time. He tried many thousands of materials before he found success. He attributed his success to his perseverance. He is famous for saying, "Genius is 1% inspiration and 99% perspiration." In his life he patented more than a thousand inventions. In 1928 President Calvin Coolidge awarded Thomas Edison the Congressional Gold Medal, one of the highest honors in America. Thomas Edison was truly an amazing inventor.

Bibliography

Eibling, Harold H., John G. Gilman, and Anna M. Skehan. *Great Names in Our Country's Story*. Sacramento: California State Department of Education, 1962.

If students will include a quotation, be sure they understand that even though they only note a few words from it on their outline, when they add the quotation to their paragraph, they must copy all the words exactly as they are in the source text and place them inside quotation marks.

Key Word Notes

Take notes on your own paper formatted like this.

Topic: Great Inventors: Thomas Edison

Source 1: "The Wizard of Menlo Park"

1. *mid 1800s–1900s, T. Edison, prolific, inventor*
2. *created, research, lab, w/team*
3. *> fame, Menlo Park, NJ, "invention factory"*
4. *> 1000 patented, inventions*
5. *ex., phonograph (favo), 💡, movie cam.*
6. *perseverance, "⊘ failed . . . 10,000 ways, ⊘ work"*
7. *called, "Wizard of Menlo Park"*

Source 2: "An Amazing Inventor"

1. *T. Ed., > famous, Amer., inventor*
2. *success, b/c, ⊘, gave up*
3. *ex., talking mach., laugh, ⊘, stop*
4. *phonograph, 1st rec, "Mary had a little lamb"*
5. *= worked, 2 yrs. 💡, tested, 1000s materials*
6. *believed, perseverance = success*
7. *"Genius, 1% inspiration, 99% perspiration"*

Choose some of the notes you took from both sources, and put them in a logical order.

Fused Outline

I. *T.Ed., > famous, Amer, inventor*

1. *w/team, patented, > 1000 inv.*
2. *💡, phonograph, movie cam.*
3. *successful, b/c, ⊘, quit*
4. *ex, ppl, laughed, talking machine*
5. *phonograph 1st rec, "Mary had . . ."*
6. *2 yrs, tested 1000s mat., 💡*
7. *"Genius, 1% inspiration, 99% perspiration"*

Clincher

Banned Adjectives: *Good* and *Bad*

You have already learned to avoid boring and overused adjectives such as *pretty*, *ugly*, and *big*. From this lesson forward you must also avoid *good* and *bad*. These adjectives are vague. The SRP has lists of quality adjectives that can easily replace them. Use those lists, a thesaurus, or your own ideas to substitute adjectives for the banned adjectives in the sentences below.

1. Thomas Edison was a *good* inventor.

ingenious, adept, brilliant, exemplary, extraordinary

2. He built *good* laboratories where *good* workers helped him.

productive, unequalled; skilled, top-notch, capable

3. He did not view failures as *bad* events.

disastrous, ineffectual, detrimental, ruinous, harmful

Brainstorm #4 -ing Openers

Finish each sentence by adding an -ing phrase at the beginning. Place a *4* in the left margin because this is how you will indicate a #4 -ing opener in your paragraph.

4 *Knowing that perseverance is the key to success*, Thomas Edison did not give up.

4 *Thinking such a thing impossible*, some of Edison's team laughed at him when he wanted to make a talking machine.

Other Ideas:

Working tirelessly, inventors like Edison have accomplished great things.

Unit 6: Summarizing Multiple References

Lesson 17 Checklist: Great Inventors: Thomas Edison

Name: ______________________________

STRUCTURE

☐	MLA format (see Appendix I)	_____ (6 pts)
☐	Title centered and repeats or reflects 2–3 key words from clincher	_____ (1 pt)
☐	Topic-clincher repeats or reflects 2–3 key words (highlighted or bold).	_____ (5 pts)

STYLE Each paragraph must contain at least one of each element of style.

	Dress-Ups (underline one of each)	**(3 pts each)**
☐	-ly adverb	_____ (3 pts)
☐	*who-which* clause	_____ (3 pts)
☐	strong verb	_____ (3 pts)
☐	quality adjective	_____ (3 pts)
☐	www.asia.b clause	_____ (3 pts)
	Sentence Openers (numbered; one of each as possible)	
☐	[2] prepositional	_____ (3 pts)
☐	[3] -ly adverb	_____ (3 pts)
☐	[4] -ing ,	_____ (3 pts)
	Decorations ("dec" in margin or italics if typed) (Choose one.)	**(5 pts each)**
☐	alliteration *(allit)*, simile, or metaphor	_____ (5 pts)

MECHANICS

☐	capitalization, punctuation, spelling, grammar	_____ (4 pt)
☐	banned words: go, went, say, said, pretty, ugly, big, good, bad	_____ (-1 pt)

	More Advanced Additions (optional unless your teacher requires them of you)	
☐	vocab word(s) (Label voc or bold.)	_____
☐	dual adj, verbs, or -ly adverbs	_____

Total: __________/ 45

Custom Total: __________/___

Teachers are free to adjust a checklist by requiring only the stylistic techniques that have become easy, plus one new one. "EZ+1." Reproducible checklists are available (see blue page).

Lesson 18: Great Inventors: Alexander Graham Bell

Structures: Unit 6: Summarizing Multiple References

Style: reviewing stylistic techniques

Writing Topics: Alexander Graham Bell

Optional Student Reading Assignment: during Lessons 16–20: *Rifles for Watie*

UNIT 6: SUMMARIZING MULTIPLE REFERENCES

Lesson 18: Great Inventors: Alexander Graham Bell

Begin with Vocabulary Quiz 4.

Review

Read the topic sentence and clincher of your Thomas Edison paragraph from Lesson 17. Did you remember to highlight the two to three key words that tell the topic? In this lesson you will write the second paragraph of a 3-paragraph report about American inventors.

The Assignment

Day 1:

1. Read Source 1, "A Man of Honor," on page 140. On your own paper, formatted like page 142, write three key words to help you remember each of the facts you think are the most interesting or most important. Limit yourself to seven facts.
2. Repeat Step 1 with Source 2, "Thank You, Alexander Graham Bell," on page 141. Do not note facts that you already noted from the first source.
3. Once you have notes from both sources, you will have to organize them into one fused outline on page 142. Remember that report paragraphs need topic sentences. What main idea about Alexander Graham Bell would make a good topic sentence?
4. To make your fused outline, under the topic line, note seven facts. Arrange the notes in an order that makes sense.
5. Use the fused outline to tell back in complete sentences the ideas you will include in your paragraph.

Days 2–4:

1. Polish your Civil War paragraph from Lesson 16.
2. Use your fused outline (not your notes) to write a paragraph about Alexander Graham Bell. Follow and attach the checklist.
3. There are no new vocabulary words for Lesson 18. Review all.

Option for experienced Level B students: Find a third source text of your own from which to take notes. Fuse those notes into the fused outline from class before writing your paragraph. You may also learn a new decoration, the triple extension, from the *U.S. History-Based Writing Lessons Blackline Masters*.

Students will likely need much help. Teachers should model the note taking process and help students limit the facts they choose. Help them look for the interesting or important ideas and facts. Ask them which facts they can do without. Write sample notes on the whiteboard.

While Bell's work with the deaf is interesting, it is not vital to the main topic of inventing the telephone, so it can be left out. Help students focus on facts that best support the topic of the paragraph.

Source Text 1

A Man of Honor

Alexander Graham Bell was born on March 3,1847, in Edinburgh, Scotland, but moved to America as a young man. At age sixteen he became a teacher and from his father learned to teach and communicate better with deaf students. He supported deaf education all his life. This is probably because both his mother and wife were deaf. He also met Helen Keller, a young girl who was deaf, mute, and blind. He helped her parents find a good teacher for her. However, he is most famous for inventing the first practical telephone in 1876.

The idea of transmitting voices over wires came to him while he was working on improving the telegraph. When Thomas Watson joined him, he became interested in the idea, too. Together they succeeded, and Bell promoted the invention in many public exhibitions. At one such event, the emperor of Brazil was so surprised that he shouted, "My God, it talks!" Soon the Bell Telephone Company was organized, and over the next ten years more than 150,000 Americans owned telephones. At first people had to shout to be heard, but Thomas Edison invented a microphone to solve this problem. In 1915 Bell made the first phone call all the way across the country, from New York to California. When he died on August 2, 1922, the phone system was shut down for one minute to honor him. Also, in his honor, the units that measure how loud sounds are were named after him: the bel and the decibel.

Bibliography

"Alexander Graham Bell." *famousscientists.org.* N.p. 14 Sept. 2014. Web. 20 April 2016.

When noting quotations, write only a few words inside quotation marks. Tell students that when they write their paragraph, they must copy the exact words and use quotation marks.

Lesson 18: Great Inventors: Alexander Graham Bell

Source Text 2

Thank You, Alexander Graham Bell

Alexander Graham Bell was a Scottish-born inventor most famous for inventing the first practical telephone, but he patented many inventions. He once said, "An inventor ... wants to improve whatever he sees; he wants to benefit the world." From a young age Bell enjoyed problem solving. For example, when he was twelve, he noticed that the grain mill in his town was very slow at husking wheat. He went home and invented a machine to speed up the process, and the town used his machine for years.

In 1871 after he had moved to Boston, Bell began work on improving the telegraph. He wanted to be able to send several messages over the same wire. This sparked his interest in transmitting voices over wires. However, the men funding his work were concerned that this was distracting him from working on the telegraph, so they hired Thomas Watson to work with Bell and keep him focused. Soon, though, Watson was just as intrigued with the idea of transmitting voices. In 1876 they built the first practical telephone. By 1886 more than 150,000 people had telephones. Later he predicted, "The day will come when the man at the telephone will be able to see the distant person to whom he is speaking." How right he was! We can thank Mr. Bell for our phones.

Bibliography

Biography.com Editors. "Alexander Graham Bell." *Biography.com*. A & E Television Network. N.d. Web. 20 April 2016.

There is much information about Bell in the source texts. Remind students to focus on facts related to Bell as an inventor, especially as the inventor of the telephone.

There are no brainstorming pages for this assignment. Choose elements of style that your students seem to have the most difficulty with, and discuss possible ideas. Write them on a whiteboard. These will likely be the #2 prepositional opener, the #4 -ing opener, and the decorations. Examples:

2 *In 1871 Bell worked to improve the telegraph.*

4 *Hoping to be able to transmit voices over wire, he and Watson worked tirelessly.*

(allit) *Bell toiled tirelessly with trying to transmit voice over wire.*

Unit 6: Summarizing Multiple References

Key Word Outline

(Remember, only choose facts that relate to the topic.)

Topic: Great Inventors: Alexander Graham Bell invents the telephone.

Source 1: "A Man of Honor"

1. *born, 1847, Scotland, Amer., yn man*
2. *fame, 1st, practical, telephone, 1876*
3. *💡 voice → wire, w/telegraph*
4. *w/Thomas Watson, succeeded, pub, demos*
5. *1st, shout, T. Edison, microphone*
6. *1915, Bell, 1st call, Amer., (NY → CA)*
7. *xx, Aug. 2, 1922, phones, off, 1 min., honor*

Source 2: "Thank You, Alexander Graham Bell"

1. *patented, > inventions, "inv. ⊙ ⊙ world . . ."*
2. *1871, worked, improve, telegraph*
3. *wanted, > messages, same,*
4. *T. Watson, hired, focus, telegraph*
5. *instead, helped w/phone*
6. *by 1886, > 150,000 ppl w/phone*
7. *predicted, ppl, ⊙ ⊙, talk, to*

Choose some of the notes you took from both sources, and put them in a logical order.

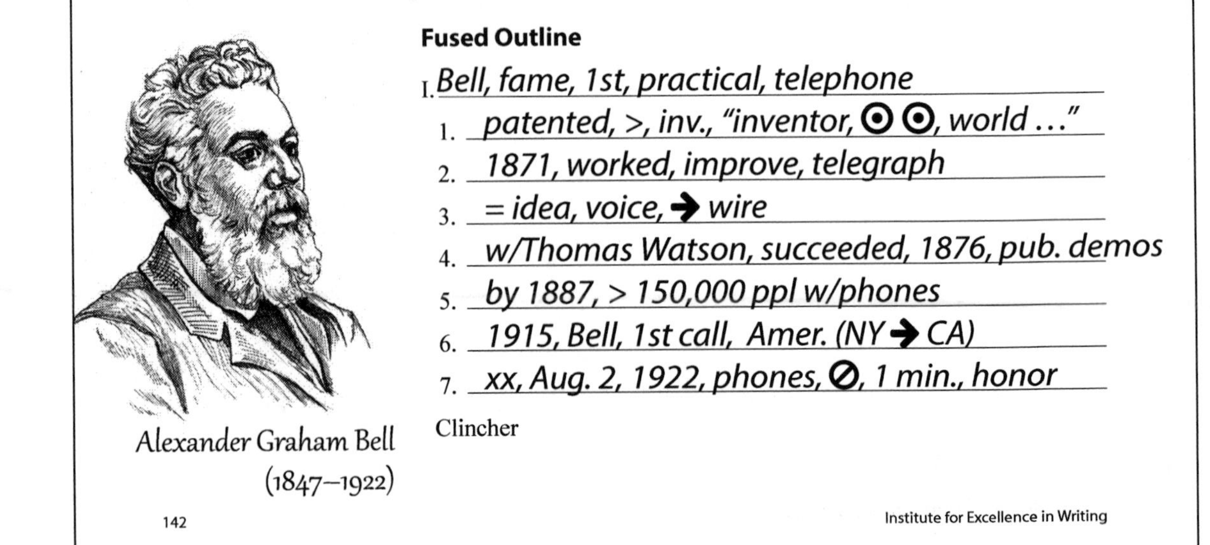

Fused Outline

I. *Bell, fame, 1st, practical, telephone*

1. *patented, >, inv., "inventor, ⊙ ⊙, world . . ."*
2. *1871, worked, improve, telegraph*
3. *= idea, voice, → wire*
4. *w/Thomas Watson, succeeded, 1876, pub. demos*
5. *by 1887, > 150,000 ppl w/phones*
6. *1915, Bell, 1st call, Amer. (NY → CA)*
7. *xx, Aug. 2, 1922, phones, ⊘, 1 min., honor*

Clincher

Alexander Graham Bell (1847–1922)

142 Institute for Excellence in Writing

Lesson 18: Great Inventors: Alexander Graham Bell

Lesson 18 Final Checklist: Great Inventors: Alexander Graham Bell

Name: ______________________________

Note: This paragraph will be graded when it is placed within the 3-paragraph report assigned in Lesson 19.

STRUCTURE

☐	MLA format (see Appendix I)	____ (4 pts)
☐	Title centered and repeats or reflects 2–3 key words from clincher	____ (1 pt)
☐	Topic-clincher repeats or reflects 2–3 key words (highlighted or bold).	____ (5 pts)

STYLE Each paragraph must contain at least one of each element of style.

	Dress-Ups (underline one of each)	**(3 pts each)**
☐	-ly adverb	____ (3 pts)
☐	*who-which* clause	____ (3 pts)
☐	strong verb	____ (3 pts)
☐	quality adjective	____ (3 pts)
☐	www.asia.b clause	____ (3 pts)
	Sentence Openers (numbered; one of each as possible)	**(2 pts each)**
☐	[2] prepositional	____ (2 pts)
☐	[3] -ly adverb	____ (2 pts)
☐	[4] -ing ,	____ (2 pts)
	Decorations ("dec" in margin or italics if typed) (Choose one.)	**(5 pts each)**
☐	alliteration *(allit)*, simile, or metaphor	____ (5 pts)

MECHANICS

☐	capitalization, punctuation, spelling, grammar	____ (4 pts)
☐	banned words: go, went, say, said, pretty, ugly, big, good, bad	____ (-1 pt)

More Advanced Additions (optional unless your teacher requires them of you)

☐	vocab word(s) (Label voc or bold.)	____
☐	dual adj, verbs, or -ly adverbs	____
☐	triple extension	____

Total: ________/ 40

Custom Total: ________/___

Teachers are free to adjust a checklist by requiring only the stylistic techniques that have become easy, plus one new one. "EZ+1." Reproducible checklists are available (see blue page).

Lesson 19: Great Inventors: The Wright Brothers

Structures: Unit 6: Summarizing Multiple References
Skill: compiling a bibliography
Writing Topics: the Wright Brothers
Optional Student Reading Assignment: during Lessons 16–20: *Rifles for Watie*

Return the Edison paragraph. Do not collect the Bell paragraph. Students will need it for their homework.

UNIT 6: SUMMARIZING MULTIPLE REFERENCES

Lesson 19: Great Inventors: The Wright Brothers

Review

In this lesson you will write the final paragraph of the 3-paragraph report about great inventors. Then, you will put all three paragraphs into one report. If your teacher assigns it, you will also add a bibliography.

The Assignment

Day 1:

1. Follow the procedure taught in Lessons 17 and 18 to write a paragraph about the Wright Brothers. Use pages 146–148.
2. Go to page 149 to see how to put all three paragraphs together. See pages 149–150 to see how to add a bibliography.

Days 2–4:

1. Polish your Thomas Edison paragraph from Lesson 17. You will include this in your 3-paragraph report. (See page 149.)
2. Use your fused outline (not your notes) to write a paragraph about the Wright Brothers. Follow and attach the checklist on page 151.
3. Put all three great inventor paragraphs together into one report. (See page 149.) Follow the checklist on page 152 carefully.
4. If your teacher assigns it, use pages 149–150 to help you add a bibliography.
5. There are no new vocabulary words for this lesson.
6. Be sure to save this report because you will need it in Lesson 25.

Orville Wright (1871–1948)

Wilbur Wright (1867–1912)

Unit 6: Summarizing Multiple References

Source Text 1

The Age of Flight Begins

Orville and Wilbur Wright are famous for building and flying the first motorized airplane. While neither formally graduated from high school, both were intelligent and enjoyed working with machines. When they became interested in flight, they first experimented with gliders. They built a wind tunnel and tirelessly tested many different wing shapes until they found the one they believed was the best. Then they built a huge glider and took it to Kitty Hawk, North Carolina, to test. It flew amazingly well, so they decided to work on adding a motor to it. Of course, they built their own engine. They named their plane *The Wright Flyer I.* It had a wing span of forty feet and weighed about six hundred pounds.

The Wrights continued to work to improve their invention. Even after a horrible crash in which Orville almost died, they did not stop. Their flights became longer and longer, and they flew demonstration flights all over the world. The age of flight had begun.

Bibliography

Hobar, Linda Lacour. *The Mystery of History, Volume IV*. Dover: Bright Ideas Press, 2014. Print.

Lesson 19: Great Inventors: The Wright Brothers

Source Text 2

Great Americans

As boys, Orville and Wilbur Wright were fascinated with machines. They made and sold small mechanical toys. While still in their twenties, they began to rent and sell bicycles. Soon they also manufactured bikes. They became interested in studying flight. They began building and experimenting with gliders. In 1900 and 1901 they went to Kitty Hawk, North Carolina, to test their first gliders that could carry a man, but they could not get the lift they wanted. So they built a 6-foot wind tunnel and experimented with lots and lots of model wings. They were able to develop a much better wing design. They returned to Kitty Hawk and made almost a thousand flights in their new glider, perfecting the balance and control of the craft. They were then ready to add power to it.

When they returned to Kitty Hawk in 1903, they had added a motor to their glider. Four men and one boy witnessed their historic flights on December 17. Orville made the first flight of 120 feet. Wilbur had the longest flight of 852 feet. The public took little interest in their achievement, but the brothers continued to quietly work on improving their machine. By 1915 their craft could fly over 24 miles. The age of flight began. Both Orville and Wilbur were elected into the Hall of Fame for Great Americans because of their contributions to the advancement of flight.

Bibliography

Bilstein, Roger E. "Wright Brothers." *World Book Encyclopedia*, 1988 ed. Print.

There is much information about the Wright brothers in the source texts. Remind students to focus on facts related to building the first motorized airplane. That is the topic of the paragraph.

Key Word Outline

(Remember, only choose facts that relate to the topic.)

Topic: Great Inventors: The Wright Brothers invent a motorized airplane.

Source 1: "The Age of Flight Begins"

1. *fame, 1st, motor, airplane*
2. *machines, began, exp. w/gliders*
3. *wind tun., test, > wings*
4. *built, glider, → Kitty Hawk, NC*
5. *added, motor,* Wright Flyer I, *600 lbs.*
6. *Dec. 17, 1903, 1st flt, Orville, 120 ft, 12 sec.*
7. *Wilbur, longest, 852 ft., 59 sec.*

Source 2: "Great Americans"

1. *1st gliders, ⊘, lift 6 ft. wind tun.*
2. *better, wings, glider*
3. *1000 flts, perfected, control*
4. *1903, added, motor → Kitty Hawk*
5. *by 1915, fly, 24 mi.*
6. *age, flt, began*
7. *both, Hall of Fame, > Amer., b/c flt*

Choose some of the notes you took from both sources, and put them in a logical order.

Fused Outline

I. *Wright bros., fame, 1st, motor, plane*

1. *machines, exp, w/gliders*
2. *6 ft, wind, tun., tested > wings*
3. *built, glider, > 1000 flts, perfect*
4. *added, motor,* Wright Flyer 1, *600 lbs*
5. *Kitty Hawk, NC, Dec. 17, 1903, 1st flt*
6. *Orville, 120 ft., 12 sec.; Wilbur, longest, 852 ft., 59 sec.*
7. *age, flt, began*
8. ______

Clincher

Lesson 19: Great Inventors: The Wright Brothers

Putting It All Together

Once you have written the paragraph about the Wrights, you will have three paragraphs about great inventors. You can now combine these paragraphs into one report. To do so, simply move them all to the same page. Place the Edison paragraph first, then the Alexander Graham Bell paragraph (remember to indent), and finally the Wright Brothers paragraph (again, indent). You will end the report with a bibliography page that lists the sources of information you used. Below and on the next page, see how to do this.

Creating Your Title

Your report will have one title, taken from two to three key words in the last sentence of the paragraph about the Wrights. Try to make the title general enough to apply to all the inventors, not just the Wrights. In order to do this, you might have to change your clincher a little. For example, you might have ended the Wright Brothers paragraph with something like this:

> *Orville and Wilbur Wright are remembered for their work in making flight possible.*

You could add words about them being great inventors to that sentence to help you make a title that will apply to all three inventors:

> *Orville and Wilbur Wright were great inventors who are remembered for their work in making flight possible.*

Now your title could reflect the words "great inventors" and apply to all the inventors you wrote about.

Bibliography

A bibliography is a list of the sources that were used to write a research report. It is placed as the last page of the report. See the SRP for instructions on how to format a bibliography.

In order to practice listing various types of sources, pretend that you actually used the sources given at the bottom of each source text. If you used other sources, include those in your bibliography as well.

Bibliographic Information

Be sure students understand that to complete their bibliography on the last page of their report, they must add the rest of the information about each source by looking at the bottom of each source text. If they used sources of their own, they must add those as well.

Internet Articles

Internet articles can be tricky to list. Here is how to format an Internet article listing:

Author's last name, first name. [If no author given, just skip this.] "Title of Article." [in quotes] *Title of website. [in italics]* Publisher or Sponsor. [Put n.p. if not given.] Date posted. [n.d. if not given.] Web. Date you looked at the site [day month year].

The primary sources for Alexander Graham Bell are Internet sources and are given in the above format for you. If you used other Internet sources, you will need to study this format closely.

Preparing to Write Your Bibliography

On the lines below, list the first words of each entry from this book in alphabetical order. If the author is known, the author's last name should be the first word of the entry. If the author is not known, the title of the book (in italics) or title of the Internet article (in quotation marks) should be first. Listing them in order here will help you know the order in which to place them in your bibliography.

"Alexander Graham Bell" (Note: Article title should be in quotation marks.)

Bilstein, Roger E.

Biography.com Editors (Note: Names of websites are italicized.)

Eibling, Harold H., John Gilman, and Anna Skehan

Hobar, Linda Lacour

Newman, John J. and John H. Schmalbach

Lesson 19: Great Inventors: The Wright Brothers

Lesson 19 Final Checklist: Great Inventors: The Wright Brothers

Name: ____

(Place this paragraph in your 3-paragraph report of great inventors.)

STRUCTURE

☐	MLA format (see Appendix I)	_____ (6 pts)
☐	Title centered and repeats or reflects 2–3 key words from clincher	_____ (1 pt)
☐	Topic-clincher repeats or reflects 2–3 key words (highlighted or bold).	_____ (5 pts)

STYLE Each paragraph must contain at least one of each element of style.

	Dress-Ups (underline one of each)	**(3 pts each)**
☐	-ly adverb	_____ (3 pts)
☐	*who-which* clause	_____ (3 pts)
☐	strong verb	_____ (3 pts)
☐	quality adjective	_____ (3 pts)
☐	www.asia.b clause	_____ (3 pts)
	Sentence Openers (numbered; one of each as possible)	
☐	[2] prepositional	_____ (3 pts)
☐	[3] -ly adverb	_____ (3 pts)
☐	[4] -ing ,	_____ (3 pts)
	Decorations ("dec" in margin or italics if typed) (Choose one.)	**(5 pts each)**
☐	alliteration *(allit)*, simile, or metaphor	_____ (5 pts)

MECHANICS

☐	capitalization, punctuation, spelling, grammar	_____ (4 pts)
☐	banned words: go, went, say, said, pretty, ugly, big, good, bad	_____ (-1 pt)

	More Advanced Additions (optional unless your teacher requires them of you)	
☐	vocab word(s) (Label voc or bold.)	_____
☐	dual adj, verbs, or -ly adverbs	_____
☐	triple extension	_____

Total: _________/ 45

Custom Total: _________/___

Teachers are free to adjust a checklist by requiring only the stylistic techniques that have become easy, plus one new one. "EZ+1." Reproducible checklists are available (see blue page).

Unit 6: Summarizing Multiple References

Lesson 19 Final Checklist 2: Three-Paragraph Report: Great Inventors

Name: ______________________________

STRUCTURE

☐	MLA format (see Appendix I)	_____ (10 pts)
☐	Title centered and repeats or reflects 2–3 key words from clincher	_____ (2 pts)
☐	Topic-clincher repeats or reflects 2–3 key words (highlighted or bold).	_____ (10 pts)

BIBLIOGRAPHY

☐	Entries are in alphabetical order.	_____ (3 pts)
☐	Entries are in proper format.	_____ (5 pts)

OTHER

☐	Checklists for Lessons 17–19 attached	_____ (5 pts)

Total: __________/ 35

Custom Total: __________/___

Lesson 20: The Statue of Liberty: Hopes and Dreams, Part 1

Structures: Unit 7: Inventive Writing

Style: #5 clausal opener (www.asia.b)

Writing Topics: hopes and dreams for your future

Optional Student Reading Assignment: during Lessons 16–20: *Rifles for Watie*

Teaching Writing: Structure and Style

Watch the sections for Unit 7: Inventive Writing.
At IEW.com/twss-help reference the TWSS Viewing Guides.

UNIT 7: INVENTIVE WRITING

Lesson 20: The Statue of Liberty: Hopes and Dreams, Part 1

Review

Play a vocabulary review game from the Teacher's Manual.

In the following lessons you will learn how to structure a basic 4- or 5-paragraph essay in response to a prompt. In this lesson you will also learn a new sentence opener, the #5 clausal opener (www.asia.b).

Notes from the Brain

In the next few lessons, you will write essays without the help of source texts, but you will still need to make a key word outline of notes to organize your ideas. So, where are you going to get your notes? You are going to get them from your brain! To do so, you must learn to ask yourself questions. Memorizing some question starter words and phrases will help you.

What? Who? Where? When? Why? How? Best/Worst? Problems? Value? Meaning?

You will practice using these question words to give you ideas for what to write in response to the prompt below.

Prompt

The Statue of Liberty was a gift from France to America. The statue symbolizes the freedom and opportunity that America is known for all over the world. Lady Liberty was placed in New York harbor where she holds a torch in one hand and the Declaration of Independence in the other. Broken chains are at her feet. The Statue of Liberty represents the hopes and dreams of a bright future for the many immigrants who have come to America since 1886.

What hopes and dreams do you have for your future? In other words, what things do you hope to do or accomplish in either the near or far future?

Write two body paragraphs this week. You will add an introduction and conclusion in Lesson 21.

Before you begin, though, learn a new sentence opener, the #5 clausal opener (www.asia.b).

p.54

Unit 7: Inventive Writing

The #5 Clausal Opener: www.asia.b

You have been using the www.asia.b clause as a dress-up. You know that a www.asia.b clause begins with one of these words: *when, while, where, as, since, if, although,* or *because*.

Now you must use this type of clause as a sentence opener as well as a dress-up. In other words, you must begin at least one sentence of each paragraph with a www.asia.b clause in addition to having such a clause in the middle of a sentence as a dress-up.

Remember, a clause that begins with one of the www.asia.b words cannot be a complete sentence by itself. Look at the sample sentences below. Each has a www.asia.b clause plus another complete thought.

If the clause is at the beginning of a sentence, it is a #5 opener, and a *5* indicates it in the left margin. Notice that a www.asia.b clause at the beginning of a sentence is always followed by a comma.

When the www.asia.b clause is used as a sentence opener, it is simply numbered 5 in the left margin. It is not underlined as when it is used as a dress-up.

5 *While I am in college, I want to study robotics and compete in a national robot contest.*

5 *As I traveled the world, I would learn to scuba dive at the Great Barrier Reef.*

Practice

Write a sentence with a #5 clausal opener (about anything). Don't forget the comma.

5 *When a clausal opener is used, follow it with a comma.*

Lesson 20: The Statue of Liberty: Hopes and Dreams, Part 1

The Assignment

Day 1:

1. Since you need two body paragraphs, you need two topics to write about. As a class discuss several possible ideas.
2. The teacher should model the question process by choosing one of the topics to outline together. She should ask questions and encourage specific details and examples. Students should not copy the class KWO, but they should notice the process. Study the sample on the following page.
3. Paragraphs must follow the topic-clincher rule. Keep in mind that you will be adding a paragraph of introduction and a paragraph of conclusion in Lesson 21.
4. See page 158 for help with adding details to your paragraphs.
5. Look at the vocabulary words for Lesson 20. Try to use some in your essay.

Days 2–4:

1. Complete the outline and essay about your hopes and dreams. Remember to ask yourself plenty of questions to get ideas about what to say. Also, try to include specific examples and descriptions. See page 158.
2. Remember to add the new sentence opener, a #5 www.asia.b clause.
3. Follow the checklist on page 160.
4. Cut out and learn the vocabulary words for Lesson 20. Try to use some in your essay.
5. If you are reading the suggested literature, obtain *Hattie Big Sky* by Kirby Larson for next week.

Do not collect the body paragraphs from Lesson 20. Students will add introduction and conclusion paragraphs in the next lesson.

Unit 7: Inventive Writing

Sample

Topic A	want, travel, Amer, nature landscapes
Who?	1. w/family
How?	2. RV, 1 yr
What?	3. redwood forest
Why?	4. Gen. Sherman, pic
Where?	5. camp, Yellowstone, geysers
How feel?	6. anticipation, excitement
Other ideas?	7. AK, glaciers, northern lights, awe
Clincher	

Here is a sample paragraph from the above outline.

I would love to visit as many of *America's* national parks and *beautiful landscapes* as possible. I would like my family to rent a spacious RV for a whole year and drive wherever we choose. The redwood and sequoia forests are some of the first places I would want to see. Certainly I would be in awe of the towering trees, and I would be sure to snap a picture of us driving through giant General Sherman. Next I would want to head for Yellowstone National Park to camp. I would love to hike and camp and see the beauty of nature. I have never seen a real geyser, so I think anticipating seeing Old Faithful spray hot steam into the air would be exciting. I would also hope to see the moose and bison there. Alaska would be next. I want to climb a massive, sparkling glacier and see the northern lights splash colors across the sky. I think I would be awestruck. There are *many breathtaking sights* to see and experience across *our great land.*

Key Word Outline

I. Topic A: *want, be, nurse*

1. *work, w/children*
2. *hospitals, often, ☹*
3. *dark, stinky, w/crying*
4. *kids, afraid, lonely*
5. *want, make, ☺, hope*
6. *fill, rooms, balloons*
7. *story, time, surprises*

Clincher A

II. Topic B: *also, want, b, mom*

1. *5, children*
2. *homeschool, learning, fun*
3. *teach, love, siblings*
4. *teach, help, others*
5. *take, field, trips*
6. *+ fun, trips (Disney), see, ☺*
7. *mom, > love, + love*

Clincher B

Brain-Helping Questions

Who?
Where?
What?
How?
Why?
What kind?
How big?
How many?
Favorite?
How feel?
Worst?
When?
Other ideas?

Look at the sample paragraph on page 156. Notice it does not simply say, "Old faithful would be exciting." What does it add that tells how or why it would be exciting? Then, have students find general ideas on their outlines and fill in specific details to explain the how and why. Let them share their ideas with the class.

Stretch Your Ideas

For some students adding specific details and descriptions is the most difficult part of writing essays, but both are important. To help with this, do the following.

1. Add *specific* details or examples to one or more of the ideas in your outline.

   For example, if you said something like *Sky diving would be fun*, you could add something like the following:

   Sky diving would be the ultimate thrill. As you stand at the door of a plane thousands of feet above the ground, you hold your breath in suspense. Then, it's your turn, and you free fall. Your heart pounds as the ground gets closer and closer, and the wind contorts your face. You have to let out a scream of thrill or fright. Then, you pull the cord and—whoosh! Up you zoom, then you descend slowly.

   Sky diving would be fun by itself is vague. It is boring. It says little. The addition is much more specific. It tells *how* and *why* sky diving would be fun. It is much more engaging.

   Try to add such detail to an idea you have for one of your paragraphs. Be *specific*.

   ____

   ____

2. Look for things to describe with five-senses words. For example, which of the following sentences is more descriptive and, therefore, more vivid?

   I love to camp. At night we sit around a fire and roast marshmallows for s'mores. They are delicious.

   I love to camp. At night we sit around a crackling fire listening to the hoots of the owls in the forest. We roast marshmallows until the sweet smell of the burning sugar fills the air. Then the white gooey blobs melt the dark, yummy chocolate to make delicious s'mores.

   Highlight the five-senses words in the example above. Then, add at least three five-senses words to an idea you have for your essay. What might you see, hear, feel, smell, or taste? Think of adjectives, verbs, and -ly adverbs that appeal to the senses. Write ideas below.

   First, find five-senses words in the sample paragraph on page 156.

   Then, have students find places in their outlines where they can add

   five-senses words. Let them share their ideas with the class.

   ____

Lesson 20: The Statue of Liberty: Hopes and Dreams, Part 1

#5 Clausal Opener

Don't forget to add a #5 clausal opener. It, too, can help you add more details to your ideas. Write two ideas for a #5 clausal opener that you could use in your essay, each for a different paragraph.

1. *5 If I were a nurse, I could bring smiles to sick children.*

2. *5 Although I am young, I would like to help other children.*

Unit 7: Inventive Writing

Lesson 20 Checklist (Body Paragraphs): The Statue of Liberty: Hopes and Dreams, Part 1

Name: ______________________________

STRUCTURE

☐	MLA format (see Appendix I)	_____ (4 pts)
☐	Topic-clincher repeats or reflects 2–3 key words (highlighted or bold). No title.	_____ (8 pts)

STYLE Each paragraph must contain at least one of each element of style.

¶ 1	¶ 2	Dress-Ups (underline one of each)	(1 pt each)
☐	☐	-ly adverb	_____ (2 pts)
☐	☐	*who-which* clause	_____ (2 pts)
☐	☐	strong verb	_____ (2 pts)
☐	☐	quality adjective	_____ (2 pts)
☐	☐	www.asia.b clause	_____ (2 pts)

¶ 1	¶ 2	Sentence Openers* (numbered; one of each as possible)	
☐	☐	[1] subject	_____ (2 pts)
☐	☐	[2] prepositional	_____ (2 pts)
☐	☐	[3] -ly adverb	_____ (2 pts)
☐	☐	[4] -ing ,	_____ (2 pts)
☐	☐	[5] clausal , (www.asia.b)	_____ (2 pts)

*** The number of sentence openers required depends on the number of sentences present in the paragraph.**

		Decorations ("dec" in margin or italics if typed) (one per paragraph)	(2 pts each)
☐	☐	alliteration *(allit)*, simile, or metaphor	_____ (4 pts)

MECHANICS

☐	capitalization, punctuation, spelling, grammar	_____ (4 pts)
☐	banned words: go, went, say, said, pretty, ugly, big, good, bad	_____ (-1 pt)

More Advanced Additions (optional unless your teacher requires them of you)

☐	vocab word(s) (Label voc or bold.); dual adj, verbs, or -ly adverbs; trip. ext.	_____

Total: _________/ 40

Custom Total: _________/___

Teachers are free to adjust a checklist by requiring only the stylistic techniques that have become easy, plus one new one. "EZ+1." Reproducible checklists are available (see blue page).

Lesson 21: The Statue of Liberty: Hopes and Dreams, Part 2

Structures: Unit 7: Inventive Writing

Style: adding introduction and conclusion paragraphs

Writing Topics: hopes and dreams for your future, cont.

Optional Student Reading Assignment: during Lessons 21–23: *Hattie Big Sky*

Do not collect the body paragraphs from Lesson 20. Students will add an introduction and conclusion to them in this lesson.

Lesson 21: The Statue of Liberty: Hopes and Dreams, Part 2

UNIT 7: INVENTIVE WRITING

Lesson 21: The Statue of Liberty: Hopes and Dreams, Part 2

Review

1. Play a review game such as Tic-Tac-Toe from the Teacher's Manual.
2. What are the question starter words that help you think of details to add to your paragraphs?
3. Read your topic sentences and clinchers for Lesson 20 paragraphs. Then share part of one of the paragraphs where you purposely added specific details or description.

what? who? where? when? why? how? best/worst? problems? value? meaning?

In this lesson you will outline and add a paragraph of conclusion and a paragraph of introduction to the paragraphs you wrote in Lesson 20 about your hopes and dreams.

Conclusions and Introductions

The job of the conclusion is to remind the reader of the topics and then to clarify what is the most important thing to remember about the subject and why. It should end with an essay clincher that ties to the beginning of the introduction.

The job of the introduction is to introduce the topics of the essay. But the introduction has another just as important purpose. An introduction must grab the reader's attention—it must entice him to keep reading. If you begin with something boring, it is likely that your reader will put down the essay without finishing it.

It is often easier to outline and write the conclusion directly after writing the body. This is because the conclusion must flow smoothly from the final body paragraph, and the details in the body paragraphs will be fresh on your mind as you move to the conclusion. For these reasons, we will outline the conclusion before the introduction. Outline and write the introduction last.

Follow the assignment instruction to outline a conclusion and an introduction for your hopes and dreams essay.

The Assignment

Day 1:

1. First, read the sample introduction and conclusion on page 163.
2. With a teacher fill in the blank outline on page 164 for a conclusion. Read your notes as complete sentences to be sure you understand how to use your outline to write a conclusion.
3. Do the same for an introduction, using page 165.

Days 2–4:

1. Polish your "Great Inventors" report from Lesson 19.
2. Using the class outlines as guides, add an introduction and conclusion to the beginning and end of the paragraphs you wrote about your hopes and dreams in Lesson 20. In other words, put all four paragraphs together into one essay. Follow and attach the checklist on page 166. Also attach the body checklist, page 160.
3. Cut out and learn the vocabulary words for Lesson 21. Try to use some in your essay.

Literature Suggestion

Read *Hattie Big Sky* by Kirby Larson with Lessons 21–23.

Lesson 21: The Statue of Liberty: Hopes and Dreams, Part 2

Sample Introduction

[Grab attention] America is beautiful and diverse. **[Subject and background]** Our landscapes are filled with awe-inspiring beauty and grandeur. Our cities are filled with culture and history. We can read all about our great land in books, or see it on TV and the Internet, but it would be much more exciting to experience it. I would love to spend an entire year traveling across America. **[A]** First I would camp, hike, and backpack in many of our national parks and forests. **[B]** Next I would enjoy the culture and history of some of our major cities.

Sample Conclusion

[Topics A, B] It would be wonderful to be able to take a year off from everyday life and experience the rich and diverse landscapes and cities of America. **[Most significant]** Such a trip would give me a deep appreciation for the country as well as unforgettable memories. **[Why]** It would be a real education, not a textbook or Internet education. **[Essay clincher]** Perhaps someday soon I will be on the road with all of America's splendor before me.

Conclusion

Even though the introduction will come first in your essay, we will outline the conclusion first, as explained on page 161.

Restate the topics: Write a sentence about each topic, or list them in one sentence.

The most significant and why: What is the most important thing about your topic and why? What is the most important thing to remember about all your topics? Why? For example, do you believe your hopes and dreams will become real? What will you do to make them happen? Why do you believe they are important?

Essay clincher: Because the essay clincher and the "grab attention" of the introduction should repeat or reflect 2–3 key words, try to do them together.

If you have a great idea for ending your conclusion, use 2–3 key words from that idea at the beginning of your introduction. If you have a great idea for a "grab attention" to begin the introduction, use 2–3 key words from that idea to help you think of an essay clincher. Use a thesaurus if you need help. What words are reflected in the sample opening sentence and essay clincher on page 163?

Remember the title rule: The title repeats or reflects 2–3 key words from your final sentence.

Outline for Conclusion

Topic A ___*study, hard, nurse*___

Topic B ___*hope, be, mom*___

Most significant ___*love, children, be ☺*___

____

____

Why? ___*☺ children →, ☺ adults*___

___*+, ☺, spreads*___

Essay clincher repeats or reflects 2–3 key words from the first sentence of the introduction.

Lesson 21: The Statue of Liberty: Hopes and Dreams, Part 2

Introduction

Grab your reader's attention: Begin your report with something intriguing that will make your reader want to read on. Is there something especially exciting about your subject? If you have already written an essay clincher in the conclusion, how can you repeat or reflect two to three key words from it to begin your introduction?

Introduce the subject, and give background information: Tell your reader the subject of the essay, but do not say anything similar to *"This essay is about."* Simply make a general statement about the subject. Something as basic as *Everyone has hopes and dreams for the future* might work as would anything related to what your dream is.

Then, give any background information you think would be helpful. What makes you desire the things you will write about? (Notice how the sample introduction does this.)

Mention the topics: The simplest way to meet this requirement is to list the topics, but a list is not very interesting reading. Try to write one complete sentence for each of your topics; tell the main idea of each body paragraph. You may need to add phrases or sentences to connect these ideas smoothly.

Outline for Introduction

Grab attention.	*love, little, children*
Subject/Background	*have, siblings, 2 y.o., 4 y.o.*
	babysit, + church nursery
	fun, play, w/
	☹, when, child, hurts
Topic A	*want, b, nurse, sick*
Topic B	*+ mom, w/ lots, children, ♥*

Unit 7: Inventive Writing

Lesson 21 Final Checklist (Introduction and Conclusion) The Statue of Liberty: Hopes and Dreams, Part 2

Name: ______________________________

STRUCTURE

☐ Title centered and repeats or reflects 2–3 key words from essay clincher	____	(2 pts)
Introduction Paragraph		
☐ Opening grabs attention.	____	(5 pts)
☐ Subject and background information	____	(5 pts)
☐ Topics mentioned	____	(6 pts)
Body Paragraphs		
☐ (Attach checklist, page 160.)	____	(4 pts)
Conclusion Paragraph		
☐ Restate topics.	____	(6 pts)
☐ Most significant and why	____	(5 pts)
☐ Essay clincher (Reflect the beginning of the introduction.)	____	(2 pts)

STYLE Each paragraph must contain at least one of each element of style.

Dress-Ups (underline one of each)		**(1 pt each)**
☐ ☐ -ly adverb	____	(2 pts)
☐ ☐ *who-which* clause	____	(2 pts)
☐ ☐ strong verb	____	(2 pts)
☐ ☐ quality adjective	____	(2 pts)
☐ ☐ www.asia.b clause	____	(2 pts)
Sentence Openers* (numbered; one of each as possible)		
☐ ☐ [1] subject	____	(2 pts)
☐ ☐ [2] prepositional	____	(2 pts)
☐ ☐ [3] -ly adverb	____	(2 pts)
☐ ☐ [4] -ing ,	____	(2 pts)
☐ ☐ [5] clausal , (www.asia.b)	____	(2 pts)

*** The number of sentence openers required depends on the number of sentences present in the paragraph.**

Decorations ("dec" in margin or italics if typed) (one per paragraph)		**(3 pts each)**
☐ ☐ alliteration *(allit),* simile, or metaphor	____	(6 pts)

MECHANICS

☐ capitalization, punctuation, spelling, grammar	____	(4 pts)
☐ banned words: go, went, say, said, pretty, ugly, big, good, bad	____	(-1 pt)

Total: ________/ 65

Custom Total: ________/___

Lesson 22: World War I: Soldiers

Structures: Unit 7: Inventive Writing

Style: no new stylistic techniques

Writing Topics: soldiers

Optional Student Reading Assignment: during Lessons 21–23: *Hattie Big Sky*

UNIT 7: INVENTIVE WRITING

Lesson 22: World War I: Soldiers

Review

Some students should read their introduction and conclusion from Lesson 21 to the class. The class should identify each required component (*Introduction*—attention getter, subject and background, Topic A and Topic B. *Conclusion*—topics, most significant and why, essay clincher that reflects two to three key words from the introduction).

The Assignment

Follow the instructions below to write a 4- or 5-paragraph essay responding to the following prompt. A third body paragraph is an optional advanced addition. Your teacher will decide whether you must write it.

Prompt

World War I was horrific. Many young American soldiers headed to Europe with grandiose visions of quick victory and glory. But what they discovered was disease, death, and destruction everywhere. WWI introduced terrifying weapons such as poisonous gases, flamethrowers, tanks, machine guns, and improved artillery. In addition, much of the war was fought in muddy trenches, which protected soldiers from some of the weapons but made life miserable. Soldiers could be in trenches no more than 6 feet wide for months at a time. Disease spread rapidly in these trenches. Soldiers of WWI endured unspeakable hardships. But they did so to fight for what they believed in and to protect their countries.

Write four or five paragraphs about American soldiers (or soldiers in general). Remember that this is not a report. Do not go to sources for help. Write your own thoughts and ideas about soldiers.

Since the prompt asks for four or five paragraphs, you will need two or three body paragraphs plus an introduction and conclusion.

1. First, determine the topics of each of your body paragraphs. Here are some suggestions, but you may think of others.

the life and sacrifices of a soldier	soldiers you know personally
why we need soldiers	famous soldiers

2. Take out a sheet of paper for each topic you will write about. Format each paper as shown on the next page. Please note: For the 5-paragraph essay, the introduction is Roman numeral I, body paragraphs are II–IV, and conclusion is V.

Unit 7: Inventive Writing

II. *soldiers, brave, noble*

1. *most, vol., serve, country*
2. *know, → war*
3. *risk, life, defend, U.S.*
4. *→, enemy, territory*
5. *face, fire, boldly*
6. *willing, sacrifice, self*
7. *for, us, + liberty*

Clincher

III. *life, soldier, difficult*

1. *rigorous, training, discipline*
2. *away, from, family*
3. *example, @ war, year*
4. *families, live, world*
5. *friend, Egypt, 3 yrs.*
6. *never, know, where*

Clincher

IV. (optional) *famous, = nation , great*

1. *George Washington, encouraged, solds.*
2. *→, win, independence*
3. *→, great, country*
4. *Gen. Grant, Civil War*
5. *fought, keep, U.S. together*
6. *w/o, > soldiers, U.S., Ø, >*

Clincher

Brain-Helping Questions

Who?

Where?

What?

How?

Best?

Worst?

Why?

What kind?

How big?

How many?

How feel?

When?

Value?

Other ideas?

(> = great)

Lesson 22: World War I: Soldiers

3. For each body paragraph (paragraphs II, III, and possibly IV), get ideas about what to say by asking yourself questions using the question starter words (see page 153). Write your ideas in key word notes on your outline.
4. Use your outlines to help you write the body paragraphs of your essay. Add all the elements of Structure and Style that are on the checklist on page 170.
5. Once you have written your body paragraphs, outline a conclusion and an introduction.
6. Put all four or five paragraphs together in one essay. Be sure you have followed and attached the checklists on pages 170–171.

Outline for Conclusion

Topic A	*soldiers, valiant*
Topic B	*give up, normal*
(Topic C)	*> soldiers = >nation*
Most significant	*soldiers, keep, free*
Why?	*feel, safe, home*

Essay clincher repeats or reflects 2–3 key words from first sentence of the introduction.

Outline for Introduction

Grab attention.	*Would, u, die, 4, country?*
Subject/Background	*soldiers, willing*
	U.S., many, enemies
	despise, freedom
Topic A	*soldiers, noble, brave*
Topic B	*sacrifice, much, protect*
(Topic C)	*> soldiers, preserve, nation*

Unit 7: Inventive Writing

Lesson 22 Final Checklist 1 (Body Paragraphs): World War I: Soldiers

Name: ______________________________

STRUCTURE

- ☐ Topic-clincher repeats or reflects 2–3 key words (highlighted or bold). _____ (8 pts)
- ☐ MLA format (see Appendix I) _____ (2 pts)

STYLE Each paragraph must contain at least one of each element of style.

Dress-Ups (underline one of each) **(2 pts each)**

- ☐ ☐ -ly adverb _____ (4 pts)
- ☐ ☐ *who-which* clause _____ (4 pts)
- ☐ ☐ strong verb _____ (4 pts)
- ☐ ☐ quality adjective _____ (4 pts)
- ☐ ☐ www.asia.b clause _____ (4 pts)

Sentence Openers* (numbered; one of each as possible)

- ☐ ☐ [1] subject _____ (4 pts)
- ☐ ☐ [2] prepositional _____ (4 pts)
- ☐ ☐ [3] -ly adverb _____ (4 pts)
- ☐ ☐ [4] -ing , _____ (4 pts)
- ☐ ☐ [5] clausal , (www.asia.b) _____ (4 pts)

*** The number of sentence openers required depends on the number of sentences present in the paragraph.**

Decorations ("dec" in margin or italics if typed) (one per paragraph) **(3 pts each)**

- ☐ ☐ alliteration *(allit)*, simile, or metaphor _____ (6 pts)

MECHANICS

- ☐ capitalization, punctuation, spelling, grammar _____ (4 pts)
- ☐ banned words: go, went, say, said, pretty, ugly, big, good, bad _____ (-1 pt)

More Advanced Additions (optional unless your teacher requires them of you)

- ☐ vocab word(s) (Label voc or bold.) _____
- ☐ dual adj, verbs, or -ly adverbs _____
- ☐ triple extensions _____
- ☐ third body paragraph _____

Total: __________/ 60

Custom Total: __________/___

Lesson 22: World War I: Soldiers

Lesson 22 Final Checklist 2 (Introduction and Conclusion) World War I: Soldiers

Name: ______________________________

STRUCTURE

☐	Title centered and repeats or reflects 2–3 key words from essay clincher	_____ (3 pts)
	Introduction Paragraph	
☐	Opening grabs attention.	_____ (4 pts)
☐	Subject and background information	_____ (4 pts)
☐	Topics mentioned	_____ (6 pts)
	Body Paragraphs	
☐	(Attach checklist, page 170.)	_____ (3 pts)
	Conclusion Paragraph	
☐	Restate topics.	_____ (6 pts)
☐	Most significant and why	_____ (5 pts)
☐	Essay clincher (Reflect the beginning of the introduction.)	_____ (2 pts)

STYLE Each paragraph must contain at least one of each element of style.

¶ 1	¶ 4 or 5	Dress-Ups (underline one of each)	(2 pts each)
☐	☐	-ly adverb	_____ (4 pts)
☐	☐	*who-which* clause	_____ (4 pts)
☐	☐	strong verb	_____ (4 pts)
☐	☐	quality adjective	_____ (4 pts)
☐	☐	www.asia.b clause	_____ (4 pts)
¶ 1	**¶ 4 or 5**	**Sentence Openers* (numbered; one of each as possible)**	
☐	☐	[1] subject	_____ (4 pts)
☐	☐	[2] prepositional	_____ (4 pts)
☐	☐	[3] -ly adverb	_____ (4 pts)
☐	☐	[4] -ing ,	_____ (4 pts)
☐	☐	[5] clausal , (www.asia.b)	_____ (4 pts)

*** The number of sentence openers required depends on the number of sentences present in the paragraph.**

		Decorations ("dec" in margin or italics if typed) (one per paragraph)	(3 pts each)
☐	☐	alliteration *(allit)*, simile, or metaphor	_____ (6 pts)

MECHANICS

☐	capitalization, punctuation, spelling, grammar	_____ (6 pts)
☐	banned words: go, went, say, said, pretty, ugly, big, good, bad	_____ (-1 pt)

Total: _________/ 85

Custom Total: _________/___

Unit 7: Inventive Writing

Lesson 23: Nationalism: The American Flag

Structures: Unit 7: Inventive Writing

Style: #6 very short sentence (VSS); decoration – three short, staccato sentences (3sss)

Writing Topics: the flag of the United States of America

Optional Student Reading Assignment: during Lessons 21–23: *Hattie Big Sky*

If you will assign the More Advanced Addition in the Blackline Masters, obtain one or more of the following: *Who Was Thomas Edison?* by Margaret Frith, *Who Was Alexander Graham Bell?* by Bonnie Bader, and *Who Were the Wright Brothers?* by James Buckley.

UNIT 7: INVENTIVE WRITING

Lesson 23: Nationalism: The American Flag

Review

Play a vocabulary game from the Teacher's Manual to prepare for Quiz 5.

In this lesson you will write a 1-paragraph essay. You will learn to write in first person, and you will learn a new sentence opener (#6 very short sentence.) You will also learn to use the #6 sentence in a special way as a decoration.

#6 VSS

Before beginning the new essay for this lesson, learn the last sentence opener: a #6 VSS. This is simply a sentence with at least two words, but no more than five words. It is a very short sentence (vss). Remember that variety in sentence structure and length is important to good writing. In each paragraph, you should have some sentences that are long, some that are of medium length, and some that are short. With all of the dress-ups and openers you have learned, you may end up with too many long sentences. Purposely adding a very short sentence will solve this problem.

The very short sentence is best placed in a spot that you would like to emphasize because it will stand out. Here are two samples. These are passages from *Hattie Big Sky* by Kirby Larson and *Journey to Topaz* by Yoshiko Uchida. Note that they are indicated with a *6* in the left margin. Notice how each stands out among the longer sentences.

"It was not illness but loneliness gnawing at my bones. I missed Mattie's songs, Fern's giggles, the baby's sweet smell, reading to Chase at bedtime, and sitting squashed around
6 *the supper table. I missed my family."*

"They sat in silence, listening in disbelief as the newscaster continued to tell of the
6 *attack. Yuri shuddered. The news was like a burden of darkness suddenly blotting out the light of day."*

The 3sss

The name 3sss stands for three short, staccato sentences. The 3sss is simply the use of three #6 very short sentences in a row. Using short sentences this way, especially among longer sentences, can be a powerful stylistic technique. It is one of the IEW decorations. Here is a sample:

Boot camps try to break new recruits, and only those who persevere become our soldiers.
dec They are the strong. They are the determined. They are then ready.

***Caution*:** Very short sentences must be complete sentences. Do not create fragments.

The Assignment

As in previous lessons, you will write from your own ideas; however, this lesson requires only one paragraph, and your topic sentence is given to you.

Prompt

The years following WWI were times of great nationalism. Leaders of Germany, Italy, and Japan believed their nations were superior to other nations and tried to take over the world. During WWII the German Nazi flag became despised and feared across much of Europe. To America, the Japanese flag represented aggression in Asia.

One of the most prominent WWII victories for America was the 1945 battle for the Japanese island, Iwo Jima. The memory of this victory is captured in Joe Rosenthal's iconic image of American troops planting the U.S. flag over Mt. Suribachi. The American flag stands for liberty and is a great symbol of the U.S.

Pretend you are the American flag. Write one paragraph about where you have been, what you have seen, and what you mean to people who see you. Write in first person. (Use "I," not "you.")

Day 1:

1. Read the sample student essay on page 237.
2. In groups, brainstorm ideas on page 175. Groups may share ideas with the class.
3. Each student should then begin to outline his paragraph, page 176.

Days 2–4:

1. Polish your hopes and dreams essay from Lesson 21.
2. Use your outline to write your paragraph. Add all the elements on the checklist on page 178. Remember to use a #6 vss and a 3sss decoration. (Since this is only a 1-paragraph essay, you may count one of the 3sss sentences as your #6 VSS opener on the checklist.)
3. If you are reading the literature, finish *Hattie Big Sky.*
4. If you are reading the suggested literature, obtain one or more of the following. They will be very helpful for Lesson 25 if you will add the assignment from the Blackline Masters.

   Who Was Thomas Edison? by Margaret Frith

   Who Was Alexander Graham Bell? by Bonnie Bader

   Who Were the Wright Brothers? by James Buckley

Study for Vocabulary Quiz 5. It will cover words from Lessons 1–21.
(There are no new words for Lessons 22–23.)

Lesson 23: Nationalism: The American Flag

Brainstorming

Before you outline, answer the questions below as if you were the American flag. Choose a different place and time for each group of questions.

Where and when are/were you? *Fourth of July*

Who saw/sees you? *young and old; Americans; families*

What do you stand for? *freedom, opportunity*

How do they feel? You feel? *proud, patriotic*

Five senses to describe the scene *glittering fireworks exploding*

bands blaring, laughing, bbq sizzling

Where and when are/were you? *casket, fallen, soldier*

Who saw/sees you? *widow, family, friends*

What do you stand for? *ultimate, sacrifice, country*

How do they feel? You feel? *proud, sad*

Five senses to describe the scene *muffled, sobs, bugle, "Taps," 21 blasts*

Where and when are/were you? *Olympics*

Who saw/sees you? *spectators, around, world*

What do you stand for? *USA victorious, athletes' hard, work*

How do they feel? You feel? *proud*

Five senses to describe the scene *"Star Spangled Banner" blaring, cheers, smiles, gold medals dangling*

Where and when are/were you? *9-11, emergency vehicles*

Who saw/sees you? *ppl watching in horror, united in hope*

What do you stand for? *USA united against enemies*

How do they feel? You feel? *glad to unite and give hope*

Five senses to describe the scene *woeful cries, black smoke billowing, sirens blaring*

Key Word Outline

I. Topic sentence: I am the American flag.

1. *rep., freedom, opportunity, all*
2. *fly, proudly, 4th July*
3. *fireworks, light, sky, ppl, ☺, rememb.*
4. *@ battle, inspire, soldiers*
5. *@Olympics, instill, pride*
6. *@ schools, children, pledge*
7. *@ sports, sing, Nat'l Anthem, as 1 ppl*
8. *@ tragedy, unite, Amer.*
9. *ex, 9-11, everywhere, I, = ♥, country*

Clincher

Lesson 23: Nationalism: The American Flag

Brainstorming Style

Write an idea for a 3sss. (One of the sentences may count for your #6 vss on the checklist.)

Bands play. Fireworks explode. Everyone celebrates freedom.

Write an idea for a sentence with a *who-which* clause.

Widows, who mourn the loss of their loved one, find a little bit of comfort in my stars and stripes.

Write an idea for a sentence with a www.asia.b clause, either as a dress-up or a sentence opener.

When "The Star Spangled Banner" *begins, they stand at attention and salute me.*

Lesson 23 Final Checklist: Nationalism: The American Flag

Name: ______________________________

STRUCTURE

☐	MLA format (see Appendix I)	______ (3 pts)
☐	Title repeats or reflects 2–3 key words from clincher.	______ (3 pts)
☐	Topic-clincher repeats or reflects 2–3 key words (highlighted or bold).	______ (5 pts)

STYLE Each paragraph must contain at least one of each element of style.

Dress-Ups (Underline one of each; abbreviate in right margin.) **(3 pts each)**

☐	-ly adverb	______ (3 pts)
☐	*who-which* clause	______ (3 pts)
☐	strong verb	______ (3 pts)
☐	quality adjective	______ (3 pts)
☐	www.asia.b clause	______ (3 pts)

Sentence Openers* (numbered: one of each as possible)

☐	[1] subject	______ (3 pts)
☐	[2] prepositional	______ (3 pts)
☐	[3] -ly adverb	______ (3 pts)
☐	[4] -ing ,	______ (3 pts)
☐	[5] clausal , (www.asia.b)	______ (3 pts)

*The number of sentence openers required depends on the number of sentences present in the paragraph.

Decorations (Italicize or "dec" in margin. Choose one.)

☐	alliteration *(allit)*, simile or metaphor, or 3sss	______ (3 pts)

MECHANICS

☐	capitalization, punctuation, spelling, grammar	______ (6 pts)
☐	banned words: go, went, say, said, pretty, ugly, big, good, bad	______ (-1 pt)

Total: __________/ 50

Teachers are free to adjust a checklist by requiring only the stylistic techniques that have become easy, plus one new one. "EZ+1." Reproducible checklists are available (see blue page).

Lesson 24: Civil Rights: Freedom of Religion

Structures: Unit 7: Inventive Writing

Style: no new stylistic techniques

Writing Topics: freedom of religion or celebration of holidays

Optional Student Reading Assignment: during Lessons 24–27: *Journey to Topaz*

UNIT 7: INVENTIVE WRITING

Lesson 24: Civil Rights: Freedom of Religion

Begin with Vocabulary Quiz 5

In this lesson you will write one more essay from your brain. This essay will be a personal essay, meaning it will be about you. In this essay you will write in first person (use *I*, not *you*.) Here is the prompt.

Prompt

One of the rights guaranteed to all Americans in the First Amendment of the Bill of Rights is freedom of religion. This means that Americans may practice their faith freely without fear of persecution. It also means that the government cannot force a particular faith on anyone; it cannot force a person to celebrate religious holidays, nor can it tell him how to celebrate holidays, including those associated with religions.

Write a 5-paragraph essay about how you practice your freedom of religion. If you are not religious, you may write about how you celebrate your favorite holidays.

The Assignment

Follow the instructions below to write three body paragraphs responding to the prompt.

1. First determine the topics of each of your paragraphs. What three main ways do you practice your faith or celebrate holidays? Below are some possibilities. You might be able to think of others as well. Choose three below if you are religious:

   a. attending church, synagogue, or mosque (could include worship, prayer, singing)

   b. attending religious studies or youth groups

   c. praying anytime, anywhere

   d. studying a holy book

   e. obeying the guidelines of your faith in your daily life

   f. celebrating holidays in ways that honor your faith

If you are not religious, write about three topics.

   a. three holidays you celebrate

   b. three ways you celebrate one holiday. For example, if you chose Christmas, you might break into topics such as family traditions, picking out gifts, picking out a Christmas tree, seeing relatives, preparing favorite foods, or helping others.

2. Take out a sheet of paper. Format it as shown on the next page.

Unit 7: Inventive Writing

II. *Christmas, traditions*

1. *pick, tree, w/Dad*
2. *home, decorate, fav., ornaments*
3. *lights, star, top*
4. *mom, yummy, cookies*
5. *hot, choc.*
6. *listen, Christmas, music*

Clincher

III. *Christmas, gifts*

1. *really, wanted, BMX, bike*
2. *jump, spin, speed*
3. *⊘, look, under, tree*
4. *parents, hid, tub*
5. *☺, hug, grateful*
6. *never, forget*
7.

Clincher

IV. *Christmas, giving*

1. *Christmas Eve, Rescue Mission*
2. *w/church, youth, group*
3. *kitchen, serve, homeless*
4. *turkey, mashed, potatoes*
5. *enjoy, seeing, ☺, thankful*
6. *hope, make, difference*
7.

Clincher

Brain-Helping Questions

Who?
Where?
What?
How?
Best?
Worst?
Why?
Problems?
What kind?
How big?
How many?
How feel?
When?
Value?
Meaning?
Other ideas?

Lesson 24: Civil Rights: Freedom of Religion

3. For each body paragraph, get ideas about what to say by asking yourself questions using the question starter words. Write your ideas in key word notes on your outline.

   Important Note: Remember that this is a personal essay about you—what you personally do. It is not a report about your religion or about a holiday or what other people do. What is special about what *you* do? Use *I* and *my*, not *you* or *your*.

4. Once you have outlined your body paragraphs, use the blank outlines on the next page to outline a conclusion and an introduction.

Days 2–4:

1. Polish your soldier essay from Lesson 22.
2. Finish outlining the body, conclusion, and introduction. If you get stuck, ask yourself questions, or ask a parent to ask you some. Use your outline to help you write your essay about celebrating holidays or practicing freedom of religion. Include everything on both checklists, pages 183–184.

Option for Advanced Level B students: Read one or more of the following: *Who Was Thomas Edison?*, *Who Was Alexander Graham Bell?*, or *Who Were the Wright Brothers?* They will be helpful for the advanced assignment in the Blackline Masters for Lesson 25.

If you are not doing the advanced assignments, you may begin *Journey to Topaz* by Yoshiko Uchida. A critique of this book is assigned in Lesson 28. If you opt not to read *Journey to Topaz*, you will need to substitute another book that you can critique in Lesson 28.

Outline for Conclusion

Topic A	*love, Christmas, traditions*
Topic B	*love, receiving, gifts*
Topic C	*love, giving*
Most significant	*brings, fam., friends, tog.*
Why?	*creates, memories*
	encourages, good, will

Essay clincher repeats or reflects 2–3 key words from the beginning of the introduction.

Outline for Introduction

Grab attention.	*America, free, celebrate*
Subject/Background	*celeb., Christmas, my, way*
	gov't, ⊘, dictate, how
Topic A	*fam., traditions, begin, tree*
Topic B	*receive, gifts, esp. parents*
Topic C	*give, to, others*

Lesson 24: Civil Rights: Freedom of Religion

Lesson 24 Final Checklist 1 (Body Paragraphs): Civil Rights: Freedom of Religion

Name: ______________________________

STRUCTURE

☐	Topic-clinchers repeat or reflect 2–3 key words (highlighted or bold).	_____ (6 pts)
☐	MLA format (see Appendix I)	_____ (3 pts)

STYLE Each paragraph must contain at least one of each element of style.

			Dress-Ups (underline one of each)	**(2 pts each)**
☐	☐	☐	-ly adverb	_____ (6 pts)
☐	☐	☐	*who-which* clause	_____ (6 pts)
☐	☐	☐	strong verb	_____ (6 pts)
☐	☐	☐	quality adjective	_____ (6 pts)
☐	☐	☐	www.asia.b clause	_____ (6 pts)
			Sentence Openers* (numbered; one of each as possible)	
☐	☐	☐	[1] subject	_____ (6 pts)
☐	☐	☐	[2] prepositional	_____ (6 pts)
☐	☐	☐	[3] -ly adverb	_____ (6 pts)
☐	☐	☐	[4] -ing ,	_____ (6 pts)
☐	☐	☐	[5] clausal , (www.asia.b)	_____ (6 pts)
☐	☐	☐	[6] vss (2–5 words)	_____ (6 pts)

*** The number of sentence openers required depends on the number of sentences present in the paragraph.**

	Decorations (Italicize or "dec" in margin. Choose three.)	**(3 pts each)**
☐	alliteration *(allit)*, simile or metaphor, or 3sss	_____ (9 pts)

MECHANICS

☐	capitalization, punctuation, spelling, grammar	_____ (6 pts)
☐	banned words: go, went, say, said, pretty, ugly, big, good, bad	_____ (-1 pt)

More Advanced Additions (optional unless your teacher requires them of you)

☐	vocab word(s) (Label voc or bold.)	_____
☐	dual adj, verbs, or -ly adverbs	_____
☐	triple extensions	_____

Total: _________/ 90

Custom Total: _________/___

Unit 7: Inventive Writing

Lesson 24 Final Checklist 2 (Introduction and Conclusion)
Freedom of Religion

Name: ______________________

STRUCTURE

- [ ] Title centered and repeats or reflects 2–3 key words from essay clincher ____ (1 pt)

I. Introduction Paragraph

- [ ] Opening grabs attention. ____ (3 pts)
- [ ] Subject and background information ____ (3 pts)
- [ ] Topics mentioned ____ (3 pts)

II.–IV. Body Paragraphs

- [ ] (Attach checklist, page 183.) ____ (3 pts)

V. Conclusion Paragraph

- [ ] Restate topics. ____ (3 pts)
- [ ] Most significant and why ____ (3 pts)
- [ ] Essay clincher (Reflect the beginning of the introduction.) ____ (3 pts)

STYLE

Each paragraph must contain at least one of each element of style.

Dress-Ups (underline one of each) **(2 pts each)**

- [ ] [ ] -ly adverb ____ (4 pts)
- [ ] [ ] *who-which* clause ____ (4 pts)
- [ ] [ ] strong verb ____ (4 pts)
- [ ] [ ] quality adjective ____ (4 pts)
- [ ] [ ] www.asia.b clause ____ (4 pts)

Sentence Openers* (numbered; one of each as possible)

- [ ] [ ] [1] subject ____ (4 pts)
- [ ] [ ] [2] prepositional ____ (4 pts)
- [ ] [ ] [3] -ly adverb ____ (4 pts)
- [ ] [ ] [4] -ing , ____ (4 pts)
- [ ] [ ] [5] clausal , (www.asia.b) ____ (4 pts)
- [ ] [ ] [6] vss (2–5 words) ____ (4 pts)

*** The number of sentence openers required depends on the number of sentences present in the paragraph.**

Decorations (Italicize or "dec" in margin. Choose two.) **(3 pts each)**

- [ ] [ ] alliteration *(allit),* simile or metaphor, or 3sss ____ (6 pts)

MECHANICS

- [ ] capitalization, punctuation, spelling, grammar ____ (3 pts)
- [ ] banned words: go, went, say, said, pretty, ugly, big, good, bad ____ (-1 pt)

More Advanced Additions (optional unless your teacher requires them of you)

- [ ] vocab word(s) (Label voc or bold.) ____
- [ ] dual adj, verbs, or -ly adverbs ____
- [ ] triple extensions ____

Total: ________/ 75

Custom Total: ________/___

Lesson 25: Expanding Unit 6 Summaries

Structures: Unit 8: Formal Essay Models

Style: no new stylistic techniques

Writing Topics: introduction and conclusion to inventor paragraphs from Lessons 17–19

Optional Student Reading Assignment: during Lessons 25–27: *Journey to Topaz*

Teaching Writing: Structure and Style

Watch the sections for Unit 8: Formal Essay Models. At IEW.com/twss-help reference the TWSS Viewing Guides.

UNIT 8: FORMAL ESSAY MODELS

Lesson 25: Expanding Unit 6 Summaries

Unit 7 taught you how to write a 5-paragraph essay using notes from your brain. You can use the same structure to write report-type essays. In this lesson you will add a paragraph of conclusion and a paragraph of introduction to the report you wrote in Lessons 17–19.

The Assignment

Day 1:

1. So that the details are fresh in your mind, read the inventors report you wrote in Lessons 17–19.
2. With a teacher, fill in the outline on page 186 for a conclusion. Study page 187.
3. With a teacher, fill in the outline on page 186 for an introduction. Study page 187.

Days 2–4:

1. Polish your flag essay from Lesson 23.
2. Use your outlines to add a conclusion and an introduction to your inventor report. Follow the checklist on page 188.

Read Chapters 1–6 of *Journey to Topaz* by Yoshiko Uchida if you have not yet started it.

Option for experienced Level B students: Complete the lesson in the Student Book first. If your teacher assigns it, learn how to add the anecdotal opener and closer to your essay.

Unit 8: Formal Essay Models

Outline for Conclusion

Topic A	*Edison, > 1000, inventions*
Topic B	*Bell, phone, + 30*
Topic C	*Wright bros., airplane*
Most significant	*worked, hard, ⊘, quit*
Why?	*examples, greatness, possible*

Essay clincher repeats or reflects 2–3 key words from the first sentence of the introduction.

Outline for Introduction

Grab attention.	
Subject	*great, inventors, mid-1800s–1900s*
	modern, conveniences, granted
Background	*2day, ⊘, think, lights, on*
	talking, friends, listening
	inventors, made, possible
Topic A	*T.Edison, 💡, sound, movie*
Topic B	*Bell, phone*
Topic C	*Wright bros., flight*

Read the following sample conclusion and introduction for a report about Benjamin Franklin. They may helpful in understanding how to put the requirements of each into a paragraph.

Lesson 25: Expanding Unit 6 Summaries

Sample Conclusion

[Topics A–C] Benjamin Franklin was a successful writer, printer, inventor, community helper, diplomat, and statesman. **[Most significant and why]** He was successful in all that he did because he had a desire to help and serve those in his community and his country. His life enriched those around him, and his leadership helped give America two great documents, the Declaration of Independence and the Constitution. After a long, prosperous life, this great American died on April 17, 1790.

Sample Introduction

[Grab attention] Some have called Benjamin Franklin the first great American. **[Subject/Background]** He was born in Boston in 1706. Although he only attended school for two years, he became one of the wisest and greatest Americans of his time. He is one of America's founding fathers. **[Topic A]** He was first successful as a printer and writer. **[Topic B]** When he retired from that, he worked hard in many ways to improve life in the colonies. **[Topic C]** When the colonies struggled against England, Franklin was America's best diplomat and statesman. With all his many accomplishments, he is probably most famous for helping write the Declaration of Independence and the Constitution.

Lesson 25 Final Checklist: Great Inventors with Introduction and Conclusion

STRUCTURE

☐	Title centered and repeats or reflects 2–3 key words from essay clincher	_____ (1 pt)

I. Introduction Paragraph

☐	Opening grabs attention.	_____ (3 pts)
☐	Subject and background information	_____ (3 pts)
☐	Topics mentioned	_____ (3 pts)

II.–IV. Body Paragraphs

☐	Three inventor paragraphs from Lesson 19 are placed between the introduction and conclusion. Bibliography is placed after the conclusion.	_____ (3 pts)

V. Conclusion Paragraph

☐	Restate topics.	_____ (3 pts)
☐	Most significant and why	_____ (3 pts)
☐	Essay clincher (Reflect the beginning of the introduction.)	_____ (3 pts)

STYLE Each paragraph must contain at least one of each element of style.

		Dress-Ups (underline one of each)	(2 pts each)
☐	☐	-ly adverb	_____ (4 pts)
☐	☐	*who-which* clause	_____ (4 pts)
☐	☐	strong verb	_____ (4 pts)
☐	☐	quality adjective	_____ (4 pts)
☐	☐	www.asia.b clause	_____ (4 pts)

		Sentence Openers* (numbered; one of each as possible)	
☐	☐	[1] subject	_____ (4 pts)
☐	☐	[2] prepositional	_____ (4 pts)
☐	☐	[3] -ly adverb	_____ (4 pts)
☐	☐	[4] -ing ,	_____ (4 pts)
☐	☐	[5] clausal , (www.asia.b)	_____ (4 pts)
☐	☐	[6] vss (2–5 words)	_____ (4 pts)

*** The number of sentence openers required depends on the number of sentences present in the paragraph.**

		Decorations (Italicize or "dec" in margin. Choose two.)	(3 pts each)
☐	☐	alliteration *(allit)*, simile or metaphor, or 3sss	_____ (6 pts)

MECHANICS

☐	capitalization, punctuation, spelling, grammar	_____ (3 pts)
☐	banned words: go, went, say, said, pretty, ugly, big, good, bad	_____ (-1 pt)

More Advanced Additions (optional unless your teacher requires them of you)

☐ vocab word(s); dual adj, verbs, or -ly adverbs; trip. ext.; anecdotal open-close

Total: __________/ 75

Lesson 26: The Space Race, Part 1

UNIT 8: FORMAL ESSAY MODELS

Lesson 26: The Space Race, Part 1

Review

What are the components of a basic 5-paragraph essay?

The Space Race

In the next two lessons, you will write a research essay. You will use the basic 5-paragraph essay model that includes an introduction, three body paragraphs, and a conclusion. The subject will be something related to the space race. This lesson provides you with one source text of general information to get you started. It is on page 192. Read it. However, you will need to find other sources on your own specific to the subject you are assigned. Learning to find appropriate sources is a valuable skill to practice.

First, you need to choose your specific subject. Here are some options:

1. the space race
2. a famous American astronaut
3. space probes
4. space shuttles and their missions

If your teacher assigns astronauts as the subject, here are some of the most famous American astronauts you may want to choose from:

Alan B. Shepherd, Jr.	One of the original seven NASA astronauts; first American in space
Gus Grissom	One of the original seven NASA astronauts; died tragically in a fire during pre-flight tests
Ed White	First American astronaut to spacewalk; also died in the pre-flight fire with Gus Grissom
John Glenn, Jr.	First American to completely orbit the earth
Neil Armstrong	First man to walk on the moon; one of the *Apollo 11* astronauts
Edwin (Buzz) Aldrin	Second man to walk on the moon; one of the *Apollo 11* astronauts
Michael Collins	The only *Apollo 11* astronaut who did not walk on the moon, but on a previous mission he was able to spacewalk
James Lovell, Jr.	Made four trips into space; commander of the *Apollo 13* mission; famous for calmly stating on that mission: "Houston, we have a problem."; played by Tom Hanks in the movie *Apollo 13*
Sally Ride	First American female astronaut
Sharon Christa McAuliffe	First American civilian (teacher) selected to go into space. She was killed when the space shuttle *Challenger* exploded in 1986.

Unit 8: Formal Essay Models

Once you know the subject you will research, find at least three sources of information about it. History textbooks, Internet articles (especially those googled "for kids"), encyclopedia articles, and children's short books will make the best sources. Your parents or a librarian should help you choose short, easy sources. The difficulty of this essay will be determined largely by the difficulty of the sources you use.

Choosing Topics

Once you decide on a subject, you will need to familiarize yourself with it by skimming your sources. Your goal in this will be to determine three topics. If you will write about the space race, your topics could be similar to those of the source text on page 192:

A. first satellites in space

B. first men in space

C. first men on the moon

If you will write about an astronaut, the following topics will work for most choices:

A. path to becoming an astronaut

B. astronaut

C. life after being an astronaut

Look at the topics your sources cover, and choose ones that will work best.

Lesson 26: The Space Race, Part 1

The Assignment

Day 1:

1. In class, take out three sheets of paper. Format each like page 193. When you know the topics of each of your body paragraphs, write them on the Topic line. You will use the first two papers this week and the third next week.
2. Discuss in detail the remaining assignment (Days 2–4).

Days 2–4:

1. Polish your essay from Lesson 24.
2. At home on your first sheet of paper, take key word notes for Topic A. Do so by reading the paragraphs in all your sources that contain information about your first topic, for example, *the path to becoming an astronaut.*
3. Once you have notes from all of your sources for Topic A, you must organize them into one fused outline. Use page 194. Begin with words for a topic sentence. Then choose the facts from your notes that you want in your paragraph, and write them in an order that makes sense.
4. Repeat Steps 2 and 3 for Topic B. Fuse the notes you wrote on your own paper onto page 195.
5. Use the fused outlines (pages 194 and 195) to write the first two paragraphs of your research essay. You will add the remaining paragraphs in Lesson 28. Follow the checklist on page 201 (with Lesson 27).
6. Read Chapters 7–11 of *Journey to Topaz.*
7. Bring your sources to class next week. If they are Internet articles, print them out.

Source Text

The Space Race

Following World War II, the Soviet Union and the United States focused on developing rockets. Why? First, even though the two superpowers were not officially at war, they did not trust each other. They were in what is called the "Cold War." Each was hoping to launch satellites into space that could spy on the other. Second, both nations wanted to be first to explore outer space. This competition between America and the Soviet Union is called "the Space Race." So, who won the race?

The Soviets had the first successes. In 1957 they sent two man-made satellites into orbit around the earth: *Sputnik I* and *II*. *Sputnik II* carried a dog named Laika. Their early success shocked Americans and prompted the government to form the National Space and Aeronautics Administration (NASA) in 1958. Soon NASA launched its own satellites. The first successful one was named *Explorer I*. On a later test in 1961, America sent a chimpanzee named Ham into space to see if it would survive. It did.

The first man in space was a Soviet. His name was Yuri Gagarin. He circled the earth in 108 minutes in *Vostok I*. One month later the first American to enter space blasted off. He was Alan B. Shepherd. The race heated up. President John F. Kennedy set a goal of "landing a man on the moon and returning him safely to earth." Who would succeed in doing this?

It was America's turn to be first. Neil Armstrong was the first man to walk on the moon. He and two other astronauts, Buzz Aldrin and Michael Collins, launched on July 16, 1969. They were part of NASA's Apollo program, and their mission was named Apollo 11. The craft that landed on the moon was named the *Eagle*, so when it touched down, Armstrong said, "The *Eagle* has landed." After a while he opened the door and climbed down the ladder with his camera. About six million people watched on TV as he proclaimed the words he is famous for: "That's one small step for man; one giant leap for mankind." Buzz Aldrin stepped out next and said, "Beautiful view!" The astronauts left a plaque and an American flag on the moon. They splashed down to Earth on July 24, 1969. All of these brave early astronauts opened the way to future space travel.

Lesson 26: The Space Race, Part 1

Prepare three sheets of paper for note taking by copying this format onto each.

Topic ______________________________

Source 1

1. ______________________________
2. ______________________________
3. ______________________________
4. ______________________________
5. ______________________________
6. ______________________________

Source 2

1. ______________________________
2. ______________________________
3. ______________________________
4. ______________________________
5. ______________________________
6. ______________________________

Source 3

1. ______________________________
2. ______________________________
3. ______________________________
4. ______________________________
5. ______________________________
6. ______________________________

Unit 8: Formal Essay Models

Fused Outline A

Choose facts from the notes you took on your own paper from all sources for Topic A. Put them in an order that makes sense.

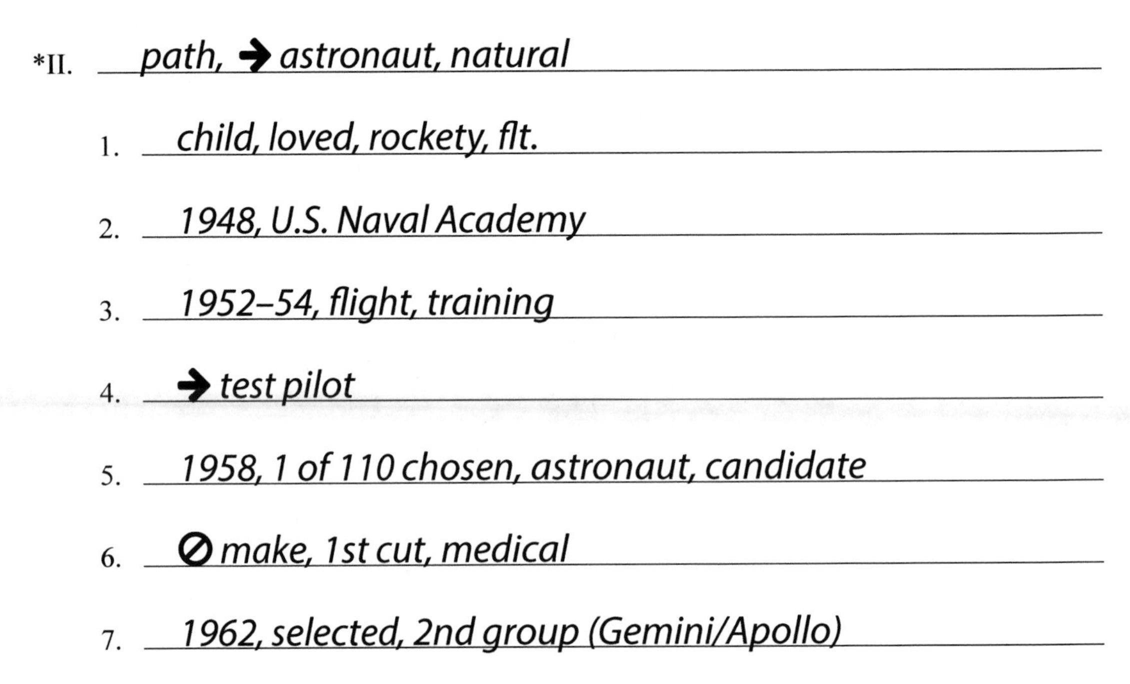

*II. *path, → astronaut, natural*

1. *child, loved, rockety, flt.*
2. *1948, U.S. Naval Academy*
3. *1952–54, flight, training*
4. *→ test pilot*
5. *1958, 1 of 110 chosen, astronaut, candidate*
6. *⊘ make, 1st cut, medical*
7. *1962, selected, 2nd group (Gemini/Apollo)*

Clincher

The checklist is on page 201 with Lesson 27.

*Topic A is paragraph II because a paragraph of introduction will be placed in front of it in Lesson 27.

Lesson 26: The Space Race, Part 1

Fused Outline B

Choose facts from the notes you took on your own paper from all sources for Topic B. Put them in an order that makes sense.

*III. *1st, space, flt., Gemini 7, 1965*

1. *record, 14 days, space*
2. *1st command, Gemini 12, 1966*
3. *Apollo 8, 1st ➔ moon*
4. *10 orbits, 2 hours*
5. *Genesis 1, returned, Christmas*
6. *radio, "There is a Santa Claus"*

Clincher

The checklist is on page 201 with Lesson 27. You will work on Topic C in Lesson 27.

*Topic B is paragraph III because a paragraph of introduction will be written in Lesson 27.

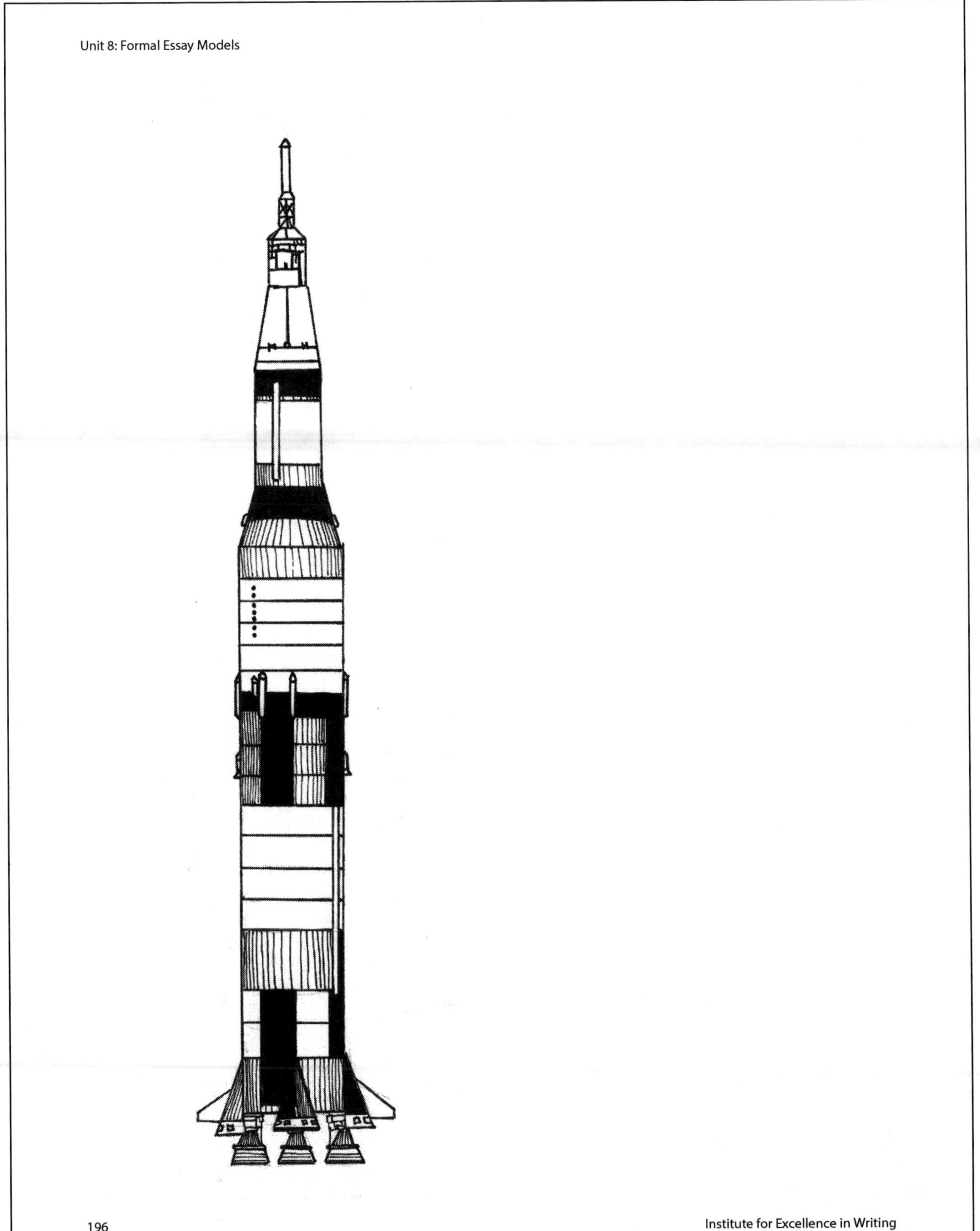
Unit 8: Formal Essay Models
196
Institute for Excellence in Writing

UNIT 8: FORMAL ESSAY MODELS

Lesson 27: The Space Race, Part 2

Review

Read the topic sentence and clincher of each of the two body paragraphs you wrote last week.

Play a vocabulary review game from the Teacher's Manual.

You have learned to write basic introductions and conclusions. It is likely that the most challenging part of the introduction is the very first sentence—the sentence that should grab your readers' attention. In this lesson you will learn one technique that may help you with this.

Dramatic Openers: Very Short Sentence

Dramatic openers are designed to grab a reader's attention. One type of dramatic opener is a #6 sentence (vss), used as the first sentence in an essay. When a vss is used in this way, we call it a "hook." Remember that this is a sentence with 2–5 words. Short sentences stand out. They draw attention to themselves.

The prompt paragraph on page 167 begins with a vss. Read it.

The sample introduction in Lesson 21 on page 163 also begins with a vss. Turn there and read it.

When you use a vss as a hook, you might have to add a sentence or two between the dramatic short sentence and the sentence that introduces the subject in order to make the sentences flow smoothly. Be sure your paragraph flows well.

If you begin your essay with a very short sentence, you will want to end the entire essay with another very short sentence that reflects it. This is called a dramatic closer. The dramatic opener and closer go together to frame the report.

Look at page 163 again. If I wanted to frame my report, I could add a dramatic closer to the conclusion that would reflect the vss at the beginning. One possibility is this:

America, here I come.

You can see an entire sample essay, "Celebrating Freedom," with a vss open and close on pages 238–239.

VSS page 167

World War I was horrific.

VSS page 163

America is beautiful and diverse.

In the student essay, "Celebrating Freedom," pp. 238-239, the vss open and close are these:

Open: *America means freedom.*

Close: *I'm glad America is free.*

The Assignment

Day 1:

1. You will use the sheet of paper you prepared in Lesson 26 for Topic C to take notes from all your sources for Topic C. (See page 193.) You will fuse those notes into one outline as you did for Topics A and B. Do so on page 199. Your teacher will decide whether to have you begin this in class. If not, be sure you understand what you are to do.
2. With the help of your teacher, complete the outlines for a conclusion and an introduction for your research essay (page 200). Use the sources you brought and page 192, if applicable to your subject, for help.
3. In the SRP, review how to format a bibliography. Begin a bibliography.

Days 2–4:

1. Polish your essay from Lesson 25, "Great Inventors," if necessary.
2. Finish taking notes from at least two sources for your third space topic.
3. Use page 199 to fuse your notes into an outline for one paragraph. Remember to note key words for a topic because this is the outline from which you will write your paragraph.
4. Use your fused outline to write one paragraph about Topic C. Follow the checklist on page 201.
5. Use the outlines on page 200 to write a conclusion and an introduction to your research essay. Also follow Checklist 2 on page 202.
6. Add a bibliography page by listing all of the sources you used. If you used the source in this book (page 192), here is how to cite it:

   Verstegen, Lori. "The Space Race." *U.S. History-Based Writing Lessons*.

   Locust Grove: Institute for Excellence in Writing, 2016. Print. 192.
7. Put all five paragraphs together into one essay, followed by the bibliography page. Be sure you have followed and attached both checklists, pages 201–202.
8. Finish reading *Journey to Topaz*.

Lesson 27: The Space Race, Part 2

Fused Outline

Choose facts from the notes you took from all sources for Topic C. Put them in an order that makes sense.

*IV. *Apollo 13, mission, 1970*

1. *supposed, land, moon*
2. *problem, O2, tank, fire*
3. *abort, mission*
4. *lunar module, "lifeboat"*
5. *re-adjust, course, home*
6. *➔ farthest, earth, ever*
7. *portrayed, T. Hanks, movie*

Clincher

*Topic C is paragraph IV, that is, the third body paragraph after the introductory paragraph.

Unit 8: Formal Essay Models

Outline for Conclusion

Topic A — *knew, loved, space*

Topic B — *missions, w/Gemini, Apollo projects*

Topic C — *Apollo 13, > famous, dangerous*

Most significant — *brave, smart, determined*

Why? — *overcame, obstacles*

farthest, human, earth

Essay clincher repeats or reflects 2–3 key words from the first sentence of the introduction after the vss opener.

VSS closer repeats or reflects key words from the vss opener.

Outline for Introduction

VSS opener — *space, "the final frontier"*

Subject — *many, men, dream, ➔*

Background — *few, do*

Jim Lovell, 4x, total, 29 days

Topic A — *childhood, intrigued, w/flight*

Topic B — *astronaut, 1965, w/Gemini, Apollo*

Topic C — *final, fateful, Apollo 13*

Lessons 26–27 Final Checklist (Body Paragraphs): The Space Race

Name: ______________________________

STRUCTURE

☐	Topic-clinchers repeat or reflect 2–3 key words (highlighted or bold).	_____ (5 pts)

STYLE

Each paragraph must contain at least one of each element of style.

¶ 2	¶ 3	¶ 4	**Dress-Ups (underline one of each)**	**(2 pts each)**
☐	☐	☐	-ly adverb	_____ (6 pts)
☐	☐	☐	*who-which* clause	_____ (6 pts)
☐	☐	☐	strong verb	_____ (6 pts)
☐	☐	☐	quality adjective	_____ (6 pts)
☐	☐	☐	www.asia.b clause	_____ (6 pts)
¶ 2	**¶ 3**	**¶ 4**	**Sentence Openers* (numbered; one of each as possible)**	
☐	☐	☐	[1] subject	_____ (6 pts)
☐	☐	☐	[2] prepositional	_____ (6 pts)
☐	☐	☐	[3] -ly adverb	_____ (6 pts)
☐	☐	☐	[4] -ing ,	_____ (6 pts)
☐	☐	☐	[5] clausal , (www.asia.b)	_____ (6 pts)
☐	☐	☐	[6] vss (2–5 words)	_____ (6 pts)

*** The number of sentence openers required depends on the number of sentences present in the paragraph.**

	Decorations ("dec" in margin or italics if typed)	**(3 pts each)**
☐	alliteration *(allit)*	_____ (3 pts)
☐	simile or metaphor	_____ (3 pts)
☐	3sss	_____ (3 pts)

MECHANICS

☐	capitalization, punctuation, spelling, grammar	_____ (4 pts)
☐	banned words: go, went, say, said, pretty, ugly, big, good, bad	_____ (-1 pt)

Total: _________/ 90

Custom Total: _________/___

Teachers are free to adjust a checklist by requiring only the stylistic techniques that have become easy, plus one new one. "EZ+1." Reproducible checklists are available (see blue page).

Unit 8: Formal Essay Models

Lesson 27 Checklist: Introduction and Conclusion

STRUCTURE

- [ ] Title centered and repeats or reflects 2–3 key words from essay clincher _____ (4 pts)

I. Introduction Paragraph

- [ ] Subject and background information _____ (3 pts)
- [ ] Topics mentioned _____ (3 pts)

II.–IV. Body Paragraphs

- [ ] (Attach checklist, page 201.) _____ (3 pts)

V. Conclusion Paragraph

- [ ] Restate topics. _____ (3 pts)
- [ ] Most significant and why _____ (3 pts)
- [ ] Essay clincher (Reflect the beginning of the introduction.) _____ (3 pts)

STYLE Each paragraph must contain at least one of each element of style.

Dress-Ups (underline one of each) **(2 pts each)**

- [ ] [ ] -ly adverb _____ (4 pts)
- [ ] [ ] *who-which* clause _____ (4 pts)
- [ ] [ ] strong verb _____ (4 pts)
- [ ] [ ] quality adjective _____ (4 pts)
- [ ] [ ] www.asia.b clause _____ (4 pts)

Sentence Openers* (numbered; one of each as possible) **(2 pts each)**

- [ ] [ ] [1] subject _____ (4 pts)
- [ ] [ ] [2] prepositional _____ (4 pts)
- [ ] [ ] [3] -ly adverb _____ (4 pts)
- [ ] [ ] [4] -ing , _____ (4 pts)
- [ ] [ ] [5] clausal , (www.asia.b) _____ (4 pts)
- [ ] [ ] [6] vss (2–5 words) _____ (4 pts)

*** The number of sentence openers required depends on the number of sentences present in the paragraph.**

Decorations (Italicize or "dec" in margin.) **(3 pts each)**

- [ ] [ ] alliteration *(allit),* simile or metaphor, or 3sss _____ (6 pts)
- [ ] [ ] vss dramatic opener and closer _____ (3 pts)

MECHANICS

- [ ] banned words: go, went, say, said, pretty, ugly, big, good, bad _____ (-1 pt)

More Advanced Additions (optional unless your teacher requires them of you)

- [ ] vocab word(s) (Label voc or bold.) _____
- [ ] dual adj, verbs, or -ly adverbs _____
- [ ] triple extensions _____

Total: __________/ 75

Custom Total: __________/___

Lesson 28: *Journey to Topaz*

Structures: Unit 9: Formal Critique

Style: no new stylistic techniques

Writing Topics: internment of Japanese-Americans

Optional Student Reading Assignment: If not completed, finish *Journey to Topaz.*

Teaching Writing: Structure and Style

Watch the sections for Unit 9: Formal Critique.
At IEW.com/twss-help reference the TWSS Viewing Guides.

UNIT 9: FORMAL CRITIQUE

Lesson 28: *Journey to Topaz*

Review

Play a vocabulary game from the Teacher's Manual.

The Critique Model

This lesson begins a new unit, one in which you will be combining the skills of two previous units. You have learned the elements of a well-written story: the Story Sequence Chart. You have learned to write essays' conclusion and introduction paragraphs. In this unit you are going to use these skills to help you write critiques of literature.

When you critique a story, you do not retell it. Instead, you give your opinion about it. You tell what you like or do not like about it. Before you do though, you explain the most important aspects of the Story Sequence Chart—just enough so your reader can follow your discussion of your opinion. This is the body of the critique.

A critique follows the basic essay model with an introduction, three body paragraphs, and a conclusion. The body paragraphs follow the Story Sequence Chart, and the elements required in the introduction and conclusion are specific to critiques.

Here is a model of the structure for a critique:

I. Introduction (title, author, publisher, background)

II. Setting and Characters

III. Conflict or Problem

IV. Climax/Resolution

V. Conclusion (your opinion)

This model can be used to critique any type of story: short stories, movies, novels, plays, TV shows—anything that tells a story.

The most important part of a critique is also the most difficult to write: the conclusion. Here you should tell what you like or dislike about the story, but do not say anything like "I think " or "in my opinion." For example, if you say, "It was a suspenseful story with plenty of thrilling action," your readers will know your opinion, but it will sound much more convincing than, "I think it was a good story."

The following page is a sample critique. Can you tell whether the author liked the story? How?

Note also that while the body paragraphs have clear opening sentences for *setting and characters*, *conflict*, and *climax*, they do not have clinchers. This is because the paragraphs move through the events of the story as each element of the Story Sequence Chart is discussed.

Sample Critique

History Made Fun

"A Message for King George" by Jonathan Verstegen was written for his IEW writing class in 2003. It is historical fiction based on the Boston Tea Party. As the story begins, Verstegen immediately creates a mood of suspense. An anxious crowd suggests that something important is about to happen, but Verstegen does not reveal what it is. Instead, he lets the reader watch through the eyes of the main character.

The story takes place in Boston in 1773. The characters in this story include a British officer and the American Sons of Liberty. We are first introduced to the British officer who is on board the *Dartmouth*, where crates of English tea are waiting to be unloaded. Although his name is not given, he is the only character who is developed. He is smug and he does not like or trust the Americans. The colonists, most of whom are part of the Sons of Liberty, are indignant over the taxes that King George has placed on them. They are determined to stand against what they believe are injustices.

The conflict of the story is that the king and his royal governor in America insist that the shipment of tea from England be unloaded and sold in the colonies, but the Americans refuse it. They are angry over what they believe are unfair taxes placed on it. The British officer guarding the tea sees a crowd gathering and wonders what they are planning. Both know that the deadline for unloading the tea is very near.

The climax happens when the Sons of Liberty, dressed as Indians, board the ship. With little resistance from the surprised guard, they dump all of the tea into the ocean. The problem is resolved—Americans will not buy the tea. Their actions convey the message of the story: This type of *audacious* action was the only way to make King George understand the colonists' *animosity* over what they believed was unfair taxation.

"A Message for King George" is an enjoyable, easy-to-read story that helps bring an event in history to life. Since most accounts of this incident are written from the colonists' viewpoint, Verstegen's use of the British soldier to tell the story gives it a unique perspective. It also helps him create the suspenseful mood because the soldier had to just watch and wonder what would happen. Words like "ominously" and "anxious" also enhance the mood. To add interest, historical facts and famous people are woven into the story. For example, John Hancock and Sam Adams are mentioned. The theme that this kind of action was the only action King George would understand is important because it helps readers understand how *obstinate* King George was, and, therefore, why the Revolutionary War was *inevitable*. "A Message for King George" is a fun and informative perspective of an important historical event.

Lesson 28: *Journey to Topaz*

The Assignment

Note: This assignment is lengthy, so younger students may spend two weeks on it. They should outline and write paragraphs II–IV first, followed by paragraph V, and finally, the introduction.

1. With your teacher's help, use the blank outline on page 206 as a guide to write a key word outline for the middle three paragraphs of your critique about *Journey to Topaz*. Try to include the words *setting*, *characters*, *conflict*, and *climax* in the opening sentences.
2. Using page 207, outline a conclusion with your teacher's help.
3. Using page 208, outline the introduction of the critique.
4. Once you have finished the outlines, use them to write a 5-paragraph critique. Follow the checklist on page 209.

Advanced lesson: Use the *U.S. History-Based Writing Lessons Blackline Masters* to practice avoiding "you." In addition, refer to the SRP for tips on critique vocabulary.

Unit 9: Formal Critique

Critique Outline

Use this page as a guide to outline on your own paper.

SETTING AND CHARACTERS	II. *western, U.S., WWII, Sakane Fam.*
place	1. *Yuki, 11-y-o, Jap.-Amer., girl*
time	2. *story, her, perspective*
mood	3. *parents, born, Japan*
Describe main characters.	4. *bro., Ken, → college, responsible*

PLOT OR PROBLEM	III. *Pearl Harbor, bombed, Japan*
State the problem or want.	1. *Father, → FBI*
What causes the problem or want?	2. *rest, → camp, racetrack*
What happens next?	3. *live, horse, stables*
What do the characters do, say,	4. *→ Topaz, prison, UT*
think, and feel before the climax?	5. *> hardships (weather, disease)*
	6. *Y- & friend, father, joins*

CLIMAX AND RESOLUTION	IV. *father, secures, job*
What leads to the conflict working out as it did?	1. *Dad, pass, → Topaz*
What happens next?	2. *move, new, home*
What is the end result?	3. *theme = fear, horrible*
	4. *regretful, events, US, history*

UNIT 9: FORMAL CRITIQUE

The Conclusion

In the conclusion discuss what you like or dislike about the story and why. It is the most difficult part to write because it requires you to analyze. The following questions should help you fill in the outline.

What did you think of the story? Begin your conclusion with a general statement that reveals your overall impression or opinion of the story. Use specific adjectives. Do not use vague adjectives like *good*, *interesting*, *wonderful*, and the like. Do not say *I*, *my*, or *you*. Here is a template that may help:

Journey to Topaz is a ____________________ story that ___________________________.

Support your opinion by discussing some of the following:

Characters

What makes the characters interesting to read about or to relate to?

Conflict or Problem

Are the conflict and problem intriguing? Why or why not?

Climax and Resolution

How would you describe the climax, e.g., was it surprising, exciting, predictable, dull?

Theme

Is there a lesson or truth communicated? What was most effective, least effective, and why?

End with your overall impression, an essay clincher. (Reflect two to three key words from the first general statement of this paragraph.)

Outline for Conclusion

CONCLUSION	V.	*sad, events, Jap.-Amer., vs./U.S., defense*
What do you think of the story?	1.	*char., realistic, likable, strong*
Things you like or dislike	2.	*angry, US, gov't, conditions, camps*
Why? Examples from story	3.	*neighbors, supported*
	4.	*⊘ all, Amer., prejudiced*
	5.	*end, abrupt, succeed, ?, rtn., CA?*
Discuss the theme(s).	6.	*theme, fear, prej. → horrible*
Most effective, least? Why?	7.	*must, rememb., ⊘ repeat*
Never use "I."	8.	____________

Essay clincher (reflect your opinion) → Title

The Introduction

The critique introduction differs from the introductions you have written in previous lessons. It should contain basic information about the source: title, a sentence about the background of the author and his literary time, the period in which the story is set, the publisher, and date of publication. Page count, quality of illustrations, and story type might also be discussed.

Recall that a dramatic opener is designed to grab your reader's attention. In Lesson 27 you learned one dramatic opener, the #6 sentence (vss) used as the first sentence in an essay. We called it a "hook." With only two to five words, the vss stands out! It is optional to start the critique introduction with a hook.

Outline for Introduction

INTRODUCTION	I. *WWII, hit, home, esp. Japanese*
Grab attention (optional).	1. *Journey to Topaz, Yoshiko Uchida, Heyday Bks., 1971*
title, author, publisher, date	2. *hist. fict., based, author's, real*
type of story	3. *reveals, difficult, period, Amer., hist.*
background	4. ______

Lesson 28: *Journey to Topaz*

Lesson 28 Final Checklist: *Journey to Topaz* Critique

Name: ______________________________

GENERAL

- ☐ MLA format (see Appendix I) _____ (4 pts)
- ☐ Title centered; reflects 2–3 key words of essay clincher _____ (1 pt)

INTRODUCTION

- ☐ Attention getter (optional) _____ (10 pts)
- ☐ Includes name of author and title of story _____ (10 pts)
- ☐ Includes type of story, author and story background information _____ (15 pts)

BODY

- ☐ 3 paragraphs follow Story Sequence Model (Unit 3). _____ (30 pts)

CONCLUSION

- ☐ Your opinion of the story: well written or not, like/dislike, and why. You may also include character development, theme, style of writing, effect of story on reader. _____ (20 pts)
- ☐ No "I" or "we" _____ (1 pt)
- ☐ Final sentence reflects the title. _____ (5 pts)

STYLE

- ☐ **Dress-Ups.** Underline one of each in every paragraph (1 pt each):
  - -ly adverb (not first word)
  - *who-which*
  - strong verb
  - quality adjective
  - www.asia.b word (not first word)

  _____ (25 pts)
- ☐ **Sentence Openers* (numbered; one of each as possible)** (1 pt each):
  - [1] subject
  - [2] prepositional
  - [3] -ly adverb
  - [4] -ing opener ,
  - [5] clausal , (www.asia.b)
  - [6] vss (2–5 words)

  _____ (30 pts)

*** The number of sentence openers required depends on the number of sentences present in the paragraph.**

Decorations ("dec" in margin or italics if typed) (one per paragraph) **(3 pts each)**

- ☐ alliteration *(allit)*, simile or metaphor, 3sss _____ (15 pts)

MECHANICS

- ☐ capitalization, punctuation, spelling, grammar _____ (4 pts)
- ☐ banned words: go, went, say, said, pretty, ugly, big, good, bad _____ (-1 pt)

More Advanced Additions (optional unless your teacher requires them of you)

- ☐ vocab word(s); dual adj, verbs, or -ly adverbs; trip. ext.; anecdotal open-close

Total __________/170

Custom Total: __________/___

Unit 9: Response to Literature

Lesson 29: Character Analysis

Structures: Response to Literature
Style: no new stylistic techniques
Writing Topics: character from a book you have read this year

Teaching Writing: Structure and Style

Watch the sections for Unit 9: Writing about Literature.
At IEW.com/twss-help reference the TWSS Viewing Guides.

Lesson 29: Character Analysis

UNIT 9: RESPONSE TO LITERATURE

Lesson 29: Character Analysis

Modifying the Critique Model: Character Analysis

In Lesson 28 you learned to write a basic critique. In this lesson, you will use and modify this model in order to focus on analyzing a character in one of the stories you have read this year. Praiseworthy from *By the Great Horn Spoon!* would be an excellent choice, but you may choose any character from any book you have read. This type of composition is similar to a critique, but we call it a response to literature. The model you will follow is modified a bit from last week to allow for a paragraph to discuss a character of a story. Here is the model you will follow:

I. Introduction (grab attention, title, author, publisher, background)

II. Setting, Characters, Conflict/Plot, Climax/Resolution

III. Character Analysis

Clincher

Notice that in the above model you will summarize the story sequence in one paragraph, rather than in three as before. This means that you will have to discuss only the most important elements, and do so very briefly. You will have to leave much out. You will not retell all the details of the story.

Character Analysis: TRIAC

To help you structure the character analysis paragraph, we will learn a trick called TRIAC. TRIAC stands for five elements that should be part of your analysis paragraph. It is explained on the following page.

Unit 9: Response to Literature

TRIAC Paragraph

Topic	Begin with a topic sentence that describes the character.
Restrict	Restrict to a specific reason to support what you said.
Illustrate	Illustrate your reason with a passage from the story.
Analyze	Explain the passage.
Restrict	Restrict to another reason to support the topic.
Illustrate	Illustrate your reason with a passage from the story.
Analyze	Explain the passage.
Clincher	Reflect key words from the topic sentence.
Conclude:	Tell what is most significant about the character and the story.

Sample TRIAC Paragraph

It includes a quote from *Hattie Big Sky*, but that is not required. It is an advanced addition.

[Topic] Hattie is courageous and determined, but a bit naive. **[Restrict]** First of all, at sixteen she heads to Montana all by herself to try to prove up on her uncle's homestead claim. **[Illustrate]** She admits that all she could see was "the chance to leave Aunt Ivy and the feeling of being the one odd sock left behind." She was following her dream to have a place to belong. **[Analyze]** She does not really think through the difficulties she might encounter. She just gathers her few belongings and leaves, determined to have a place of her own. That is both brave and naive. **[Restrict]** Once she arrives, she faces many serious challenges, but she never gives up. **[Illustrate]** The winter is brutally cold, her "house" is no more than a shack, she must set 480 rods of fence, and she must grow crops on the land in order to keep it. **[Analyze]** None of these hardships stop her. She presses on. And while in the end she does not succeed in proving up, she does succeed in finding a "family," the Muellers. **[Clincher]** Her courage, perseverance, and dreams pay off. **[Concluding statement]** *Hattie Big Sky* should inspire us all to chase our dreams.

Lesson 29: Character Analysis

The Assignment

Day 1:

1. Choose a character to analyze from a story you have read. We will use Praiseworthy from *By the Great Horn Spoon!* See the sample in Appendix III, page 243.
2. Using the blank outline on pages 214–215 as a guide, write a key word outline together.

Days 2–4:

1. If you will write about Praiseworthy, you may use the class outline, but you may wish to tweak the final paragraph to include your own ideas. For example, you may choose different passages to illustrate your points than the class chose. If you will write about a different character, write an outline for that book and character in the same way we did for Praiseworthy in *By the Great Horn Spoon!* in class.
2. Use your outline to write a response to literature. Use present tense.

   Praiseworthy is (not was) humorously clever.
3. In the final paragraph you must label the TRIAC in the same way the sample does. However, if you do not want to type the complete words, you may use [T], [R], [I], [A], and [C].
4. There are no new vocabulary words.

Advanced option: Add quotes from the story in the "illustrate" sections.

Unit 9: Response to Literature

Key Word Outline: Story of Choice

I. Introduction

Attention getter Title and author Type of story Background	*By the Great Horn Spoon!* *Sid Fleischman* *Little, Brown, and Co., 1988* *historical fict.* *CA, gold rush*

II. Story Sequence Chart

Setting and Characters Conflict Climax/ Resolution	*1849, sea, CA, Jack, 12-y-o* *Praiseworthy, ☺, devoted, resourceful* *save, Aunt Ara, 🏠* *→ CA, find, gold* *lose, gold, find, Ara., CA* *live, ☺, new, home* *teaches, value, ☺ attitude, humor*

Lesson 29: Character Analysis

Key Word Outline: Story of Choice

III. Character Analysis

Note: Because the notes are your own thoughts, you may use more than three words per line. You may also write more than one line in each box. Develop your thoughts.

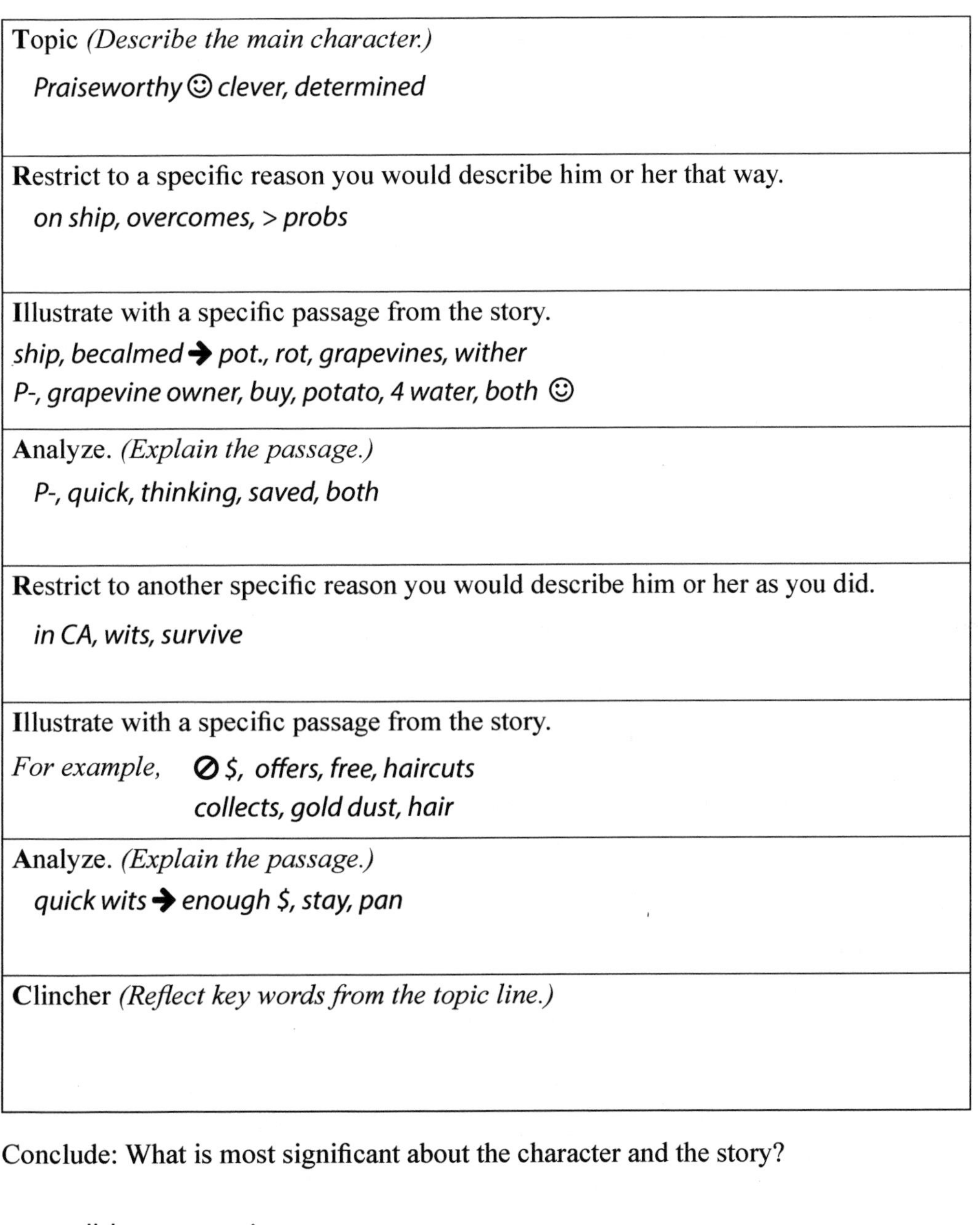

Topic *(Describe the main character.)* *Praiseworthy ☺ clever, determined*
Restrict to a specific reason you would describe him or her that way. *on ship, overcomes, > probs*
Illustrate with a specific passage from the story. *ship, becalmed → pot., rot, grapevines, wither* *P-, grapevine owner, buy, potato, 4 water, both ☺*
Analyze. *(Explain the passage.)* *P-, quick, thinking, saved, both*
Restrict to another specific reason you would describe him or her as you did. *in CA, wits, survive*
Illustrate with a specific passage from the story. *For example,* *⊘ $, offers, free, haircuts* *collects, gold dust, hair*
Analyze. *(Explain the passage.)* *quick wits → enough $, stay, pan*
Clincher *(Reflect key words from the topic line.)*

Conclude: What is most significant about the character and the story?

all, learn, use, wits, overcome

Unit 9: Response to Literature

Lesson 29 Checklist: Character Analysis

Name: ______________________________

GENERAL

☐	MLA format (see Appendix I)	_____ (4 pts)
☐	Title centered; reflects 2–3 key words of essay clincher	_____ (1 pt)

INTRODUCTION

☐	Attention getter (optional)	_____ (10 pts)
☐	Includes name of author and title of story	_____ (10 pts)
☐	Includes type of story, author and story background information	_____ (10 pts)

ELEMENTS OF STORY'S SEQUENCE (UNIT 3)

☐	Setting, characters, conflict/problem, climax/resolution	_____ (30 pts)

CHARACTER ANALYSIS

☐	TRIAC model	_____ (20 pts)
☐	Topic-clincher repeats or reflects 2–3 key words.	_____ (5 pts)
☐	Clincher reflects the title.	_____ (4 pts)

STYLE

☐ **Dress-Ups.** Underline one of each in every paragraph (1 pt each):

-ly adverb (not first word)
who-which
strong verb
quality adjective
www.asia.b word (not first word)

_____ (15 pts)

☐ **Sentence Openers* (numbered; one of each as possible)** (1 pt each):

[1] subject
[2] prepositional
[3] -ly adverb
[4] -ing opener ,
[5] clausal , (www.asia.b)
[6] vss (2–5 words)

_____ (18 pts)

*** The number of sentence openers required depends on the number of sentences present in the paragraph.**

Decorations ("dec" in margin or italics if typed) (3 pts each)

☐	alliteration *(allit)*, simile or metaphor, 3sss	_____ (9 pts)

MECHANICS

☐	capitalization, punctuation, spelling, grammar	_____ (4 pts)
☐	banned words: go, went, say, said, pretty, ugly, big, good, bad	_____ (-1 pt)

More Advanced Additions (optional unless your teacher requires them of you)

☐	vocab word(s); dual adj, verbs, or -ly adverbs; trip. ext.; quote

Total _________/140

Custom Total: _________/___

Teachers are free to adjust a checklist by requiring only the stylistic techniques that have become easy, plus one new one. "EZ+1." Reproducible checklists are available (see blue page).

JUST FOR FUN

Lesson 30: Vocabulary Story

Vocabulary Story

Toward the end of the year, I like to have a "just for fun" assignment. My classes have always enjoyed writing vocabulary stories. Not only are they a fun way to end the year, but they serve as a great review of the vocabulary words you have learned.

The instructions are simple: Write a story using as many vocabulary words as you can. You may write a familiar story (such as an Aesop fable or fairy tale), or make up your own story, using the Story Sequence Chart as a guide. There are only two rules:

1. Words must be used correctly and fit naturally.
2. You may not put more than three adjectives in front of one noun.

There is no checklist for this assignment, but tickets will be given as follows:

one ticket for each vocabulary word used well

three tickets for each decoration used well

If your teacher is not using tickets, she will decide how to reward you for using the above.

Read the sample story in the Appendix, page 245, to get the idea.

The Assignment

Day 1:

1. With a partner discuss ideas for a story. Make a list of familiar stories, as you did for Lesson 8. Choose one.
2. Begin filling out the outline on page 218 and discussing ideas for adding vocabulary words.

Days 2–4:

1. Polish the *Journey to Topaz* critique from Lesson 28.
2. Write your story, adding as many vocabulary words as you can. Bold or all cap each. Also, try to include some decorations (label). These will make the story more enjoyable to read.

Vocabulary Story

The Story Sequence Chart

Characters and Setting

Who is in the story? What are they like? Where do they live/go? When does it happen?	I. ______ 1. ______ 2. ______ 3. ______ 4. ______

Conflict or Problem

What do they need/want? What do the characters do, say, think, and feel? What happens before the climax?	II. ______ 1. ______ 2. ______ 3. ______ 4. ______

Climax and Resolution

What leads to the conflict being solved (the climax)? What happens as a result? What is learned? (message, moral)	III. ______ 1. ______ 2. ______ 3. ______ 4. ______

Story clincher ➔ Title

Appendices

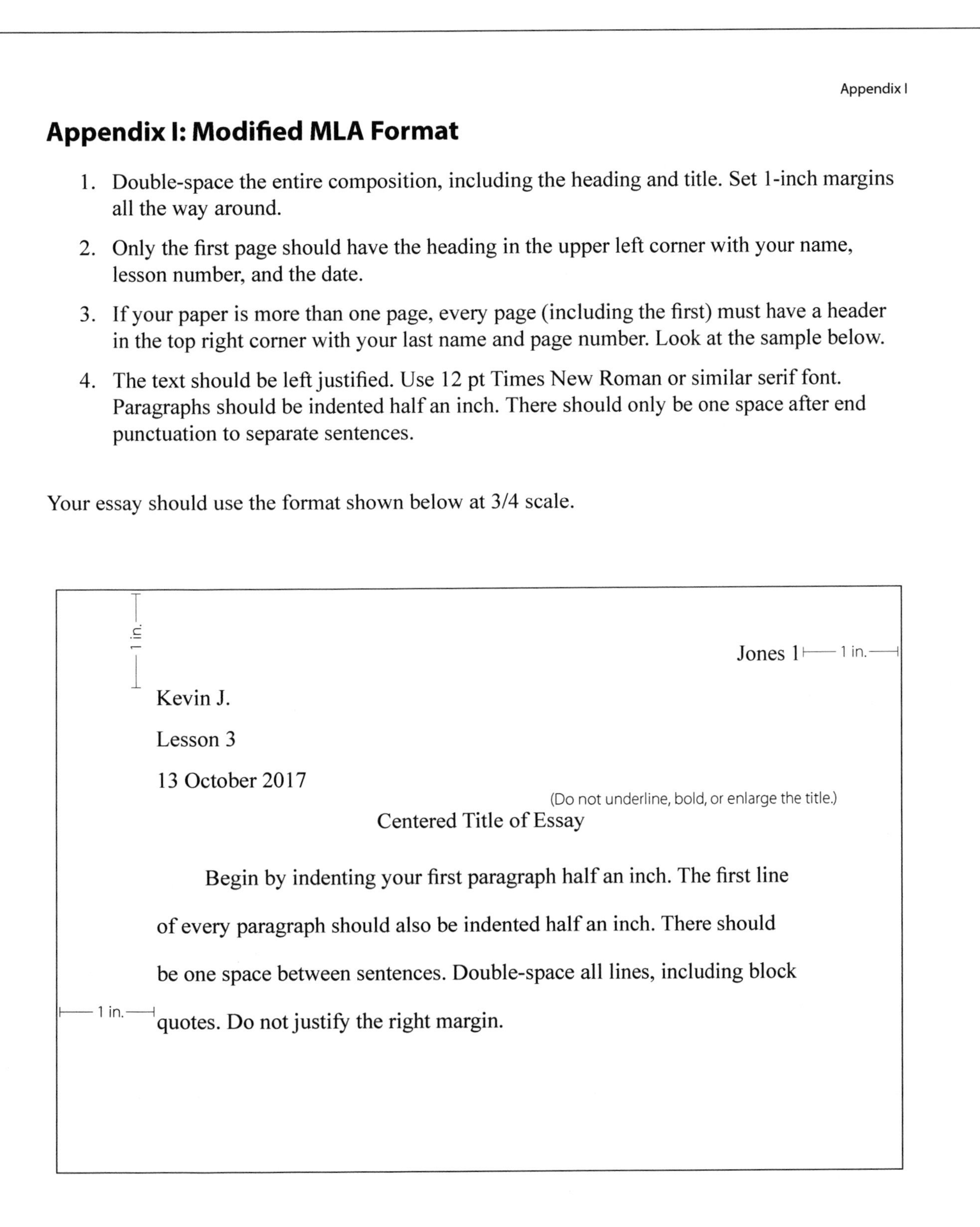

Appendix I: Modified MLA Format

1. Double-space the entire composition, including the heading and title. Set 1-inch margins all the way around.
2. Only the first page should have the heading in the upper left corner with your name, lesson number, and the date.
3. If your paper is more than one page, every page (including the first) must have a header in the top right corner with your last name and page number. Look at the sample below.
4. The text should be left justified. Use 12 pt Times New Roman or similar serif font. Paragraphs should be indented half an inch. There should only be one space after end punctuation to separate sentences.

Your essay should use the format shown below at 3/4 scale.

1 in.

Jones 1 — 1 in.

Kevin J.

Lesson 3

13 October 2017

(Do not underline, bold, or enlarge the title.)

Centered Title of Essay

Begin by indenting your first paragraph half an inch. The first line of every paragraph should also be indented half an inch. There should be one space between sentences. Double-space all lines, including block

— 1 in. — quotes. Do not justify the right margin.

Appendix I: Modified MLA Format

Appendix II: Polished Draft Notebook and Keepsake

Students should polish and illustrate each of their final drafts as soon as they have been checked and returned by a teacher.

To polish a final draft, students should make the corrections noted. Parents should help their student understand the reason for each correction. This last draft is referred to as "the polished draft" and does not have to be labeled.

The following page is the checklist that should be attached to each polished draft if teachers require them to be turned in. To check, teachers simply make sure that each correction marked on the final draft has been made and that a picture has been added.

Once returned, polished drafts should be kept in a half-inch binder in clear sheet protectors *with the original, labeled final drafts hidden behind the first page of each polished draft.* At the end of the year, students will have a fine collection of a variety of types of compositions that move through major themes in U.S. history.

Each student also may do an "About the Author" page as his title page. This can either be a paragraph about himself or an acrostic poem. For the poem option, each student writes his name in large, bold letters in a column down the page. He then uses each of the letters of his name as the first letter of each line of the poem describing himself. With either option, students should include a picture of themselves.

Also, I make a picture collage of the class for each of the students to put in the front of their notebooks. The students also sign one another's books on blank paper placed at the end of the notebook (like a year book) in a clear sheet protector.

All these things make the polished draft notebook a wonderful keepsake of the year.

In a class setting, I display the polished draft notebooks at the end of the year at our Parent Day party.

Important: Teachers should periodically require the students to bring their polished draft notebooks to class, so you can check that they are keeping up with them.

Make sixteen copies of this page. You will need one checklist for each lesson.

Polished Draft Checklist

Each item is worth 5 points.

- ☐ Polished draft is in clear sheet protector(s) with the original final draft and checklist hidden behind the first page.
- ☐ Composition is neat and double-spaced.
- ☐ Elements of style missing on final draft have been added.
- ☐ Grammar and spelling corrections have been made.
- ☐ Picture is added.
  (You may draw, or you may cut and paste from a periodical.)

***Note*:** Polished drafts do not have to be relabeled.

Total ___________

Polished Draft Checklist

Each item is worth 5 points.

- ☐ Polished draft is in clear sheet protector(s) with the original final draft and checklist hidden behind the first page.
- ☐ Composition is neat and double-spaced.
- ☐ Elements of style missing on final draft have been added.
- ☐ Grammar and spelling corrections have been made.
- ☐ Picture is added.
  (You may draw, or you may cut and paste from a periodical.)

***Note*:** Polished drafts do not have to be relabeled.

Total ___________

Appendix III

Appendix III: Student Samples

Appendix III: Student Samples

UNIT 2 SAMPLE

Lesson 3: Jamestown

This student added some information from her own studies, which is great!

Tessa A.

Grade 5

A New World Colony

In April of 1607 Englishmen, who were searching for **prosperity**, traveled to the New World. It was springtime. Weeks later they reached America, and 105 anxious men disembarked from three small wooden ships. **Reverently**, they named the new land Jamestown after King James. These weary settlers struggled for survival. Winter was progressing, and few of them knew how to farm, grow food, build shelter, or work. Many died, but the **frivolous** gentlemen only **endeavored** to find gold. The red-bearded **pillar** of the colony, Captain John Smith, was **appalled** and resolved to take control. Wisely, he coaxed them with a new law, "He who will not work shall not eat." By enforcing this law, Captain Smith made sure Jamestown would not fail. Eventually, they discovered tobacco, which helped them **prosper**. Jamestown became the first successful English colony in the New World.

UNIT 2 SAMPLE

Lesson 4: The *Mayflower* Mishap

(Bold words include vocabulary words from this and previous years.)

Nathan E.

Grade 7 (third year IEW)

Enduring the Elements

In the year of 1620, a group of English Separatists and workmen traveled to America. The Separatists underwent the journey so that they could worship God in their own way. They are collectively known as the Pilgrims. These **devout** men made their voyage on the *Mayflower*, an old, worn ship. But before they had gone far, dark, threatening clouds loomed on the horizon. **Presently**, the ship sailed under the angry, sinister clouds, so the Pilgrims huddled in the gun deck while the sailors **toiled** to keep their boat afloat. Rain drummed on the deck, drenching the courageous sailors who battled the fury of the elements. The vicious wind howled through the tattered sails, its glacial breath sending salty sea foam into the faces of the spluttering mariners. The waves **towered** over the ship, then crashed down with **massive** impact. The storm raged furiously. The Pilgrim men were on their knees in prayer, anxiously **pleading** for God to save them. The mothers cradled their babies tightly, as their infants bawled inconsolably. Throughout the ship, all were shivering with the cold thought of a watery grave.

Inside the gun deck, a Pilgrim named John Howland was pacing around. He was totally bored. He wanted to be free, to escape the leaky, wooden room, so he scampered up onto the main deck. Suddenly, a wave smashed into the side of the ship, sending the *Mayflower* reeling and rocking **perilously**. John Howland lost his balance. He was thrown against the railing, and as his thigh hit it, he flipped over and toppled into the icy sea. As he fell, John Howland clutched wildly at a rope hanging from the ship's side. The cold water engulfed him, only to **subside**, and then soak him again. Desperately, he gasped for breath as the frothy seawater filled his mouth. The wind itself, <u>which</u> was shrieking around worse than ever, seemed as if it was trying to blow him off, furiously sending mighty gusts to slam into him again and again. The rain hammered him **mercilessly**. He squeezed the rope with all his might, hoping that he would survive the day. As John Howland held tightly onto his life-saving rope, he spotted the distant sailors waving and shouting frantically to him. The sailors scooped a boat hook into the water to **extract** the bedraggled Pilgrim from the foamy sea. John Howland, who was dripping wet and shivering uncontrollably, sighed in relief and thanked all the sailors **profusely** with many a hearty handshake. Back under the deck, the Pilgrims shed tears of joy to see John Howland safe and in one piece. They all knew that the remainder of the journey would be no safer, but they thanked God for sparing John Howland. The *Mayflower* struggled on. Eventually, the brave little ship broke free from the raging tempest. Behind them, far away, thunder **bellowed** <u>wrathfully</u> at losing its **perseverant** targets.

UNIT 3 SAMPLE

Lesson 6: The Boston Tea Party

(vocabulary words bolded)

Samuel E.

Grade 4 (second year IEW)

Robert Lux-Whiskers and the Boston Tea Party

The planks of the docked ships groaned eerily in the chilly wind. Sweetly, the spicy aroma of tea filled the air. The *orb-like* moon illuminated the vast crowd, which was milling about gravely. Overhead, a flock of noisy seagulls squawked. Midnight mist lazily drifted about. Many mice paws incessantly pitter-pattered on the rough pavement. I should know. I was there on December 1773 at the Boston Harbor. My name is Robert Lux-Whiskers, and I am an American mouse.

I heard the colonists mutter through clenched teeth something along these lines, "*I won't buy any more tea now that there are taxes on it!*" I also heard someone with twisted brows indignantly growl, "*Send the tea back.*" Viciously, one man complained, "*The pompous governor refuses to send back the tea. He demands we obey the king. The governor made a deadline to unload the tea by December 16th, which is tonight!*" After listening to the colonists, I, Robert Lux-Whiskers, did **resolve** to side with the Americans against the English. May God bless America!

As I scampered down the ropes on the ship *Dartmouth*, I counted at least one hundred "Indians" climb onto the boat. The Sons of Liberty disguised themselves as Mohawk Indians to protect their identity. *With war whoops*, the Indians ran down into the ship's cargo holds and lugged up three hundred crates of tea. They swung their **massive**, shiny, sharp axes, hacked all the crates to splinters, and tossed the tea into the sea. Slowly, the tea **subsided** to the bottom of the ocean. The crowd loudly raised their voices and started to cheer:

Appendix III: Student Samples

"Rally Indians!

Bring your axes,

And tell King George

We'll pay no taxes!"

The Sons of Liberty, who claimed victory that night, danced and stomped their feet upon the creaking timbers of the boats. I squeaked with joy. I, Robert Lux-Whiskers, knew that King George would understand the message of the Boston Tea Party: Americans refuse to pay unfair English taxes.

UNIT 3 SAMPLE

Lesson 8: Borrowing a Conflict

Luke V.

Grade 4

A Colorful Flyer

Once upon a time, in colonial Maine, there was a forest of *tremendous towering trees*, and inside one of those trees, the tallest one of all, there was a family of mealworms, ten to be exact. Their names were Wiggly, Wormy, Mealy, Crawly, Creepy, Curly, Cubby, Charlie, Squiggly, and Clyde. They all <u>shared</u> the same home, ate the same foods, and looked <u>basically</u> alike. That is, except for Clyde. He was different. Instead of a brownish-gold color, <u>which</u> most mealworms have, he had bright stripes of yellow, black, and white with antennae on his head and legs behind him! Mealworms don't have these! Clyde's brothers made fun of the way he looked and called him names like Stripy, Bumblebee, Many Legs, Twighead, and many others. <u>Because</u> they were so jealous of him, they wouldn't even let him play in their games. Clyde felt so **<u>secluded</u>**. And so it went, day after day.

A few months later, springtime <u>arrived</u>, <u>which</u> meant it was time for all the mealworms to change into beetles. They all **<u>diligently</u>** climbed down from their safe little home and dug deep into the dirt for a little nap. Clyde, on the other hand, thought digging in the dirt was ridiculous. He found a tree limb where he decided to hang upside-down. He thought it was a much safer and cleaner way to nap.

Finally, summer was here and all the mealworms turned into black beetles that had exoskeletons, <u>which</u> looked like hard, shiny armor. They looked plain and simple. At that moment, Clyde joined his brothers. They all stared at him with their eyes wide opened. They were **<u>transfixed</u>** <u>because</u>, instead of turning into a plain old beetle, Clyde had <u>transformed</u> into a

Appendix III: Student Samples

beautifully colored butterfly. This was *baffling* to his *boring brothers*. Clyde was more beautiful than they were. They immediately felt sorry for all the awful names they had called him. Clyde quickly forgave his brothers, and they all lived happily ever after.

UNIT 4 SAMPLE

Lesson 9: Colonial Life: Church

Note the topic sentence and clincher key words.

A Life That Contradicts Ours

Church was strict and taken very seriously in colonial days. The colonists, who believed that the Bible was **imperative** and their guide, **resolved** to make the children **reverently** read it many times. Every Sunday, the people would **venture** to a **secluded** church, known as the meetinghouse. Sermons lasted from two to five hours. Two sermons were given on Sunday, one in the morning and one in the afternoon. There was a **diligent** man named the tithing-man, who carried a punishment stick. The *strong,* ***savage*** *stick* had a hard ball at one end and a fox's tail on the other. The tithing-man **warily** watched for misbehaving children to **confront** and bop with the ball and for sleeping adults to tickle with the fox tail. If anyone whispered or smiled, he or she would be **hostilely** fined. Because church was strict and long, people understood the **gravity** of church life in colonial times.

Appendix III: Student Samples

POETRY

Lesson 11: The "America" Poem

(cover for Polished Draft Notebook)

AMERICA,

~~~~~~~~

Land of.........

Sunlit, dazzling seashores
With radiant and soft sunsets

Dense, lush forests
With fragrance and grace

Misty, magestic mountains
That tower bravely

Rolling, golden plains
With placid and immeasurable space

Icy, raging rivers
With sparkling and rythmic waters

AMERICA, land of....

Proud, diverse people
Who strive for liberty

Heroic, patriotic people
Who love their country

"The free and the brave."

"GOD BLESS AMERICA, MY HOME SWEET HOME"

Julianna Gilson, grade 8
2009 - 2010
~~~~~~~~

UNIT 5 SAMPLE

Lesson 13: The Gold Rush

(includes some advanced additions)

California

John and Mary could not believe their eyes—gold in California! Was this the answer to their problems? They, like so many others, had been struggling to live in bustling Boston because it had become so expensive. The crowd, which pushed around them to read more details on the poster, became increasingly more excited.

"*We're heading to California! We're gonna be rich!*" a man hollered. John looked at Mary. "*What do you say we go, too?*"

"*I'm with you!*" she exclaimed. So they packed up their wagon that day and headed to California to find gold and **prosperity**.

Before long they reached a *roaring, raging river*. "We'll have to cross it," John told Mary, "because there's no way around it." Then he hopped off the wagon to lead the horses, which were jittery and spooked. Mary grasped the rope with her nervous, sweaty hands and muttered a prayer. The wagon rocked and moaned as the river pushed hard against it. It was **endeavoring** to stay upright, and a few times Mary was sure it was going to topple over, but it didn't. John **adeptly** guided them safely to the other side. Now the raging waters were behind them.

Finally, after weeks and weeks, they arrived in California. However, they were not greeted by a booming town full of excited gold diggers. Instead, the first town they reached was totally empty. *Shop windows were broken. Buildings were dilapidated. Everything was silent.* All John and Mary heard were the squeaking of the old saloon doors and the swoosh of the tumbleweeds, which were blowing in the wind.

"We are too late," Mary **distraughtly** cried as she looked at the ghost town.

"Well, maybe for this town," John replied, "but there is more of California for us to see!"

Appendix III: Student Samples

UNIT 6 SAMPLE

Lesson 16: The Civil War

America's Bloodiest War

[2] From 1861–1865 the deadliest American war was fought in our land, the Civil War. [3] Tragically, it killed more American men and boys than any other war because Americans fought against Americans. The South, which depended on slave labor, wanted to leave the Union. The people there believed that President Lincoln and the northerners wanted to outlaw slavery. [2] In order to protect their way of life, they formed their own country called the Confederate States of America. President Lincoln was **resolved** to keep the Union together. He **obstinately** left Union soldiers in the South. The *South savagely attacked the soldiers at Fort Sumter*. The bloodiest war in American history began.

UNIT 7 SAMPLE

Lesson 23: The American Flag

Nick W.

Grade 7

The Flag

I am the flag of the United States. I represent the abundant free[illegible] the United States. I stand proudly in schools across the nation as childre[illegible] Pledge of Allegiance. [2] In the home of the president, I radiantly hang high. I have been to the moon, and I still stand there strong. I was there on the top of the Twin Towers on the morning of 9/11. I also fell to the ground as the buildings collapsed. [4] Inspiring hope, I was whirling on the back of fire trucks racing to help the victims. *[6] I helped unite Americans. [6] I gave them hope. [6] I made them strong*. [3] Happily people praise me on the Fourth of July. My red, white, and blue colors are flown on cars, bikes, and houses. I am on the military ships as they patrol our waters. I have been to wars. Many people were **transfixed** on me as I was pushed into the hot sands of Iwo Jima. I'm there swirling on thousands of monuments across the country. I am there smothering the coffins of our courageous fallen soldiers. I am folded and softly given to the widows who mourn their fallen men. I am there to greet other soldiers when they return home from war. I am praised and sung to at sporting events. I am there at the Olympic on the backs of runners. I am raised when American athletes win a competition. I am the iconic flag of the Unites States of America.

UNIT 7 SAMPLE

Lesson 24: Civil Rights: Freedom of Religion

Celebrating Freedom

America means freedom. Our Bill of Rights guarantees us the freedom to do the things we choose to do as long as we do not hurt others. [3] Thankfully the government cannot dictate what religion to follow, what school to go to, or what holidays to celebrate. Celebrating holidays is one of the freedoms I like best because I love holidays. My favorite holiday is Christmas. [A] [5] When December arrives, I look forward to our special family traditions. [B][2] Of course, I also love giving and receiving gifts. [C] I even like *giving great gifts* to the people I love.

December is my favorite time of year because I love my family's Christmas traditions. Every year my brother and I help Dad pick out a Christmas tree. We scout for one that is *fresh, full, and fragrant*. Then we carefully tie it to the top of the car and head home. [5] When we get there, Mom always has yummy cookies waiting for us. [3] Usually she and my sister have topped them with creamy frosting and colored sugar, which makes them irresistible. It is hard not to eat them all. Then we decorate the tree with ornaments, strings of popcorn and cranberries, and icicles. [2] At the top we place a silver star. [6] It is so much fun. Sometimes Dad makes a fire while Mom cooks hot chocolate with marshmallows. [4] Sitting by the fire, looking at the beautiful tree, I like to think about the gifts we will give each other. I love our Christmas traditions.

[2] For most kids, receiving presents is the best part of Christmas. I like that, too. Last Christmas I really wanted a BMX bike. [3] Diligently I had been trying to earn enough money to buy one, but I did not have near enough. [5] When I wanted to ride, I had to *beg my brother to borrow his bike*, which he did not like. *[6] I love to jump. [6]I love to spin.[6] I love to speed downhill*. [2] On Christmas morning, though, there was no bike under the tree. [4] Thinking that

I would not get a BMX, I was a little sad. [5] When I opened my last little present, there was a paper inside that read, "Look in the bath tub." I ran excitedly, and there was the most awesome BMX bike I had ever seen! I jumped up and down and *giggled like a girl*. That was the best Christmas gift ever.

[5] While receiving gifts is very awesome, I know it is better to give than to receive. One Christmas I was very excited about a gift that I found for my mom. [2] At our neighborhood garage sale in October, I discovered a beautiful heart necklace with stones, which sparkled *like black diamonds*. [3] Excitedly I bought it. [6] Mom would love it! I asked Dad to help me carefully wrap it and hide it because I did not want to lose it. Christmas was still two months away. [4] Being so happy about such a great gift, I found it hard not to tell Mom, but I kept my secret. It was fun to see her smile when she opened it. It really is better to give than to receive.

[A] [2] In America I am thankful I can freely celebrate Christmas with our special family traditions. [B, C] [3] Additionally I am thankful to be able to receive and gifts. [5] Although gifts are not what is most important about Christmas, they make Christmas fun. The most significant thing about celebrating holidays is that it brings families together, which creates special, lifelong memories. That is why no one should be able to control how families celebrate. *I'm glad America is free.*

Appendix III: Student Samples

UNIT 8 SAMPLE

Lesson 25: Inventors (Adding Introduction and Conclusion)

Leanne W.
Grade 8

Brilliant Inventors

We use amazing devices all the time, often without remembering, or even knowing, the inventors behind them. [3] Usually we do not stop to think that the things that are part of our daily life did not always exist. [2] In reality, it took people with new ideas and much determination to bring them to us. [5] When inventors see a need, they work hard to meet it. Like "*the little engine that could*," they do not give up. [A] Thomas Edison is <u>probably</u> the most famous American inventor <u>because</u> he was so <u>**prolific**</u>. [B] Alexander Graham Bell is famous, too. [6] He brought us the telephone. [C] The Wright Brothers, <u>who designed</u> airplanes with motors, brought in the modern age of flight.

Thomas Edison is arguably the most **prolific** inventor ever. [4] Realizing what is required for success as an inventor, Thomas Edison stated, "Genius is 1% inspiration and 99% perspiration." Edison was born on February 11, 1847, in Milan, Ohio. <u>When</u> he was young, Edison worked as a telegraph operator. [3] Eventually, he quit his job to work full time with his interest in electronic devices. Edison is most <u>**renowned**</u> for his invention of the light bulb, the phonograph, and the moving picture camera. However, he also created the concept of research laboratories. Edison and his research teams <u>crafted</u> over a thousand inventions while working in the numerous labs that Edison owned. [2] In 1928, he was given the Congressional Gold Medal, <u>which</u> is one of our country's greatest honors, for his accomplishments. He died on October 18, 1931, but many of his inventions are still <u>fundamentally</u> important parts of our current lives. Thomas Edison was truly an *ingenious, inspiring inventor* and a gifted man.

Alexander Graham Bell is most famous for inventing the telephone, but he <u>actually</u>

had 30 inventions patented during his lifetime. Bell was born on March 3, 1847, in Scotland. His father and grandfather were both experts on the mechanics of speech. They, with Bell's mother, who was deaf, homeschooled him for much of his school life. He was never an **adept** student, but he was a clever problem solver and inventor even from a young age. After moving to Boston, he began working on an invention that would allow telegraphs to transmit over different frequencies. He concocted the idea of transmitting sound over wires *like vibrations through metal beams*, and he decided to shift his focus to that. [3] Eventually, Thomas Watson came on board to help Bell with his invention. [2] On March 10, 1876, Watson heard Bell's voice through the machine, thus receiving the first ever telephone call. The telephone was met with public adoration, as everyone loved the concept. After he created the telephone, Bell continued to invent and experiment. [2] In 1915, Bell was invited to New York to participate in the first ever transcontinental phone call. [4] Sitting in New York, Bell talked to Watson, who was in San Francisco. Bell died on August 2, 1922, and the phone service nationwide was shut down for one minute in this brilliant and gifted inventor's honor. So, next August 2, remember, you have the great inventor Alexander Graham Bell to thank for your smartphone!

Orville and Wilbur Wright were two inventors who were fascinated by the possibility of flight. When the Wright Brothers were young, their father, Bishop Milton Wright, bought them a small helicopter built in France. It *whizzed and whirled wonderfully*. This tiny yet amusing model helicopter sparked the Wright Brothers' interest in flight. [2] As inventors, the Wright Brothers were most **renowned** for the invention of the airplane and their studies in flight. [2] On December 17, 1903, the Wright Brothers tested the first effective airplane. [4] Lasting twelve seconds and covering a distance of 120 feet, at a speed of 6.8 mph, the flight was a success. The second and third flights, which covered a distance of 175 feet and 200 feet respectively, also were a success. [3]Unfortunately, the Wright Brothers' airplane crashed during the fourth flight,

Appendix III: Student Samples

but thankfully, no one was injured and the machine was easily repaired. Once the machine was formally released to the public, the people adored the machine. These two hardworking inventors helped improve our world by aiding in making long-distance travel quick and efficient. **[Topics]** [3] Clearly, Thomas Edison, Alexander Graham Bell, and the Wright Brothers are four *brilliant, gifted, and persevering* inventors who truly made our world a better place. **[Most significant and why]** They worked hard when they had ideas and did not give up. [5] If it were not for such innovative inventors, we would not have any of the modern conveniences we take for granted today. So, let us be thankful to these inventors and others like them who have helped shape our daily lives. [6] Let us not forget them.

Bibliography

"Alexander Graham Bell." *famousscientists.org*. N.p. 14 Sept. 2014. Web. 20 April 2016.

Bilstein, Roger E. "Wright Brothers." *World Book Encyclopedia*, 1988 ed. Print.

Biography.com Editors. "Alexander Graham Bell." *Biography.com*. A & E Television Network. N.d. Web. 20 April 2016.

Eibling, Harold H., John G. Gilman, and Anna M. Skehan. *Great Names in Our Country's Story*. Sacramento: California State Department of Education, 1962.

Hobar, Linda Lacour. *The Mystery of History, Volume IV*. Dover: Bright Ideas Press, 2014. Print.

Newman, John J. and John H. Schmalbach. *United States History: Preparing for the Advanced Placement Examination*. New York: AMSCO School Publications, 2010.

Appendix III

UNIT 9 RESPONSE TO LITERATURE SAMPLE

Lesson 29: Character Analysis

Nathan E.
Grade 7

In the Gold Fields

The gold fields were a place full of treasure and riches in 1849. [6] They were also perilous! To fend off the cunningly wicked bandits and pilfering road agents one would need a four shooter, at least! *By the Great Horn Spoon!* by Sid Fleischman was published in 1963 by Little, Brown, and Company. It is a humorous historical fiction novel that captures the excitement and adventure of 1849.

Many hilarious characters spice up this story set during the California Gold Rush. The protagonist is a twelve-year-old boy named Jack, who is being raised by his aunt. He is brave and **audacious**. Praiseworthy, the family butler, accompanies him on his adventures. The butler is brilliantly clever but is also modest and optimistic. Their main nemesis is a corrupt robber named Cut-eye Higgins. The conflict in this story revolves around a question: *Will Praiseworthy and Jack save Aunt Arabella's home by striking it rich?* (5) When Aunt Arabella begins losing money, it becomes apparent that she will have to sell her estate. (2) In a gamble to save Arabella's home, her nephew and butler stow away on a ship (because their passage money was stolen) to reach California and gold. (3) Eventually, they strike it rich. (3) Disastrously, when they take a boat back to Sacramento, they lose all their gold. The climax is when Praiseworthy and Jack arrive at the wharf, only to find that Aunt Arabella has already sold the estate and come to California with Jack's sisters! The conflict is then resolved because Praiseworthy and Jack no longer have to "save" Arabella's estate. She is happy because she knows her true home is with Jack and Praiseworthy, so they all stay in California as a family.

[T] (5)While Jack might be thought of as the main character, it is Praiseworthy who adds

Appendix III: Student Samples

fun and intrigue to the story because he is likable, optimistic, and quick-witted. [R] The problems that **stymie** the heroes' progress are overcome by his fascinating and unusually humorous ways. [I] An example of the use of wits is when the *Lady Wilma* is becalmed. A storage of potatoes begins to rot, and the owner frets that he will not be able to sell them. Also, because water becomes rationed, another man's grape vines begin to wither. Praiseworthy suggests that owner of the grape vines buy the potatoes because potatoes are full of water. The two men strike a deal and Jack and Praiseworthy make two friends. [R] Praiseworthy also uses his wits to help Jack and him survive and thrive in the **adverse** environment of the Wild West. [I] (2)For example, when they are out of cash and cannot afford to buy mining supplies or food, Praiseworthy cleverly offers free haircuts and shaves to the miners. He is then able to collect the gold dust from the cut hair. [C] Praiseworthy's humorous shrewdness makes this rollicking adventure in the Wild West fun to read. [Concluding] People would do well to use their wits as Praiseworthy did when faced with **formidable** difficulties.

Lesson 30: Vocabulary Story

Nathan E.
Grade 7

Build Your House on the Rock

Once upon a time, three little pigs resided on a placid farm. But outside of the safe neighborhood, cunning and ruthless wolves prowled the forest, each aspiring to lure a plump, juicy pig into his jaws. The most prominent of these hostile predators was a formidable creature named Warrick W. Wolf. He was the antagonist of any pig who desired to pass through the forest. He ruled the forest tyrannically, compelling many pigs to leave the land.

One day, the mother of the three little pigs called them all into the kitchen.

"My precious porkers," their mother began, "you have lived here all your life. But now, it is imperative that you endeavor to be prosperous in this adverse world. So pack your things and travel away. But be warned! Warrick W. Wolf harbors animosity towards you."

The three pigs compliantly began to pack their bags. Laden with their possessions, the audacious pigs trekked out. Presently, the road split into three parts, each leading through the perilous wood. Piggies Number One and Two waltzed carelessly down their own roads. As he skipped along, Piggy Number One encountered a straw-dealer. The amiable dealer sold him a crate of straw at half-price. Presuming all would be well, the naïve pig carelessly threw up a house of flimsy straw on meadow grass. He then squandered the rest of the day playing jaunty tunes on his flute, enthralled by his own music.

Piggy Number Two resolved to build his house out of twigs on a convenient sandy riverbank, so that he could then play with his ball the rest of the day. A frivolous activity indeed!

Meanwhile, Piggy Number Three soon came to a clearing flanked by trees. He looked warily about. He scrutinized every inch of the clearing, contemplated different blueprints, and deliberated where to construct his house. He was elated at the discovery of a broad, flat rock for

Appendix III: Student Samples

the foundation of his abode. He seemed destined for success. Auspiciously, the sun smiled over him as he walked towards the general store to purchase supplies. He reveled in the thought of a potentially grand home. Diligently, he purchased the supplies and sped back to the clearing. Implementing all his building skills, Piggy Number Three began constructing his exemplary house. It was tedious, difficult work, but he persevered.

Danger was lurking right around the corner for the pigs. Inevitably, Warrick W. Wolf was slinking about the secluded forest when he met Piggy Number One. The pig let out a squeal of fright and dashed into his house.

"Little pig, little pig," growled Warrick in a solemn, coaxing, yet sinister voice, "let me come in." The villain hoped that his charisma would transfix the pig.

With trepidation, Piggy Number One squealed, "Not by the hair on my chinny chin chin!" Gaining courage, he added indignantly, "I'll not let you come in!"

"Then I'll blow your house down!" howled the wolf. Vehemently, Warrick blew with such force that he lifted the impotent straw house off its weak foundation. The piggy was awestruck. Then he quickly fathomed the gravity of the situation and took off towards his brother's house as only a distraught pig could. Piggy Number Two was confronted with the appalling scene of his brother dashing away from the snapping jaws of Warrick. The wolf's murderous intentions were not obscured in the least. Acting quickly, Piggy Number Two sheltered his brother.

"Little pigs, little pigs," Warrick growled, "let me come in."

But Piggy Number Two stated obstinately, "Not by the hair on my chinny chin chin! I'll not let you come in!"

"Then I'll blow your house down!"

The wolf's tempestuous wind did not subside until the whole house was askew and tipped off its puny foundation. The pigs were frightened at the power of Warrick W. Wolf. Seeing him

Appendix III

advancing, the frightened porkers scampered speedily off to Piggy Number Three's house. Just as Piggy Number Three laid the last brick reverently onto his wonderful house, he was amazed to spot both his brothers running at top speed towards him. But he did not waver in the least. He flung the door open and let his brothers rush in. Then he spotted Warrick.

Warrick let out his incessant call, "Little pigs, little pigs, let me come in!" but Piggy Number Three answered with the same, trite words as his brothers.

"Not by the hair on my chinny chin chin! I'll not let you come in!"

"Then I'll blow your house down!" bellowed the wolf.

The wolf blew with all his might, but the house stood firm. The pigs met privily then worked zealously to station a pot of boiling water under the chimney. They were none too soon; the wolf was provoked to rage. He clambered adeptly up a pillar and leapt down the chimney into the house. When he fell into the pot of water, he screeched in pain and crashed through the window. And that was the last anyone ever laid eyes on Warrick W. Wolf.

Now, Piggies Number One and Two affirm the philosophy espoused by the third pig: "Build your house on the rock."

Appendix III: Student Samples

Appendix IV: Adding Literature

Great literature will be a valuable addition to these lessons. The books below are suggested because most are Newberry Honor Books, and their stories provide background to the compositions students will write in these lessons. Some are easy enough for all students to read on their own, but others may be better read aloud. Audiobooks are also a wonderful option. Students can follow along in the actual book.

First Semester

Lessons	Book
1–4	***The Witch of Blackbird Pond*** **by Elizabeth George Speare** Don't let the title trouble you. There are no witches in this wonderful story of Kit Tyler, a girl who must leave her comfortable life on the island of Barbados and try to fit into the Puritan community in colonial Connecticut.
5–10	***Johnny Tremain*** **by Esther Forbes** This is the story of a young silversmith apprentice coming of age just prior to the Revolutionary War. Many exciting conflicts mingled with historical people and events, as well as lessons in character, make this book a must-read.
11–12	***The Sign of the Beaver*** **by Elizabeth George Speare** Thirteen-year-old Matt is left alone to guard his family's cabin in the wilderness of Maine in the late 1700s. When his family is delayed in returning, he must survive on his own. But help does arrive when he is befriended by an Indian chief and his grandson. This book is a wonderful way to gain some insight into the relationship between early settlers and Native Americans (consistently a class favorite).
13–15	***By the Great Horn Spoon!*** **by Sid Fleischman** This is a very fun, humorous tale of a young boy and his butler who head to California to strike it rich in the gold rush. It is jam-packed with IEW dress-ups and decorations.

Second Semester

Lessons	Book
16–20	***Rifles for Watie* by Harold Keith** Sixteen-year-old Jeff heads off to war with thoughts of glorious victories in battle, but he soon learns that war is not so glorious. He also learns that the people of the South are not the evil enemy he had imagined, and that they, too, are fighting for a just cause. This is a wonderfully realistic story about the Civil War that will help students better understand some of the issues and people involved. The reading level is more advanced than the other books, so it makes a great a read-aloud.
21–23	***Hattie Big Sky* by Kirby Larson** Orphaned sixteen-year-old Hattie has been bounced around from one distant relative to another. She longs for a home of her own, and the opportunity comes when an uncle leaves her a homesteading claim in Montana. The story is set in 1918 and is filled with insight into the challenges of those times, including homesteading, WWI, the discrimination against Germans in America, the Spanish influenza, and more.
25–27	***Journey to Topaz* by Yoshiko Uchida** (A critique of this book is assigned in Lesson 28. If you opt not to read this book, you will need to substitute another that you can critique.) Yuki and her family are Japanese-Americans who live in California when Pearl Harbor is bombed. Her father is suddenly whisked away, and she, with the rest of her family, is moved to an internment camp. This story is based on the real experiences of the author.

For Week 24, consider one or more of the following short biographies to help with the anecdotal opener assigned in the Blackline Masters of advanced additions suggested for experienced Level B students in Lesson 25:

Who Was Thomas Edison? by Margaret Frith

Who Was Alexander Graham Bell? by Bonnie Bader

Who Were the Wright Brothers? by James Buckley

If you will not be doing the advanced assignment, begin *Journey to Topaz* this week.

Appendix IV

Weekly Literature Response Sheet

Each week as you read, do the following:

1. Circle unfamiliar words or words that you particularly like and might want to use in your own writing.
2. Highlight or underline a few elements of style that you particularly like, such as dress-ups and decorations that you have learned and vivid descriptions.

   (If you are not allowed to mark in your book, use sticky notes.)

After you are finished reading each section, do the following:

At the top of a paper under your name and the date, write the book title and the chapter numbers you read. Then format your paper like this:

Vocabulary

(Under this heading, write two of the words you circled. Follow each with its definition and the sentence and page number where it was used in the book.)

Dress-Ups

(Under this heading, write one of the dress-ups you highlighted or underlined. Write the entire sentence in which it is used, and underline the dress-up.)

Other Style

(Under this heading, write a decoration or description you like. Decorations you will learn include alliteration, simile, metaphor, and 3sss. You may also include any other literary element of style you know, such as dual dress-up, triple extension, personification, or onomatopoeia. (Extra credit if you write more than one.)

Summary

(Write the most significant events of each chapter you read. Write 3–5 sentences per chapter.)

When you finish the entire book, fill out the Final Literature Response Sheet (page 252) instead of doing the above.

Appendix IV: Adding Literature

Final Literature Response Sheet

After you finish a book, use your own paper to answer the following questions. Then discuss your answers with the class.

1. What is the title, and who is the author of the book?
2. What is the setting of the book? Describe it.
3. Describe each main character (no more than four).
4. What is the main conflict of the story? (What is the main problem, want, or need of the main character?) Write in complete sentences, but be brief.
5. What is the climax? (What event leads to the conflict being solved?)
6. What is the resolution? (How do things work out in the end?)
7. What themes are present in the story? How?

   (A theme is a truth that can be applied to all times, a virtue that is upheld, or an evil that is condemned. Some common themes are courage, loyalty, redemption, faith, the power of love, good triumphs over evil, perseverance, the value of family, the evils of greed, prejudice, and lust for power.)
8. What is your favorite part of the story? Why?
9. What other things do you like or not like about the story?

Appendix V: Vocabulary

There is a sheet of four vocabulary cards for most of the lessons. In lessons that have cards, you will be instructed to cut them out and place them in a plastic bag or pencil pouch for easy reference. Each week you should study the words for the current lesson and continue to review words from previous lessons. You should try to use the vocabulary words in your compositions. For this purpose you may use any of the words, even from lessons you have not yet had if you would like to look ahead.

For convenience, the following chart shows the words that go with each lesson and where quizzes fall. Quizzes are cumulative and cover all the words listed above them.

Quizzes follow the chart. Teachers who do not want students to see the quizzes ahead of time may ask you to tear them from your books and turn them in at the beginning of the school year. This is at the discretion of your teacher.

Appendix V: Vocabulary

Vocabulary at a Glance

Lesson 1	pillar	a slender, upright column; one who strongly supports a cause
	prosperity	the state of being successful or flourishing
	transfixed	motionless with amazement or horror
	coax	to try to persuade by gentle but constant asking or other measures
Lesson 2	resolve	to make a firm decision; to bring to a conclusion
	endeavor	to make a major effort; attempt
	appalled	surprised and dismayed
	frivolous	not serious or important; silly
Lesson 3	askew	not lined up straight; awry
	presume	to suppose to be true; at act without permission or authority
	flank	to be placed at the side of
	reverently	with feelings of deep respect
Quiz 1		
Lesson 4	hostile	unfriendly; unfavorable to one's well-being
	subside	to sink or fall to the bottom; to settle; to become less in strength or violence
	perilous	dangerous
	secluded	kept apart from everything else
Lesson 5	animosity	a feeling of resentment that could lead to violence; hostility
	provoke	to make angry; to annoy; to arouse to action or feeling
	indignant	angry about something that is unfair, mean, or bad
	audacious	bold; daring
Lesson 6	warily	cautiously; suspiciously
	vehemently	intensely; strongly or violently
	destined	to be determined or established ahead of time
	confront	to come face to face with; to oppose
Quiz 2		
Lesson 7	diligent	hardworking
	squander	to waste
	waver	to be uncertain; to fluctuate; to swing back and forth
	inevitable	unavoidable; bound to happen
Lesson 8	cunning	sly or clever
	contemplate	to regard thoughtfully
	gravity	seriousness
	persevere	to keep on; to persist
Lesson 9	compliant	submissive; yielding
	obstinate	stubborn; clinging, usually unreasonably, to an opinion, purpose, or cause
	compel	to force
	deliberate	verb: to consider; to reflect upon

Lesson 10	solemn	serious and thoughtful; formal or stately
	tyrant	a cruel or brutal ruler; any oppressor
	adept	skilled; expert
	enthrall	to charm or captivate; to hold spellbound
Lesson 11	amiable	friendly; agreeable
	antagonist	an opponent; a person who is against another person
	distraught	confused and upset; agitated
	awestruck	amazed; filled with wonder mixed with fear
Lesson 12	trite	overused; not original
	formidable	causing fear or dread
	obscure	unclear; clouded
	laden	loaded; burdened
Quiz 3		
Lesson 13	incessant	unceasing; never ending
	zealous	enthusiastically devoted to something; fervent
	trepidation	fear; nervous trembling; apprehension
	exemplary	outstanding; worthy of imitation
Lesson 14		no new words
Lesson 15	fathom	to comprehend (understand) in depth
	imperative	necessary
	impotent	powerless
	placidly	calmly/peacefully
Lesson 16	prominent	well-known, leading, outstanding; attracting attention as by size or position
	privily	privately
	affirm	to declare positively; to maintain to be true
	espouse	to marry; to support or adopt a cause or theory
Lesson 17	tedious	long and tiring
	implement	to put into practice
	scrutinize	to examine closely
	potential	the capability of becoming real; possibility
Quiz 4		
Lesson 18–19		no new words
Lesson 20	aspire	to seek to attain something high or great
	elated	filled with joy and pride
	auspicious	favorable; pointing to a good result
	adverse	unfavorable; directed against a person or thing
Lesson 21	revel	to take great delight in something
	jaunty	lively; energetic
	encounter	to come upon or meet
	lure	to tempt or lead away by offering some pleasure or advantage
Lesson 22–30		no new words

Quiz 5

Appendix V: Vocabulary

Appendix V

Vocabulary Quiz 1

askew	flank	prosperity	transfixed
coax	pillar	resolve	
endeavor	presume	reverently	

Fill in the blanks with the appropriate word. Be sure to spell correctly. Words may be used more than once.

1. with feelings of deep respect — 1. ____________________
2. not lined up straight (crooked) — 2. ____________________
3. to try to persuade — 3. ____________________
4. to assume to be true — 4. ____________________
5. to be placed at the side of — 5. ____________________
6. motionless with amazement or horror — 6. ____________________
7. to act without permission or authority — 7. ____________________
8. a slender, upright column — 8. ____________________
9. the state of being successful — 9. ____________________
10. one who strongly supports a cause — 10. ____________________
11. to make a firm decision — 11. ____________________
12. to make a major effort — 12. ____________________

Vocabulary Quiz 1 Answer Key

askew	flank	prosperity	transfixed
coax	pillar	resolve	
endeavor	presume	reverently	

Fill in the blanks with the appropriate word. Be sure to spell correctly. Words may be used more than once.

1.	with feelings of deep respect	1.	*reverently*
2.	not lined up straight (crooked)	2.	*askew*
3.	to try to persuade	3.	*coax*
4.	to assume to be true	4.	*presume*
5.	to be placed at the side of	5.	*flank*
6.	motionless with amazement or horror	6.	*transfixed*
7.	to act without permission or authority	7.	*presume*
8.	a slender, upright column	8.	*pillar*
9.	the state of being successful	9.	*prosperity*
10.	one who strongly supports a cause	10.	*pillar*
11.	to make a firm decision	11.	*resolve*
12.	to make a major effort	12.	*endeavor*

Vocabulary Quiz 2

askew	frivolous	pillar	subside
appalled	hostile	presume	transfixed
audacious	indignant	provoke	vehemently
confront	perilous	secluded	warily

Fill in the blanks with the appropriate word. Be sure to spell correctly.

1. unfriendly; unfavorable to well-being 1. ____________________
2. bold; daring 2. ____________________
3. not lined up straight 3. ____________________
4. angry about something unfair or mean 4. ____________________
5. dangerous 5. ____________________
6. to make angry; to annoy 6. ____________________
7. to act without permission or authority 7. ____________________
8. to become less in strength or violence 8. ____________________
9. cautiously; suspiciously 9. ____________________
10. one who strongly supports a cause 10. ____________________
11. not serious or important 11. ____________________
12. kept apart from everything else 12. ____________________
13. intensely, strongly, or violently 13. ____________________
14. to come face to face with; to oppose 14. ____________________
15. surprised and dismayed 15. ____________________

Appendix V

Vocabulary Quiz 2 Answer Key

askew	frivolous	pillar	subside
appalled	hostile	presume	transfixed
audacious	indignant	provoke	vehemently
confront	perilous	secluded	warily

Fill in the blanks with the appropriate word. Be sure to spell correctly.

1. unfriendly; unfavorable to well-being — 1. *hostile*
2. bold; daring — 2. *audacious*
3. not lined up straight — 3. *askew*
4. angry about something unfair or mean — 4. *indignant*
5. dangerous — 5. *perilous*
6. to make angry; to annoy — 6. *provoke*
7. to act without permission or authority — 7. *presume*
8. to become less in strength or violence — 8. *subside*
9. cautiously; suspiciously — 9. *warily*
10. one who strongly supports a cause — 10. *pillar*
11. not serious or important — 11. *frivolous*
12. kept apart from everything else — 12. *secluded*
13. intensely, strongly, or violently — 13. *vehemently*
14. to come face to face with; to oppose — 14. *confront*
15. surprised and dismayed — 15. *appalled*

Vocabulary Quiz 3

adept	contemplate	gravity	perilous
amiable	cunning	indignant	squander
compel	destined	laden	trite
compliant	diligent	obstinate	waver

Fill in the blanks with the appropriate word. Be sure to spell correctly.

1. dangerous 1. ______________________
2. hardworking 2. ______________________
3. to waste 3. ______________________
4. sly or clever 4. ______________________
5. seriousness 5. ______________________
6. to regard thoughtfully 6. ______________________
7. angry about something unfair or mean 7. ______________________
8. to be uncertain; to fluctuate 8. ______________________
9. submissive; yielding 9. ______________________
10. stubborn 10. ______________________
11. to force 11. ______________________
12. skilled or expert 12. ______________________
13. friendly; agreeable 13. ______________________
14. loaded; burdened 14. ______________________
15. to be determined ahead of time 15. ______________________

Appendix V

Vocabulary Quiz 3 Answer Key

adept	contemplate	gravity	perilous
amiable	cunning	indignant	squander
compel	destined	laden	trite
compliant	diligent	obstinate	waver

Fill in the blanks with the appropriate word. Be sure to spell correctly.

1. dangerous	1. *perilous*
2. hardworking	2. *diligent*
3. to waste	3. *squander*
4. sly or clever	4. *cunning*
5. seriousness	5. *gravity*
6. to regard thoughtfully	6. *contemplate*
7. angry about something unfair or mean	7. *indignant*
8. to be uncertain; to fluctuate	8. *waver*
9. submissive; yielding	9. *compliant*
10. stubborn	10. *obstinate*
11. to force	11. *compel*
12. skilled or expert	12. *adept*
13. friendly; agreeable	13. *amiable*
14. loaded; burdened	14. *laden*
15. to be determined ahead of time	15. *destined*

Vocabulary Quiz 4

affirm	distraught	incessant	placidly	tedious
antagonist	enthrall	inevitable	prominent	trepidation
awestruck	formidable	laden	scrutinize	tyrant
deliberate	impotent	persevere	solemn	zealous

Fill in the blanks with the appropriate word. Be sure to spell correctly.

1. unavoidable; bound to happen — 1. ____________________
2. serious and thoughtful; formal or stately — 2. ____________________
3. a cruel or brutal ruler — 3. ____________________
4. to charm or captivate — 4. ____________________
5. an opponent — 5. ____________________
6. to consider; to reflect upon — 6. ____________________
7. confused and upset; agitated — 7. ____________________
8. amazed; filled with wonder mixed with fear — 8. ____________________
9. causing fear or dread — 9. ____________________
10. loaded; burdened — 10. ____________________
11. calmly; peacefully — 11. ____________________
12. unceasing; never ending — 12. ____________________
13. to keep on; to persist — 13. ____________________
14. enthusiastically devoted to something — 14. ____________________
15. fear; nervous trembling — 15. ____________________
16. well-known; leading; outstanding — 16. ____________________
17. powerless — 17. ____________________
18. to declare positively — 18. ____________________
19. long and tiring — 19. ____________________
20. to examine closely — 20. ____________________

Vocabulary Quiz 4 Answer Key

affirm	distraught	incessant	placidly	tedious
antagonist	enthrall	inevitable	prominent	trepidation
awestruck	formidable	laden	scrutinize	tyrant
deliberate	impotent	persevere	solemn	zealous

Fill in the blanks with the appropriate word. Be sure to spell correctly.

1.	unavoidable; bound to happen	1.	*inevitable*
2.	serious and thoughtful; formal or stately	2.	*solemn*
3.	a cruel or brutal ruler	3.	*tyrant*
4.	to charm or captivate	4.	*enthrall*
5.	an opponent	5.	*antagonist*
6.	to consider; to reflect upon	6.	*deliberate*
7.	confused and upset; agitated	7.	*distraught*
8.	amazed; filled with wonder mixed with fear	8.	*awestruck*
9.	causing fear or dread	9.	*formidable*
10.	loaded; burdened	10.	*laden*
11.	calmly; peacefully	11.	*placidly*
12.	unceasing; never ending	12.	*incessant*
13.	to keep on; to persist	13.	*persevere*
14.	enthusiastically devoted to something	14.	*zealous*
15.	fear; nervous trembling	15.	*trepidation*
16.	well-known; leading; outstanding	16.	*prominent*
17.	powerless	17.	*impotent*
18.	to declare positively	18.	*affirm*
19.	long and tiring	19.	*tedious*
20.	to examine closely	20.	*scrutinize*

Appendix V

Vocabulary Quiz 5

adverse	auspicious	espouse	jaunty	revel
amiable	confront	exemplary	lure	reverently
animosity	cunning	fathom	obscure	tedious
aspire	elated	imperative	obstinate	transfixed
audacious	encounter	implement	potential	warily

Fill in the blanks with the appropriate word. Be sure to spell correctly.

1. cautiously; suspiciously — 1. ____________________
2. motionless with amazement or horror — 2. ____________________
3. with feelings of deep respect — 3. ____________________
4. a feeling of resentment; hostility — 4. ____________________
5. to oppose; to come face to face with — 5. ____________________
6. bold and daring — 6. ____________________
7. to support or adopt a cause or theory — 7. ____________________
8. sly or clever — 8. ____________________
9. stubborn — 9. ____________________
10. friendly — 10. ____________________
11. unclear; clouded — 11. ____________________
12. to understand in depth — 12. ____________________
13. necessary — 13. ____________________
14. long and tiring — 14. ____________________
15. outstanding; worthy of imitation — 15. ____________________
16. the capability of becoming real — 16. ____________________
17. to tempt or lead away with a pleasure — 17. ____________________
18. to seek to attain something high or great — 18. ____________________
19. to come upon or meet — 19. ____________________
20. filled with joy and pride — 20. ____________________
21. lively; energetic — 21. ____________________
22. favorable; pointing to a good result — 22. ____________________
23. unfavorable — 23. ____________________
24. to take great delight in something — 24. ____________________
25. to put into practice — 25. ____________________

Vocabulary Quiz 5 Answer Key

adverse	auspicious	espouse	jaunty	revel
amiable	confront	exemplary	lure	reverently
animosity	cunning	fathom	obscure	tedious
aspire	elated	imperative	obstinate	transfixed
audacious	encounter	implement	potential	warily

Fill in the blanks with the appropriate word. Be sure to spell correctly.

1. cautiously; suspiciously — 1. *warily*
2. motionless with amazement or horror — 2. *transfixed*
3. with feelings of deep respect — 3. *reverently*
4. a feeling of resentment; hostility — 4. *animosity*
5. to oppose; to come face to face with — 5. *confront*
6. bold and daring — 6. *audacious*
7. to support or adopt a cause or theory — 7. *espouse*
8. sly or clever — 8. *cunning*
9. stubborn — 9. *obstinate*
10. friendly — 10. *amiable*
11. unclear; clouded — 11. *obscure*
12. to understand in depth — 12. *fathom*
13. necessary — 13. *imperative*
14. long and tiring — 14. *tedious*
15. outstanding; worthy of imitation — 15. *exemplary*
16. the capability of becoming real — 16. *potential*
17. to tempt or lead away with a pleasure — 17. *lure*
18. to seek to attain something high or great — 18. *aspire*
19. to come upon or meet — 19. *encounter*
20. filled with joy and pride — 20. *elated*
21. lively; energetic — 21. *jaunty*
22. favorable; pointing to a good result — 22. *auspicious*
23. unfavorable — 23. *adverse*
24. to take great delight in something — 24. *revel*
25. to put into practice — 25. *implement*

Appendix VI: Motivating Students: Tickets and Games

Students should be rewarded for jobs well done. Positive reinforcement is a wonderful motivator. In my classes, I have found a ticket system to be extremely effective. To use such a system, purchase a roll of raffle tickets from an office supply store. In addition, I make 5-, 10-, and 25-point tickets printed on colored paper. (A 2 columns x 5 rows table works well.)

Give tickets for any of the advanced lessons done and for anything done particularly well. I always give a ticket for each vocabulary word used. I also give three tickets for each decoration used.

Periodically I have contests for tickets, such as "Best Title" or the best of each type of decoration. I also give tickets for winning review games such as those described below. Tickets may be used in an auction twice a year: once just before Christmas and once at the end of the year.

The Auction

There are many ways to do an auction. Here is how I do mine. You will want a calculator.

1. Students bring items to auction to class. These can be new, or they can be items they have at home and think someone else would like. I sometimes fill in with items from a dollar store and with candy. Two items per student works well.
2. Students put their tickets in an envelope with their name and number of tickets written on the outside and turn them in to you.
3. Write the students' names and number of tickets on the whiteboard in order from greatest to least. Instead of having students physically hand you tickets when they buy and sell things, you can subtract and add from their totals.
4. To begin, ask the student with the most tickets which item he would like to have auctioned first. When he chooses, he is bidding, so he should choose something he would like. Bids must begin at 25 or higher.
5. Students who would like the item continue to bid. Highest bidder gets the item. His bid is subtracted from his ticket total and added to the total of the person who brought that item (maximum of 100 is added).
6. Repeat this process, letting the student listed second on the board choose next. However, students who have bought an item may not bid on another until everyone has one. (This means the last person will get what he wants of what is left for the minimum bid of 25.)
7. Once everyone has one item, it is open bidding for what is left.

Games

The best motivator I have found in all my years of teaching is playing games that teach and review concepts. Below are a few that are suggested in the lessons.

No-Noose Hangman

1. Think of anything you would like to review. Put it into a simple list or phrase. For example, if you want to remind your students to highlight the key words in their topic sentence and clincher, you might use "highlight key words" as your phrase.
2. On a whiteboard, write a blank for each letter in your phrase:

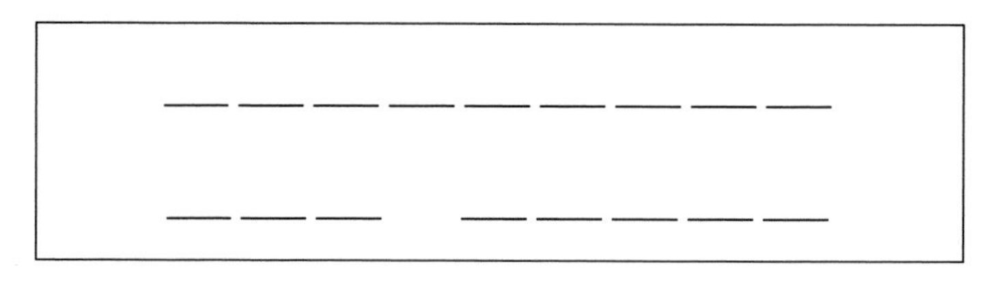

3. Students take turns guessing letters, one letter per turn. If the letter is in the puzzle, place it on the correct blank(s) and give the student a ticket for each time it is used. (Exception: Do not give tickets for vowels.) If the letter is not in the puzzle, write it on the bottom of the whiteboard, so no one else will guess it.
4. Anytime a student knows the phrase, he may raise his hand to solve the puzzle. *It does not have to be his turn.*
5. If he solves the puzzle correctly, he receives 3 tickets. If he can then answer a bonus question about the phrase, he receives 2 more. (A bonus question for the above puzzle could be, "In which sentences do you highlight the key words?")
6. Repeat with several puzzles.

Vocabulary Hangman

To play with vocabulary words, use the definition as the puzzle. When solved, the student or team who solved it must give you the matching word to receive the points.

Vocabulary Elimination or Around the World

1. Divide the class into groups of three or four students. Try to have an even number of groups. Go to one group. Read a definition of a vocabulary word. The first student in that group to shout out the matching word gets a ticket. Continue with the first group until one student has three tickets. He has eliminated the rest of his group. Repeat with the other groups.
2. Repeat with half of the winners as one group, then with the other half. Finally, repeat with the two remaining students. The winner of that round receives five extra tickets.

Around the World is similar. Start with two students. Read a definition. The first to shout the correct vocabulary word receives a ticket and moves on to challenge the next student. Continue in the same way. The winner always moves on to the next student. If one student makes it all the way "around the world" (beats everyone in the class), he gets five extra tickets.

Vocabulary Lightning

To prepare: You will need a stack of vocabulary cards (borrow from a student), a whiteboard (optional), and a timer.

To play, divide the class into two or three teams. Then, for each round, do the following:

1. Choose one or two players from one of the teams to come up in front of their team. Show them the stack of vocabulary cards with the word sides up. (They may not look at the definition side.)
2. Their job will be to try to get their team to say as many of the vocabulary words as they can in one minute. To do so, once the timer is set, they look at the first word and give their team clues, such as saying the definition, acting out the word, or describing or drawing the picture on the card. They may not say things such as what letter the word begins with or what it rhymes with. (Optional: Do not allow talking—only acting or drawing.)
3. As soon as someone from their team shouts the correct word, you (the teacher) should place the card on a table and move to the next word. If they get stuck on a word they may "pass" it after counting to five (the penalty for a pass). Be sure to place passed word cards in a separate stack from the word cards they guess correctly.
4. When the time is up, count the number of words their team guessed. Then, let the other team(s) have a turn in the same way. The team who guesses the most words wins that round. Play several rounds if you have time.

Vocabulary Pictionary

Need:
*two whiteboards (or one large one with a line sectioning it) or substitute paper and pencils
*two whiteboard markers
*a die (optional)

1. Divide the class into two teams. Assign each a whiteboard. Call one person from each team to the front of the class. Have them each roll the die to determine the number of points their team will receive if they win the round. Instruct them to write that number on the top of the whiteboard, so it is not forgotten. (The die is optional. You can just make each round won worth a point.)
2. Show the two students who came up which vocabulary word you want them to draw. (They will both draw the same word.)
3. When you say, "Go," they must draw a picture to try to get their team to say the chosen word. They may not include any letters or numbers in their drawings. The first team to guess the word receives the number of points rolled on their die. The other team erases the points they rolled. Play again with two new drawers.

The Five-Senses Game

To prepare, write the following on the whiteboard:

Looks   *Sounds*   *Feels*   *Smells/Tastes*

Divide the class into two or three teams. One person from each team comes to the front of his team. Tell each of them the same word from below (or make up your own that might be in their story or essay). Tell everyone the category of the word.

Food/Drink: popcorn, Coke, pizza, hot dog ...
Objects Outside: skyscraper, bus, train, helicopter, lawn mower ...
Inside: refrigerator, lamp, canned food, ...

The students at the front must take turns giving a five-senses word about the object. After each of the clues, the team of the student who gave it tries to guess the word. (Teacher writes the clue under the matching sense for all to see and remember.) For example, if the word is *kitten*, the student from Team A must give one five-senses word as a clue (e.g., *furry*). Then his team tries to guess the word. If wrong, the student from Team B then gives a one-word clue (e.g., *meow*), and his team guesses. Continue until a team guesses the word. That team gets a point.

Repeat with two new students and a new word. Be sure students understand that they may only say one word and that it must be a word that appeals to one of the five senses.

Sentence Stretching

On sixteen note cards write one of each of the following. (Each element of style will be on two different cards.) Omit ones you have not yet taught.

who-which clause	www.asia clause	quality adj	strong verb (replace the verb given in the sentence)
alliteration	simile	-ly adverb	3sss

To play

1. Divide the class into teams of two to four students.
2. One at a time, each team chooses three cards.
3. Each group has two minutes to stretch the basic sentence you put on the whiteboard by adding the three elements they chose. They may add more detail to the sentence in order to accomplish this. (Teachers, you may use a basic sentence from those suggested below or make up your own.)

All teams should be encouraged to add vocabulary words as well. Vocabulary words that are adjectives, verbs, or -ly adverbs may count as both when scoring if the adj, verb, or -ly adverb cards were one of the three chosen, so these words can be double points.

Sample: If a team chose simile, alliteration, and w-w clause, and the sentence on the board was *The king yelled*, they might write something like this:

> The king, who was perturbed and desperate, exploded like a violent volcano.

Scoring (Optional)

After the two minutes are up, each team must read their sentence. If they added all of their chosen elements correctly, they get 2 points for each.

Extra elements (from the eight or vocabulary), earn 2 extra points each.

Sample Scoring:

The sample sentence above uses all the required elements well (6 pts) plus it adds a vocabulary word (perturbed) and a strong verb (exploded), so they would receive 10 points. In this case, perturbed does not count double because adjective was not one of the chosen cards. (*Strong* verbs and *quality* adjectives are at the teacher's discretion.)

Repeat with more sentences. Here are some possibilities:

1. The dragon flew over the castle.
2. The knight hid behind a rock.
3. The princess danced all night.
4. The young man bowed before the king.
5. The peasant begged for mercy.

Find the Card for Vocabulary or Questions with Short Answers (a favorite!)

To prepare for vocabulary: Write each of the vocabulary words you wish to review on a separate note card. Spread them out face up on a table and let the students study them for no longer than one minute. Then turn them all face down. (In a large class, use larger cards and a pocket chart.)

To play, divide the class into three teams. Teams, in turn, do the following:

1. The teacher reads the definition of one of the words. The first team must turn over one of the word cards, trying to find the word that matches the definition.
2. If the word matches the definition, that team receives two points, and the word card is returned to its spot on the table (face down) so that all word cards remain on the table the entire game. Play would then continue with the next team and the next definition.
3. If the word card does not match the definition, the word card is returned, and the next team attempts to find the correct word for the same definition. Now the correct word is worth three points. If missed again, the next team tries for four points. Continue in this way until the correct word is found. Limit the point value to 10.

   Note: *When an incorrect word is turned over, award one point if the team that picked it can give its correct definition.*
4. Begin again with a new definition. Continue as above until all definitions have been used. The player or team with the most points wins.

For short answer questions, use questions instead of definitions, and put the answers on the cards.

Tic-Tac-Toe (or Connect Four)

Need: about twenty questions (Choose from pages 273–274.)
a whiteboard OR paper and pencil
two dice

1. Draw a tic-tac-toe board on a whiteboard or paper. Number the squares 1–9 in upper left corners.
2. Players are divided into an X team and an O team. They take turns trying to answer one of the questions. (You read one to them.)
3. If they answer correctly, place their X or O in the square of their choice. They then roll two dice.
4. The dice will determine whether they make special moves:

> *(Write this on the whiteboard for all to see.)*
>
> A total of 7 = Take an extra turn.
>
> Double 1, 2, or 3 = Erase an opponent's mark.
>
> Double 4, 5 = Erase an opponent's mark and replace it with yours.
>
> Double 6 = WILD. Go anywhere. (Can erase opponent if need be.)

5. Play until one team has three in a row or all squares are filled.
6. Repeat until one team has won two out of three or three out of five games.

For a longer game, try a 5 x 5 grid, and require four in a row to win.

21 QUESTIONS (or whatever number you desire)

To prepare:

1. Choose questions from the list below. (I usually choose 21.) Number each differently each time you play.
2. Write the numbers 1 through 21 (or however many questions you want to ask) on a whiteboard.
3. Obtain a die.

To Play:

1. Divide the class into three teams.
2. On each team's turn, they choose a number, and you read the corresponding question from your list. If a team answers correctly, they roll the die for points, and you erase the number from the board, so that question will not be chosen again.
3. If they answer incorrectly, you circle the number. The team gets no points. Now another team may choose that number for double points on their turn.
4. To add some fun, write "lose a turn" or "free roll" by two of your numbers.
5. Play until most questions have been chosen and teams have had an equal number of turns. Each player on the team with the most points receives five tickets.

QUESTIONS (You may renumber each time you play 21 Questions.)

1. What dress-ups have we learned thus far? How should you label them?
2. If you take a *who-which* clause out of a sentence, what should be left? *(a complete sentence)*
3. Give examples of 5 five-senses words, one for each sense. *(answers will vary)*
4. What do we call the time and place of a story? *(setting)*
5. What do we call the problem, want, or need of the main character of a story? *(conflict)*
6. In a story, what do we call the event that leads to the conflict being solved? *(climax)*
7. When punctuating conversation, periods and commas always go (*inside* or outside) end quotation marks.
8. What are the banned verbs? *(go, went, come, came, say, said, get, got, see, saw, look)*
9. What is alliteration? Give an example. *(three or more words that begin with the same* <u>sound</u> *(not necessarily letter) used close together: snow swept the city)*
10. What is a simile? Give an example. *(comparing one thing to another using* like *or* as: She stood as still as a statue.)
11. Where does a comma go with a *because* clause? *(after the because clause, unless there is a period there)*
12. What should each body paragraph of a report begin with? *(topic sentence)*
13. What should be highlighted in a topic sentence? *(key words that tell the topic)*
14. What should the clincher of a report paragraph do? *(repeat or reflect key words from the topic sentence)*
15. What is the topic sentence-clincher rule? *(The topic sentence and the clincher should repeat or reflect two to three key words.*
16. Do story paragraphs have topic sentences? *(no)*
17. What are the banned adjectives? *(good, bad, pretty, ugly)*
18. What is a 3sss? *(three short, staccato sentences in a row)*
19. Where does a comma go with a www.asia.b clause? *(after the entire www.asia.b clause, unless there is a period there)*
20. What are the www.asia.b words? *(when, while, where, as, since, if, although, because)*
21. What is a fused outline? *(the outline you make after you take notes from more than one source; the outline you use to write a research report paragraph)*
22. When writing a research report (using more than one source text), after you have your sources, what must you know BEFORE you begin taking notes? *(topics)*

23. Should each note page for a research report have all the notes from the *same source* or all the notes for the *same topic*? *(same topic)* Why? *(so all notes for the same paragraph are together)*
24. What sentence openers have you learned? How do you label them?
25. Give six prepositions that can begin a #2 sentence. *(see SRP)*
26. When you must write without a source text, how can you get ideas for what to say? *(ask yourself questions)*
27. What are the question starter words that can help you ask questions to think of more details to add to your writing? *(who, what, when, where, why, how, how feel, best thing, worst thing)*
28. What is the structure of a 5-paragraph report? *(introduction, three body paragraphs, conclusion)*
29. What must an introduction paragraph include? *(grab attention, introduce the subject, give background, and introduce the topics of the body paragraphs)*
30. What must a concluding paragraph include? *(reflect the topics, tell what is most significant and why, end with an essay clincher)*
31. What is the purpose of a critique? *(to give and support an opinion about a story, film, book ...)*
32. What should you not say in a critique? *("I" or "my," as in "I think" or "In my opinion")*
33. What is a #5 sentence opener? *(www.asia.b clause)* What do these letters stand for? *(when, while, where, as, since, if, although, because)*
34. What should you have as the last page of a research report? *(bibliography or list of works cited)*
35. How many words may a very short sentence contain? *(2–5)*